# KING LEAR IN BROOKLYN

# MICHAEL PENNINGTON

# KING LEAR IN BROOKLYN

OBERON BOOKS
LONDON

WWW.OBERONBOOKS.COM

First published in 2016 by Oberon Books Ltd
521 Caledonian Road, London N7 9RH
Tel: +44 (0) 20 7607 3637 / Fax: +44 (0) 20 7607 3629
e-mail: info@oberonbooks.com
www.oberonbooks.com

A catalogue record for this book is available from the British Library.

HB ISBN: 9781783193264
E ISBN: 9781783197385

Photography copyright © the individual photographers

Key to photographers for image plates i-viii / ix-xvi
David Sundberg/Esto [DS/ESTO]; Gerry Goodstein [GG]; Carol Rosegg [CR];
Prue Skene [PS]; Meredith Wheeler [MW]; Mark Pennington [MP]

Cover:
photograph of Michael Pennington as King Lear by Gerry Goodstein
design by James Illman

Printed, bound and converted by CPI Group (UK) Ltd, Croydon, CR0 4YY.

Visit www.oberonbooks.com to read more about all our books and to buy them. You will
also find features, author interviews and news of any author events, and you can sign up for
e-newsletters so that you're always first to hear about our new releases.

# ACKNOWLEDGEMENTS

There are a number of voices in this book, and several helping hands. First of all I am grateful to Nick Hern Books for permission to quote from my own *Sweet William – Twenty Thousand Hours with Shakespeare**; to Lucy Munro and Lucy Dallas at *The Times Literary Supplement* for permission to use the long section of Lucy Munro's article on the London and New York *Lears*; to Robert Cushman for digging out our correspondence on the subject; to Ian McKellen for permission to plunder our video brainstorm. To Avi Sharon, Jeffrey Horowitz and Arin Arbus, and to the actors and designers in New York who have contributed, either in their own voices or by supplementing my view of their characters; in this respect Timothy Stickney's back story of the life of the Earl of Kent was entirely his own work and I found it particularly fascinating.

Then to the brilliant team at Oberon Books, who have worked with an astonishing combination of speed and meticulousness: to James Hogan for his confidence in me and his determination never to let one of his writers pay for their own lunch; to Charles Glanville, with whom it is always a particular pleasure to make a contract; to James Illman, a wonderful designer who seems not to know the meaning of perturbability, and to George Spender, who apart from his own support has allowed me the pleasing illusion of collaborating with a true poet – his first cousin twice removed, Stephen Spender, whom I knew quite well.

In another sense this book is dedicated to Philip Franks, with whom I had been talking about *King Lear* for ten years and who has defined much of my thinking about the play.

And in another to Mark, Louis and Eve as always. And I owe a debt of gratitude way beyond any formal acknowledgement to my partner and domestic editor Prue Skene, who went through this Brooklyn adventure with me and whom I am delighted to have lured into the book as an important participant in the drama. This story, like much of what I do in life, would be half itself if it wasn't for them, and I am profoundly thankful.

*Also known as *Sweet William - A User's Guide to Shakespeare*

# THEATRE FOR A NEW AUDIENCE
## Polonsky Shakespeare Center

Jeffrey Horowitz
FOUNDING ARTISTIC DIRECTOR

Henry Christensen III
CHAIRMAN

Dorothy Ryan
MANAGING DIRECTOR

presents

# KING LEAR
by
## WILLIAM SHAKESPEARE
### In the Samuel H. Scripps Mainstage

Featuring

BIANCA AMATO* BENJAMIN COLE MARK H. DOLD* LILLY ENGLERT* JACOB FISHEL*

JASON THOMAS GRAY JONATHAN HOOKS JAKE HOROWITZ* ROBERT LANGDON LLOYD*

PATRICK McANDREW CHRISTOPHER McCANN* RYAN McCARTHY SAXON PALMER*

MICHAEL PENNINGTON* RACHEL PICKUP* RYAN QUINN* JON STEWART, JR. TIMOTHY D. STICKNEY*

IAN TEMPLE CHANDLER WILLIAMS* GRAHAM WINTON* ARIEL ZUCKERMAN

Scenic Designer
RICCARDO HERNANDEZ

Costume Designer
SUSAN HILFERTY

Lighting Designer
MARCUS DOSHI

Composer/Co-Sound Designer
MICHAËL ATTIAS

Co-Sound Designer
NICHOLAS POPE

Fight Director
B.H. BARRY

Movement
JOHN CARRAFA

Voice Director
ANDREW WADE

Dramaturg
JONATHAN KALB

Casting
DEBORAH BROWN

Production Stage Manager
RENEE LUTZ*

Production Manager
KAT THARP

General Manager
MICHAEL PAGE

Press Representative
THE BRUCE COHEN GROUP, LTD

Directed By
## ARIN ARBUS

This Production is sponsored by Deloitte.

Principal support for Theatre for a New Audience's season and programs is provided by The Polonsky Foundation, The Andrew W. Mellon Foundation, Bloomberg Philanthropies and The SHS Foundation.

Major support is provided by Robert H. Arnow, Valerie Anisko and Jeffrey Bliss, Marlène Brody, Sally Brody, William I. Campbell, Mr. and Mrs. Henry Christensen III, Judith and Alan Fishman, Ella M. Foshay and Michael B. Rothfeld, Sidney E. Frank Foundation, Gladys Krieble Delmas Foundation, The Howard Gilman Foundation, The Hearst Corporation, The DuBose and Dorothy Heyward Memorial Fund, John D. Howard, John and Nora Kerr, Kramer Levin Naftalis & Frankel LLP, The Blanche and Irving Laurie Foundation, Donna Mae Litowitz, William and Diane Lloyd, Loeb & Loeb LLP, Wendy and Robert Macdonald, Diane and Adam Max, Audrey Heffernan Meyer and Danny Meyer, Caroline Niemczyk, Janet C. Olshansky and Jeffrey Morris, Cynthia and Leon Polsky, The Rifkind Family Foundation, Theodore C. Rogers, Rolex Mentors & Protégés, Jonathan Rose Companies, Philip and Janet Rotner, The Fan Fox & Leslie R. Samuels Foundation, Robert T. and Cynthia V.A. Schaffner, The Shubert Foundation, Sol Schwartz, Starry Night Fund, The Harold and Mimi Steinberg Charitable Trust, Michael Stranahan, and Monica and Ali Wambold.

Theatre for a New Audience's season and programs are also made possible, in part, with public funds from The National Endowment for the Humanities; the National Endowment for the Arts; Shakespeare for a New Generation, a program of the National Endowment for the Arts in partnership with Arts Midwest; the New York State Council on the Arts with the support of Governor Andrew Cuomo and the New York State Legislature; and from the New York City Department of Cultural Affairs in partnership with the City Council.

*Member of Actors' Equity Association, the Union of Professional Actors and Stage Managers in the United States

# DRAMATIS PERSONAE

*(in order of appearance)*

Earl of Kent . . . . . . . . . . . . . . . . . . . . . . . . . . . . . . . . . . . . . . . . . . .TIMOTHY D. STICKNEY*
Earl of Gloucester . . . . . . . . . . . . . . . . . . . . . . . . . . . . . . . . . . . .CHRISTOPHER McCANN*
Edmund, *bastard son to Gloucester* . . . . . . . . . . . . . . . . . . . . .CHANDLER WILLIAMS*
Lear, *King of Britain* . . . . . . . . . . . . . . . . . . . . . . . . . . . . . . . . .MICHAEL PENNINGTON*
Goneril, *daughter to Lear* . . . . . . . . . . . . . . . . . . . . . . . . . . . . . . . .RACHEL PICKUP*
Regan, *daughter to Lear* . . . . . . . . . . . . . . . . . . . . . . . . . . . . . . . .BIANCA AMATO*
Cordelia, *daughter to Lear* . . . . . . . . . . . . . . . . . . . . . . . . . . . . .LILLY ENGLERT*
Duke of Albany . . . . . . . . . . . . . . . . . . . . . . . . . . . . . . . . . . . . . . . .GRAHAM WINTON*
Duke of Cornwall . . . . . . . . . . . . . . . . . . . . . . . . . . . . . . . . . . . . . .SAXON PALMER*
Duke of Burgundy . . . . . . . . . . . . . . . . . . . . . . . . . . . . . . . . . . . . . .JON STEWART, JR.
King of France . . . . . . . . . . . . . . . . . . . . . . . . . . . . . . . . . . . . . . . . . .RYAN QUINN*
Edgar, *son to Gloucester* . . . . . . . . . . . . . . . . . . . . . . . . . . . . . . . .JACOB FISHEL*
Oswald, *steward to Goneril* . . . . . . . . . . . . . . . . . . . . . . . . . . . . .MARK H. DOLD*
Knight/Old Man/Doctor . . . . . . . . . . . . . . . . . . . . . . . .ROBERT LANGDON LLOYD*
Fool . . . . . . . . . . . . . . . . . . . . . . . . . . . . . . . . . . . . . . . . . . . . . . . . . . .JAKE HOROWITZ*
Knight/Curan/Captain . . . . . . . . . . . . . . . . . . . . . . . . . . . . . . . . . . .RYAN QUINN*
Ensemble . . . . . . . . . . . . . . . . . .BENJAMIN COLE, JASON GRAY, JONATHAN HOOKS,
PATRICK McANDREW, RYAN McCARTHY, JON STEWART, JR.,
IAN TEMPLE, ARIEL ZUCKERMAN

## MUSICIANS
MICHAËL ATTIAS
PASCAL NIGGENKEMPER
SATOSHI TAKEISHI

**SETTING**: Ancient Briton

*THERE WILL BE ONE 15-MINUTE INTERMISSION.*

Assistant Stage Manager . . . . . . . . . . . . . . . . . . . . . . . . . . . . . .MARJORIE ANN WOOD*

*Member of Actors' Equity Association,
the Union of Professional Actors and Stage Managers in the United States

# CONTENTS

# AUTHOR'S NOTE

Though theatre productions travel to and fro across the Atlantic quite regularly and actors sometimes revisit their old roles in due course, it's an unusual thing to play King Lear twice within two years in two quite separate productions with two different directors and in two different countries. I thought such a thing was the privilege of John Gielgud's generation, with his six Hamlets, but now I find it's come my way. As this book comes out, I am beginning a tour of the UK in a new production of the play directed by Max Webster. However, in the spring of 2014 I played Lear in an American version directed by Arin Arbus for Theatre for a New Audience in New York. In the new staging I think I am the only one who has played their part before, and in the first I was the only foreigner.

I've written three books about individual Shakespeare plays and one about Shakespeare at large, but until now I have never wanted to tackle *King Lear*. The play can feel like a mountain shrouded in mist. Or some grandiose theatrical ritual with a vocabulary to match, albeit with stabs of almost unbearable realism. Or as a relentless machine sustained not so much by its audience's fascinated collaboration but by some energy drawn from within itself. It's difficult to do and difficult to write about.

However the experience of working on it with an American and now a European company has suggested to me a way in which such a book might be done. Beneath any text is a pattern of thought, passion and motive which may or may not tally with what the characters are saying. *King Lear in Brooklyn* offers my educated guess at what could be going on beneath the surface: twelve streams of consciousness in counterpoint with what the characters actually reveal as they struggle to survive a more or less permanent state of emergency.

The reward, I hope, will be to find within the thunderous mass of *King Lear* all the recognisable human processes of regret and obstinacy, of defiance, anguish and hope, not as a logical sequence but in continual transition, just as they are in life. An unenlightened central character shows, even from the start, intermittent humour and self-knowledge; a pair of his apparently vindictive children doubt themselves, and a third offers an uncanny image of the father. These people turn out to have a good deal in common with us after all.

My four months in New York brought me new colleagues and some sense of a new direction as well as realising the standard hope of any actor who has done a lot of Shakespeare. *King Lear in Brooklyn* celebrates, as it happens, a time of great personal happiness, despite one dramatic intrusion of farcical English concerns. If it can also open up what for many people is Shakespeare's most forbidding tragedy, admired but not always loved, I shall be well satisfied.

# INTRODUCTION

*Monday evening, 27<sup>th</sup> January, 2014*

T his is how a tree may grow in Brooklyn.

On some sidewalks the roots of the maples have pushed up so hard to find the light that the paving stones have buckled. When such a thing happens, ecology becomes more important than Health and Safety: the roots are removed only when they die and the trees threaten to fall, generally to be replaced by a less aggressive species such as the Callery Pear. Until then, the stones remain fractured and you must look out for yourself. That was my undoing.

As you walk home at night hereabouts you might, as often in New York (or London, or Madrid) develop a radar, simultaneously scanning the ground at your feet for safety and the street in front of you for any commotion ahead. After twenty-four hours in town mine hadn't been activated; so, hastening home after my first day's work on a freezing January evening, thinking I must be careful on the ice, I was distracted by a man yelling from the first-floor window of what looked like a flophouse across the street. It was a haunting and, dramatically, a completely realised sound. He seemed to be at the end of his tether, but also comic, like the guy in *Network* who yells "I'm mad as hell and I'm not going to take this any more". It was as if he wanted to murder someone but felt bitterly sorry about it; as if the saddest thing he knew was how angry he was. He sounded like King Lear when Cordelia lets him down.

Shouts like this are not uncommon in New York City. People yell at the desert air or at themselves, and the more threatening or pained it sounds the more, in general, other New Yorkers smile at it. Folks shout on the subway when it's busy to indicate they need to get past you to get off; they sometimes storm at each other for no very clear reason. But I was so startled by this cry of King Lear's that I looked across, missed my footing, and down I went, within fifty yards of home, felled by a proud lip of paving-stone, the root of a tree beneath it; not quite impaling myself on the low railings around the tree at the kerb, but giving my ribs, right elbow and both knees a good crack, and myself the aghast, winded feeling that I guessed would either go away in a minute or turn into a coronary. I was surprised, normally being quick to react if I lose my footing: a lifetime of falling down dead in the line of professional duty has left me aerodynamically quite sound; the knack has, you might say, got into my bones.

In the immediate impact (let's call it), what struck me (so to speak) was that four years previously, in early 2010, I had found myself lying flat on my back on the carpet of Theatre for a New Audience's office in Christopher Street in Greenwich Village, while Arin Arbus, a director of considerable talent and, as it happens, personal beauty, sat in a throne behind a great desk (not her style really – in rehearsals she favours yogically cross-legged on the floor), like the chairwoman of some slightly mysterious corporation. I was on the ground that time because I had exceptional sciatica, and lying down in front of the desk was the least agonising position. What the two incidents had in common was *King Lear*. Arin and I were agreeing that we were intrigued by the sado-masochistic relationship between Cornwall and Regan that leads them to pull out the Earl of Gloucester's eyes: anyone glancing into the room might have thought we were ourselves rehearsing a Jean Genet play about sexual dominance.

As I now stare into my paving stone, waiting for the outcome, cardiac or structural, my mood is jubilant despite the discomfort. It occurs to me that bright beginnings at Theatre for a New Audience seem generally to be accompanied by some degree of physical pain.

❖

What had happened in 2010 was this. I was playing in Peter Brook's *Love is my Sin*, his dramatisation of a sequence of Shakespeare's Sonnets for a man, a woman (Natasha Parry) and a musician (Franck Krawczyk). Though it originated at the Bouffes du Nord in Paris, Theatre for a New Audience (henceforward TFANA) were curating it for a season at the Duke on 42nd Street, a tiny theatre nestling among giants: the American Airlines Theatre, the New Victory, the New Amsterdam and the BB King Blues Club. At the first night party I spotted Arin talking about Shakespeare to a group of actors, including John Douglas Thompson – who, it turned out, had played Brutus in *The Emperor Jones* and Cleopatra's Antony and would soon be doing Tamburlaine for TFANA, as well as having a large Broadway success as Louis Armstrong in *Satchmo*. Like an impertinent suitor I asked Jeffrey Horowitz, the Artistic Director of TFANA, who she was, as I wanted to talk to her. It transpired that Arin was his Resident Associate and had done five consecutive Shakespeares for him to considerable acclaim – not only John's Othello and Macbeth but *Much Ado About Nothing, The Taming of the Shrew* and *Measure for Measure*; she had also done remarkable work with the long-term prisoners at the Woodbourne Correctional Facility in upstate New York on *Of Mice and Men*. Exactly, I said: I want to find out if we have anything in common.

And a few days later I did, over cake in Le Pain Quotidien in Hudson Street in the West Village. As any male and female Shakespearians are likely to do, we talked about *The Taming of the Shrew*, that black sheep among Shakespeare's comedies, with its awkward whiff of misogyny and violence which may or may not mask a deeper, more congenial meaning. I also rambled over my past and present, the changing styles I'd weathered over the last nearly fifty years: ideas that were ahead of their time in the Sixties, ideas that had fallen behind in the Nineties – things I'd changed my mind about and then changed it back again.

Then Arin looked levelly at me across the table and asked me if I realised that the marriage between Othello and Desdemona may never have been consummated, because of the dizzying Cyprus/Venice commute he's on in the first half of the play; and that in the end Desdemona, worn down, sincerely regrets marrying him and has a half an eye for Lodovico, that "very proper man", a fact which she half-seriously shares with her confidante Emilia. It hadn't struck me, and it made perfect sense. This unsentimental appreciation both of the sexual unease of a new, over-occupied older husband aware that he is an outsider, and of a woman more often played as a tiresomely innocent child than as an adult, did it for me. I'd met someone able to tell me something about Shakespeare that I hadn't thought of.

This being a first date, we agreed that it had been lovely to eat cake but that we hadn't come to the main point. When a few days later Jeffrey Horowitz mused to Arin that I'd never played Lear, he had called me shortly beforehand and invited me to think – not more than think – about doing just that. In the slightly engineered serendipity of such things – working lives in the theatre operate by a sort of calculated impulse – it was also true that Peter Brook had recently said that it was high time I took it on: a merry battle persists to this day as to which of them really godfathered the idea.

Before I left New York, Arin and I met again, on the occasion when sciatica was the third person in the room, though I forgot about it quite often. What was still clear was that while we very much liked talking and listening to each other and felt we might be good companions on a thing as huge as *Lear*, we had barely scratched the surface. In particular, Arin didn't want to be frivolous with my time, since nothing as well as everything might come of it all, and she must continue to mull over the play before committing herself. She was really saying that she might not yet be ready for *Lear*, which I took her to mean in terms of life-experience – a most unusual attitude among directors, who will normally do any good play they can get their hands on, and can also be a bit loose-lipped when they express their desire to work with you.

The scrupulousness already invested in our idea meant there was to be no possibility of bad faith. Two and a half years later, just after Hurricane Sandy, I was back in New York for a week's without-prejudice workshop on the play.

## November 2012

### ARIN ARBUS

We decided to ask Michael over for a week's work on *King Lear* with no strings attached for either of us. I hired a group of actors I knew, and since there was little point in having Michael read anything other than Lear I did what I wouldn't normally do for a workshop, cast the rest to specific parts as well, though everyone understood this was not to be an audition.

### JEFFREY HOROWITZ

In introducing Arin and Michael I was bringing together my past and my present. Many years ago I saw Michael in his company's seven-play history cycle *The Wars of the Roses* over three days in Connecticut, and they had made a lasting impression (I'm not even sure if Arin was born then). I hadn't seen him perform again until *Love is my Sin*. I couldn't ensure we would succeed, but I was introducing two people who I knew had the individual talent to realise the play: I knew each of them in ways they didn't know each other and I also cared about them both. Since there's an 'I want' and an 'I don't want' in any relationship, to be safe each had to be sure there was a connection, and if necessary respect the answer No. In other words, I needed to be a good producer to do *King Lear* for her, for him and for the play.

## RACHEL PICKUP

I did Goneril in the workshop. This was a company I'd been wanting to work with for years, a director I hugely respected and an actor I had very much admired from afar, in fact who had been a part of my life since I was knee-high. It was thrilling on that oh-so-cold November day in 2012 to walk into the studio and immediately have any fear obliterated by both Michael and Arin – easy with each other, easy with the play, with the plans for the week, with all of us. I certainly didn't consider the workshop as an audition for the ultimate production: though, unusually on such an occasion, we were each being asked to focus on a particular part which we might or might not end up playing. Much of the casting was utterly improbable (a 45-year-old Earl of Gloucester?), so, perhaps intentionally, it didn't feel like we were even being considered.

I don't think I've ever felt freer to say what I was thinking: the process was entirely liberating, exploratory, unpressurised. Well, perhaps not for Michael and Arin – they knew a production was going to happen – but for me it was a luxury: nobody watching, our circle of seven people very intimate. We could just think out loud about these characters, from their own viewpoint of course.

And Michael and Arin didn't make judgments either. Arin started the week saying this is a play about family; that that was what she was interested in, and that every single person in the play has a valid point of view. With *Lear* there are so many preconceived ideas about who's good and who's bad that you have to approach it believing that everyone is true to their own natures. Goneril is the same as the others – flawed, justified, hurting, needy; I saw that she is horribly wronged and that due to some twist in her own nature, she ends up doing terrible wrong as well. I saw this because of the way Arin and Michael set the ball rolling, with no sense that we had to serve our leaders' vision – quite a rare thing for this play, since not only directors but classical actors at the peak of their craft can become dictators.

Eight months later I was offered the part – the only member of the workshop who was – but rehearsals were not to start for another eight months. So when we finally came to rehearse I had all that Goneril-thought already inside me and knew what I wanted to prove about this woman.

## MICHAEL PENNINGTON

Actually the whole thing was something of a subterfuge – to see if Arin and I could do business at all.

I very much like working with American artists on Shakespeare: for all sorts of moving reasons, he is common ground. I once directed in Chicago and my only problem was stopping the actors listening to various experts from the UK, now reinventing their careers Stateside, who wanted to teach the handling of the language the British way. But Jacobean language was inherited by Americans at the same time as us, and their approach now is far less troubled by tradition, or the rejection of tradition, than that of the descendants of John Gielgud, Edith Evans and the rest. Their passionate access to Shakespeare is beyond question (remember Marlon Brando as Mark Antony?); all I ever had to do in Chicago was get the actors sometimes to take their foot off the gas and consider some ironic aside or second thought or momentary hesitation.

Much of this has been unearthed for both us and them by John Barton, acknowledged as the greatest influence on British Shakespearian acting in my lifetime. His gift for Shakespearian comedy in particular, his extraordinary understanding of Shakespeare's word chemistry, his analysis of how it contradicts and expands and depends on antithesis and irony, has led to his being described as a great Shakespeare swami, Shakespeare's map-reader, as a Shakespearian brass-rubber, an exemplar of the Elizabethan ideal he admires. And to profound affection. I know him as a friend and colleague and the mentor of a large part of my career; as a provocateur too – when I once told him that I was planning to do Cleopatra's Antony, he gently ribbed me by saying only an American actor was capable of playing the part, and he wasn't altogether joking. This is a rebel within the Establishment who is inclined, when asked for the most Shakespearian speech he knows, to point to the strange eloquence of the Italian anarchist Bartolomeo Vanzetti when he spoke to the court on behalf of Nicola Sacco and himself just before they were sentenced to death in 1927 for a crime of which the judge who convicted them knew they were innocent. "Something poetic happens in him; it's natural in him" John says.

Well, he is now the hero of a generation of American actors as well as British, partly for his own dauntless workshops and partly for his TV series and accompanying book, *Playing Shakespeare*, which looks at every aspect of the job. They are probably even more popular in the States than at home: I am quite often congratulated by US actors for the simple fact of having participated in them.

I also knew that the Shakespearians arriving to workshop *Lear* were used to plying the whole Eastern seaboard from Stratford Ontario to Washington DC – some of them had done *All's Well That Ends Well* two or three times, which I doubt any English actor has done; they were well at ease, and certainly didn't think of me as any special expert. A sense of ownership without deference to the Brits is actually manifest all over the States: think of Ashland Oregon, the Houston Shakespeare Festival, or the Guthrie in Minneapolis. If anything it was I who was a little jittery, friendly and welcoming as the American actors were. I was the only one from overseas, and I already had the job, if indeed there was to be a job. I spent the week in a dismal midtown hotel chosen with the best motives by TFANA, being routinely ripped off in the evenings by the restaurants in Hell's Kitchen, shuttling to and fro between them at great length before invariably making the decision to go back yet again to Gazala's Place on Ninth Avenue.

I also caught up with my own past in a way that now seems to me to have been a portent. Roger Rees was a friend of mine since we both began to flourish in the remarkable RSC company of the mid-1970s and early 1980s, about the time Barton was at his most active. We both played Hamlet, one after the other; Roger did inspired drawings for my book about crossing Siberia, *Rossya*; we also planned a joint professional autobiography but never did it, so that I still have a box of tapes of the two of us talking. Soon, with *Nicholas Nickleby* behind him, he would be on his way to a new life in New York with Rick Elice; but first they co-wrote a play, *Double Double*, which contained one of the most remarkable coups I've seen in a theatre, in which Roger fell dead down a spiral staircase from a height of about twelve feet to the ground. Then, as he lay at the bottom, the front door rang and was opened, and he came through it. (Yes, exit route half way down the rear part of the staircase and a body double to complete the final stage of the journey).

So one night after work I go to see Roger's production of *Peter and the Starcatcher*, a version written by Rick of the imagined back story of Peter Pan before he meets Wendy: this is my treat in a week of refined loneliness. I loved the show, not least for its gestures towards the style of *Nickleby*, Roger's biggest hit as an actor: if you want to make a door, get a piece of string, and hold its centre section tightly up in the air to make the top two corners; if you want to make a bird, use a rubber kitchen glove and just as suddenly throw it away afterwards. Get a company to such a point of speed and adroitness that they can sway and creak with the movement of a boat

– but really, not just nominally, as in less rigorous forms of physical theatre. Roger's company swashbuckled and morphed with a commitment, beneath the amplified assault of a Broadway musical, to the kind of rough theatre we all love. Later he told me they'd even thought of putting Peter Pan on a concealed flying-wire at the end but decided against, since everything must be visible. And to round it off, the boy playing Prentiss had a distinct look of Roger as I remember him, as well as of Stan Laurel. What I didn't know was that for a large part of the evening Roger was watching me watching the show from a stalls side door, pleased at my pleasure. Afterwards we met at Joe Allens, where Jeffrey Horowitz was sitting at the next table, hard at work on some donor, surprising each other yet again that we felt the same about so many things, and how they made us laugh.

The people you have the closest alliances with in my profession are not necessarily those you see most often or even know best in themselves. As we parted, Roger and I stood on the street corner and looked at each other in a kind of silent glee, the years rolling and wrapping over each other, amused by the ageing process we could see in each other's faces, as if to say... Look at you... do you remember... now here we are... We'd met quite rarely since he moved to New York over twenty years ago, though he had a habit of turning up, as surprisingly as his character in *Double Double*, in the least likely places – in Chichester to see *Richard II* and Stratford for *Timon of Athens*, appearing at my door when I didn't know he was even in the country. Now he is urging me towards the Lear that seems more and more like a certainty, while I go on about *Starcatcher* and also his solo Shakespeare – funny, deft, a wonderful mixture of his old affections and his modern instincts – in which he glittered like a silvery fish and reflected so much of himself. Encouraged and validated by old loyalties, I go home convinced I can play King Lear until it squeals for mercy. I hope Roger'll come to the first night.

Back at the Duke's rehearsal studios in daylight, I could see one significant difference in approach. While I talked about how interested Shakespeare always was in what happens in a vacuum – what energies can be released among the survivors when the King resigns, the father goes mad, or the centre collapses – the New York actors spoke about their own fathers, daughters and sisters. The question arose as to whether it was a reasonable or a cruel thing to make a cantankerous old man find his own way in a storm in which even the lion and the wolf prefer to keep their fur dry. On the whole, the women believed it was right that Lear should be locked out in this way, but the men were outraged. Presently everyone was on their feet, only half-amiably yelling at each other. With this energy in the room, I suddenly wanted to do the play very badly, with these people. After work, as they braced themselves for long journeys home, I would sit in a coffee house with Terry Doe and Rachel Pickup, both of whom I knew, and it seemed the most natural thing for a person on their home ground to do: I realised how hard I would take it if that pleasure wasn't to be mine regularly. Then I'd wake up in the night thinking about how many things *Lear* is about other than family. Would we cover them as well?

I also saw that I'd found a new important director – mild, cunning – in my life. The week was full of improvisations that sprang fresh as paint from Arin. Most of one afternoon was filled with Goneril and Regan finding ways of treating their ailing father, newly arrived at their house, with the utmost solicitude, nursing him and insisting – lovingly, but insisting – that he goes to bed immediately after his long journey. If I tried to sit up, their loving hands were as firm and unyielding as hospital restrainers but their faces were kindness itself. After I'd rested they gently showed me to the door and out into the storm, locking the doors after me with the same deadly attentiveness. Another time Lear had to build a castle round himself out of tables, chairs, whatever come to hand, to prevent anyone reaching or affecting him while he determinedly maintained control of everything.

## ARIN ARBUS

Michael, I now knew, is incredibly open, generous and collaborative. He is interested in what everyone in the room has to say. I am too. And yet he also has instincts which are unwavering. When we explored Act Two Scene Four, in which Regan and Goneril strip down the size of the entourage Lear needs to sustain (at their cost) to the deadly point of "What need one?", Michael portrayed a powerful man losing grip on power, losing grip on his mind and his sense of self: he embodied the terror of someone completely losing control. And he was able to sit in that kind of terror. Nobody in the room moved. We all felt it. The hairs on my arms stood up. It was electrifying, heartbreaking, astonishing and totally Lear. Instinctively I knew he could do the role, that we did work well together, and I wanted to take the plunge with him. And so we did.

## MICHAEL PENNINGTON

It was a flashpoint for both of us. After the last session we had arranged a debriefing with Jeffrey Horowitz but for one reason or another our time was reduced to about twenty minutes. Walking into the restaurant I decided to smack my cards on the table in an aggressive American way. I declared I had had a terrific week, I'd found my ideal director and I really wanted to do this, I knew this was going to work. Jeffrey's eyes swivelled over to Arin's: neither of them demurred. We spent a pleasant fifteen minutes discussing the labyrinthine process that at that time still had to be gone through with US Equity and Immigration on behalf of a British actor playing a major part for the first time in New York. Subject to that, we declared we were on, got up, embraced and parted.

### *December 2012 – January 2014*

There are many reasons why productions end up not getting done. Peter Brook once compared our best ideas to potential first-service aces that end up in the net while the tamer second ones may – just – get through. Projects can be proposed and then carelessly forgotten. Even when they start to move forward there can be a long phase when they're neither on nor not on. That is a time for unusual diligence: if you've lit a fire in your grate, you don't want to turn your back on it, even momentarily, in case you turn back to find it's gone out. Many times a contact is maintained which is really a coded enquiry for reassurance that the project is still slated: that the producer still means well, that the actor is still holding himself or herself free. A precarious good faith needs to be sustained. When Jeffrey Horowitz came on a thirty-six hour trip to see me play the Master Builder in Chichester, it wasn't simply out of love: it concealed a need to check for good and all that he really had the right man for the job.

In movies, notoriously, the money can be pulled at the very last minute: months of work and, inevitably, expenditure is squandered. In this case it's usually a bank or some corporation, indifferent to the human element, that has the second thoughts. There's no excuse for that in the theatre, which is cheaper in any case and has to be held together by plain dealing, without which everything collapses. Still, warm intentions can quietly congeal; good faith fades and the most heartfelt enthusiasm runs out of puff; within even the brightest ideas there can be an inbuilt decay. There is also insincerity and inertia, especially in the UK, especially in the Shakespearian heartlands, as I was to be reminded later when I attempted to import our *Lear* into Britain. But in the almost exactly four years between Arin and I eating cake and the first night of our *Lear* I never doubted that, short of an act of God, Homeland Security or American Equity, the production would happen. The music kept on playing, in London and New York, occasionally in person and more often on the phone and internet. The one question was whether there would be a finished theatre to play it in: Jeffrey's dream-child for TFANA, the Polonsky Shakespeare Center in downtown Brooklyn, only just got built in time.

The week beginning June 2013 was a sweet one. My 70th birthday was celebrated with a party I'll never forget, and also by my opening in Strindberg's *Dance of Death*, received with some rapture, and, to complete the hat trick, US Equity agreed to let me in for *King Lear*. This dance with Equity, though rapidly becoming out of date, is worth describing. As long as I can remember, if a British actor was invited to play in New York as a single company member in an otherwise American group – as opposed to being one of an entirely British company coming as a unit – a case had to be made to the union. For the actor it involved digging, or having someone dig out, all your best notices and publicity materials for as long as you could remember and making them into a sort of showcase, accompanied by letters of enthusiastic endorsement by figures such as Peter Hall, Richard Eyre, Trevor Nunn or Nicholas Hytner – maybe some commercial producers too – saying what a good egg you were. The tribal imperative allowed them to do this regardless of their private opinions. Michael Gambon had to do it, Glenda Jackson as well. As US Equity assessed your application, very much at their leisure, the subtext was:

> US Equity: Why should we let this Limey in when there are perfectly good US actors available and chomping for the work?

> British Equity: Because there's nobody your side of the pond capable of doing this particular part.

As you can see, neither side looked particularly good in these roles. Naturally; the argument was essentially unresolvable, and you're put in mind of wrestlers being forced to flex their biceps. The sequence of events had always been predictable: you made your case, US Equity deliberated at length and then turned you down, announcing as much in *The New York Times* to reassure their membership that they were looking after their interests. Then the two unions got on the phone to each other and started horse trading, considering the balance of US actors in the West End at that moment against UK actors in New York, and hammered out a deal. After that you could pack your bag; even in the most protectionist hearts, the principle faintly dwells that art should have no barriers and free exchange is desirable. Yes, of course. But it was tiring, and difficult not to resent. It first happened to me in 1991 when I was to play Peter Shaffer's *Gift of the Gorgon* in New York opposite Helen Mirren (who was by that time permanently approved); I got the go-ahead in the end, whereupon the producers pulled out. They'd never really wanted to do the play but didn't want to make an enemy of Shaffer; they hoped that Equity would solve the problem by excluding me, and since Peter Hall had declared he wouldn't do the play without me, they could shrug their shoulders.

However a deal was struck in the summer of 2014 that any American company that belonged to The League of Resident Theatres – an excellent association of seventy-four resident producing theatres from Seattle to Washington, from Dallas to Newhaven, perhaps akin to the repertory theatres of old in this much smaller island – could hire two aliens per season without consultation, so in fact I got in that way as well. This was what I was celebrating alongside my 70th and good notices for *Dance of Death*. A couple of days later Jeffrey Horowitz rang. He wanted a conference call with me and Arin. I looked forward to it, as probably being to do with the show's design or some such. In fact Jeffrey revealed that he'd just had confirmation that a rival *King Lear* would be playing at Brooklyn Academy of Music, some fifty metres from TFANA's new theatre, while we were rehearsing. It would feature Frank Langella in the title role with an English cast: indeed it was to be a co-production with Chichester Festival Theatre, where it would play first, in the very venue in which Chichester's director and I had sometimes discussed my doing the play. Did I, Jeffrey asked, want to proceed – not, you notice, maybe we shouldn't proceed. He sounded neutral, and I couldn't quite get at Arin's view as she was very quiet – her father Allan had just died. Quickened by panic, I swiftly said that in 1980 I had done Hamlet at exactly the same time as Jonathan Pryce and that hadn't hurt either of us or affected the gate; also, slightly implying that my life was hanging by a thread, I had to do Lear now and no later.

So we all reaffirmed our intentions. I asked Jeffrey later whether he'd come under any pressure from his Board to pull the production. Not at all, he told me, but there had been concern about its funding. Potential donors – and the two theatres would be aiming at the same people – might well ask why two neighbours were doing the same play three weeks apart, and whom they should listen to. So, to sustain his determination, he had had to see whether Arin and I would hold fast. His own view was that, whereas it would have been impossible to have such a clash on Broadway because of the scale of operations, down here *Lear* was a great enough play to survive two versions. Funders should have faith in the Polonsky, which held a quarter the number of BAM: it was a room both epic and intimate enough for Lear to consult the audience and in which it would also be possible for them to see the button on his clothes that he wants help in undoing just before he dies. He also believed that people would come because the theatre was already popular in expectation, partly because of the *Lear* package. He was rewarded by 85% ticket sales, well above the projections, and reviews which abstained from making invidious comparisons between the two shows in either direction.

And so it was that Prue Skene, formerly Executive Director of Ballet Rambert and the English Shakespeare Company (where she was thus my boss, or was I hers?), Chair of the Lottery and Dance Advisory Panels at the Arts Council and the Theatrical Management Association, the Arvon Foundation, Free Word and the Stephen Spender Trust, Commander of the British Empire, architect of that 70th birthday party and partner of my weal and woe without whom I would be even more sounding brass and tinkling cymbal than I already am, at a stroke resigned, postponed and abandoned all her freelance work for the Clore Leadership Programme and others, and with me combined Christmas shopping with letting a house and packing our bags for four months.

Her own taste in travel is audacious: in recent years she has visited North Korea, the Gobi Desert and Armenia, with which Brooklyn could hardly compare. But the length of time made up for it, as this in its small way was to be an experiment in living: fourteen weeks across a change of season in which you came to dream that home was there rather than here and you were conducting your business like citizens, not visitors. Meanwhile, shorn and ready for Lear, I got into the car taking us to Heathrow looking as if I was boarding a convict ship.

# WEEK ONE

Sixty hours ago I was sneaking out of a last-night party at the Barbican Theatre in London for the RSC's *Richard II* – all sentimental speeches and nervy quaffing and authorised self-congratulation. I'd been playing John of Gaunt – who like Mercutio in *Romeo and Juliet* and Antigonus in *The Winter's Tale*, is an early-bath part: Shakespeare perfected a line of characters who appear for the first hour or so, have one spectacular speech and then die. Perhaps he played them himself, so he was then free to keep an eye on the rest of the show, go to the pub or put the finishing touches to his next play. In this faint echo of my master, the second half of *Richard II* involved my sitting with a bottle of wine and learning page by page most of *King Lear* – the set pieces and some of the duologues mainly – in preparation for New York, much to the appreciation of my dresser. The only parts of the script I purposely postponed were some of Lear's clotted rhetoric in the first scene and the scene at Dover, in which he is, as they say, at his craziest, and is thus going to be the hardest to hold onto until I get the rhythms – I won't say of his madness, but rather of his patented sanity. I've also left much of the scenes with the Fool, because his elaborations are very difficult to understand in the abstract. Better to solve them in rehearsal, when I'll have seen the whites of his eyes and know what he and Arin Arbus need. I know who the Fool is – Jake Horowitz, who has just played Lysander in TFANA's opening production of *A Midsummer Night's Dream* (opposite my Cordelia as Hermia) and is the son of Jeffrey Horowitz, a fact that one or two of the surlier New York critics would be a little snide about – misguidedly, for Jake is very good. In fact he's broken off in his sophomore year at the California Institute of the Arts to do Lysander and now this; perhaps more to the point, his earlier schooling at La Guardia High School for the Arts allowed him to attend voice and text workshops with Cicely Berry and Andrew Wade, her successor at the RSC who now works fulltime in the US. So he is one of that new generation of American actors I mentioned who are entirely confident with and equipped for Shakespeare. The pity of it is that we in the UK don't know that: though the US imports many British classical companies, and we import many other European ones, we have only very rarely completed the compliment by bringing US Shakespeare into Britain. In which respect, the cross-cultural *Lear* we were to embark on would prove an opportunity that would be resoundingly missed by the RSC in particular, for reasons of their own. In my learning I've also skirted round the stuff with Edgar as Poor Tom (Jacob Fishel): a Poor Tom, as I found myself thirty years ago, has some *carte blanche* in how much of Shakespeare's excess of Bedlaming ought to be cut. This is a good example of being guided by what the actor finds most helpful to play.

I needed to get home early from the party because Prue and I were still only speculatively packed; I also wanted to shave off my beard in order to grow it again over the rehearsal period (actors will understand this eccentricity, which is something to do with a clean sweep). The flight to New York was early on Sunday, and, as a sop to jetlag, we were to start work on Monday afternoon rather than the morning.

It's necessary to celebrate such migrations, as it maybe is to mark all the surprises that accompany long-awaited events. A champagne breakfast the other side of Security at Heathrow Terminal Five, at Gordon Ramsays, was the merrier because it was the moment that the tenants in my house wouldn't be able to summon me back to explain the fridge or describe the fusebox again. So far so good. But the BA flight was marked, as if they were in a heated quarrel with each other, by unusual ill-humour from the surprisingly elderly cabin staff (seemingly unaware of the enormous significance of our trip), and the feeling, possibly as a consequence, that there was less leg-room than ever in Economy.

It also happened to run an hour late. This put it slap bang into competition at JFK Border Control with flights from Zurich and Beijing. That's all in a day's work; but I could hardly have expected that as we queued for fifty minutes or so, barely moving, my computer bag, unprompted by any movement, suddenly gave up the ghost, its outer pocket flapping open with a sigh, leaving the computer it housed precariously standing inside as on a narrow shelf, a whisker from falling out. It was like a bad piece of stage business. For a moment I thought I'd be arrested for seeking to detonate some novel device; but then the staff at JFK always look at you a little like that.

We'd have been going to bed in London at the time we turned off Interstate 678 onto North Conduit Avenue and then Atlantic Avenue, which cuts west from Kennedy Airport in Queens, the sole through truck route across Brooklyn. No-one could claim Atlantic Avenue as the most rapturous approach to the Brooklyn heartlands, since it is a used car lot heaven: but it does run a few blocks parallel to Fulton Street, which we'll head north across at its junction with Classon Avenue.

Brooklyn translates from the Dutch (who settled it) as "the broken land". It was dismissed by Charles Dickens as a sleeping-place for New York, and was indeed a dormitory town for Manhattan merchants in the nineteenth century; now it's so fashionable that the French have made Brooklyn an adjective. It's the home of fictional heroes such as Arthur Miller's Eddie Carbone, actuals like Bob Dylan's Joe Gallo, of Martha Wainwright and the notorious rapper B.I.G; of the film-maker Spike Lee, who has studios there; of the world heavyweight champion Mike Tyson, of Al Capone and Norman Mailer; and it's the setting of *Last Exit to Brooklyn* as well as *A Tree Grows in Brooklyn*. It's been said that if you throw a rock here you'll hit a writer – Jonathan Safran Foer, Jonathan Lethem, Paul Auster. Or the ghost of one: W.H Auden and Benjamin Britten lived with Gipsy Rose Lee in a house in Middagh Street under Brooklyn Bridge, now razed to make way for the Brooklyn-Queens Expressway (all that remains is a traffic sign reading "No Standing Anytime"). Or an Irish one: Colm Tóibín is clearly thinking of our exact area of Brooklyn in his novel of that name when he locates Elis in Cobble Hill, in a boarding house near Clinton Street – the department store where she works is on Fulton Street, and you can follow her routes. In the brilliant subsequent film the boarding-house is actually shot in Montreal but looks like a slightly earlier version of the apartment we'll be staying in. This is also the very stretch of Brooklyn where Frank McCourt lived for his first five years in his harrowing and hilarious memoir *Angela's Ashes*. He describes how his parents first met at a party on Classon Avenue; on Classon too was the playground in which he nearly fatally dropped his baby brother Malachy off a seesaw. The rooms he and his parents and siblings lived in would have been the same brownstone tenements you can see now as desirable conversions; the Italian grocer who befriends the family is across the road in Classon; it was on Myrtle Avenue (where Prue would buy me Tea tree oil for my bruising fall) that the police ran his father in for hi-jacking a truck that turned out to be full not of pork and beans but of buttons. The speakeasy from which his father didn't bring his Friday pay packet home was on Atlantic Avenue, and Mrs McCourt might run him to earth in the bars round Long Island Railroad Station or on Flatbush Avenue. These days Classon Avenue, running north and south between de Kalb Avenue and Fulton Street, is right on the edge of a wave of gentrification rolling gradually eastwards across Brooklyn. And we enter exactly the rectangle that includes these addresses as we cross Fulton Street to take possession of the desirable lower ground apartment with garden – sorry, yard – found for us by TFANA.

One of the few things I know in life is that even when it's your birthday you may still have to do the washing-up. It's a lesson King Lear could take to heart too. Imagination being a great glamoriser, it is I suppose in human nature to be disappointed by something you have long waited for. I also know that in some situations, people who are close conceal their circumstantial disappointment from each other for quite some time, since all their best efforts are being applied to making a go of it for the other person. So perhaps the truth slips out sideways this evening as Prue writes to her sister Lucy that the apartment is fine, but that the advance photographs had perhaps been taken on a quite complimentary wide-angle lens; and that there's a nice garden outside that will probably come into its own when spring does.

I agree about the garden; but for the moment the snow is thick on the ground, and it looks like a stage set for *The Snow Queen*. It's ten below and big icicles hang from the roof next door. Barely insulated wires hang out of a large junction box on the garden wall. We set off round the block in search of food, footwear inadequate to cope with banked snow and intersections of icy slush; we find the Metropolitan Supermarket, where we can get anything from organic vegetables to chicken's feet. Feeling a bit abandoned, I call Jeff Horowitz, who sounds a little surprised to hear me (I think) and seems to be in the middle of something – it turned out later that he was setting up some press interviews for me. And in fact he would become the soul of attention for the next sixteen weeks.

Classon is both homely and slightly, detectably jumpy, its project not complete. There are surprising gaps between the brownstones, as if land has been bought but the projects planned for it defeated by the recession, dark cavities where middle-class money has run out and very poor Afro-Americans stand watching what's happening to their neighbourhood. There's a big silent Episcopalian church across the road: I will never see anyone enter or leave or even unlock it. There's an allotment a few doors along in one of the cavities, diligently curated by the tenants of a rooming-house, on the stoop of which men who seem to have nowhere much to go hang about, looking with a very slight hostility at unfamiliar passers-by; but not with as much hostility as the old guys and the crazy woman outside the convenience store on the corner expend on each other all the time. A couple of blocks away, meanwhile, sits an Italian restaurant so successful that it goes under an alias and is thus almost impossible to find, unless you know that a sign saying Drugstore is actually the Locanda Vini e Olii. It's as if they didn't want you to waste time looking for them: you can rarely get a table. Coming home southwards to the apartment from Classon Avenue subway (G Line) feels a little unsafe – though there's no evidence whatever to show why, none at all – whereas coming north to it from Fulton Street, where the B26 bus stops, seems fine.

The apartment, though ostensibly in a nice conversion, has something of the same gloomy ambiguity as the street. The basement entry, through an iron gate with a security lock that seems about to fall off, takes you along a corridor past dead plants and a light that, having no switch, never goes out and reflects all night off the stone walls. A strangely unnerving unlit staircase runs up to the upper floors – who's there? I went up tonight and came face to face with someone who also jumped out of his skin – it turned out to be my own startled reflection in a mirror shrouded in the darkness. You can't put your finger on it but it's just not... easy here. A little touch of *Psycho*, especially in the night.

Perhaps the reason I feel this is that throughout this first of ninety-nine nights it sounded as if the Civil War was being refought in the bedroom. New York radiators work in the following way. Steam comes in through the larger pipe at the bottom of the radiator. The valve there has to be left open all the way, since closing it even a little will cool down the steam and turn it into water. If you don't know this and hot steam collides with colder water, there is a sort of explosion – or one of several kinds, of remarkable dynamic range: the crashing impact of hard metallic surfaces, the vicious hissing of serpents, locomotive exhalations, and the creaks, groans, grumblings, whinings and blowings of those for whom the conflict is seemingly not going so well.

Awake at 4 am, I consider the position. The radiators are hinting at four months of disturbed sleep while I tackle the toughest role in Shakespeare and Prue prepares hers as New York resident with special responsibility. All hyped up, I call the TFANA office as it opens to find that their Associate, who saw us into the apartment last night, no longer works for them – and as it was on a Sunday that she met us, perhaps she didn't even then. In fact she had confided that she was hoping for promotion to General Manager. I'm touched as I reflect on the unhappiness that would lead her to express such an ambition when she had already resigned because of its disappointment.

Instead I find myself talking to Web Begole, who has already supplied us with a choice of three apartments (with pictures and measurements and reassurances about security), cheap cell phones (no SIM card, much cheaper, all calls charged by time not destination), bus and subway routes, and whose fault none of this is. And now I'm saying we may have to be moved. As he replies calmly that he'll talk to the landlord and get back to me (without the reassurance that we can move if necessary) I sense a mash of emotions in his voice, not to mention the eyes cast heavenwards. I pile in with a bit more: neither the TV nor the WiFi work, and the temperature in the apartment is set at 75 degrees on a thermostat that I can't get at to change, as it is rather sternly locked in a little perspex cabinet on the sitting-room wall with no key. Meanwhile there is a note in the welcome pack that we must on no account open the windows and let the very cold air in. I think Web thinks I'm only doing this for some dame, but in fact Prue is far more philosophical than I am. And of course we didn't move, but we may have been the last straw for Web, who soon after moved to Madison Avenue and the world of high finance.

Cumulatively all this is making me feel like a bad-tempered and snobbish tourist rather than someone who has often been to New York before. But in another way I'm getting a flavour of what it's like to be an irritable, querulous and imperious old gentleman who will not be – is in fact frightened of being – gainsaid, but who also suspects that his sense of entitlement may be a bit of a fraud. So that's a good start: all I have to do now is learn the lines.

Complaint parked, we plunge from furnace to ice. Today's first rehearsal call is on the 9th Floor of the Duke on 42nd Street, where we played *Love is my Sin* and *Lear* had its workshop. We'll be here a week before moving down to TFANA's Polonsky Theatre in Brooklyn for the extraordinary boon of working on stage for six weeks as the set goes up around us, there being no performances since *A Midsummer Night's Dream* closed – a scheduling that would cause a British producer to need to sit down but is in the exceptional gift of TFANA in their new home.

A long-awaited event is turning out to be a normal working day of small inconveniences, bad traffic and changes of plan. The Superbowl Boulevard, the four-day party that precedes the annual Championship game in the National Football League, features tourist shopping, toboggan rides, video projections in Macy's, autograph sessions and much else; to accommodate a million-odd visitors fourteen midtown blocks will be closed to traffic, until either the Seattle Seahawks (rank outsiders) or the Denver Broncos (the reigning champions) have lifted the Vince Lombardi Trophy (the outsiders won, resoundingly). Midtown being gridlocked, the only practical way out of the small city of Times Square subway station for the Duke is from a particular exit on its west side.

My nerves tend to be deflected into secondary symptoms, like a certain imperiousness which is really fear. Today we do the readthrough and nothing else. As I reach my first line:

Attend the lords of France and Burgundy, Gloucester

I think intensely of my Mum. Well, of course. Then, after many pleasantries, I come home and, as you know, fall down in the street. Lying there and feeling more cheerful, I review my situation again. Knees, elbows, ribs. Well, the knee is a horribly complicated item; you could survive Baker's Cysts, arthritis, all sorts of inflammations, even replacement, only to crack it open on a Brooklyn sidewalk. It also bruises very heavily and heals slowly. So it will obviously be hard for me to kneel now, but then Lear doesn't do much of that – though I suppose he might, ironically, to Regan and Goneril for the maintenance of his hundred knights, and whole-heartedly to Cordelia when he rediscovers her in Act Four. However we won't be rehearsing them for a bit. He doesn't elbow people very much either, though God knows the elbow is complicated too, even if barely used. On the other hand a punctured lung is not the best place to generate the raging tirades of Lear. We'll have to see. Prue races out into the unknown in the middle of cooking soup to buy Tea tree oil at thirty dollars a bottle. Now its scent always reminds me of attending the lords of France and Burgundy.

There's a message tonight from our landlord. He explains what I already know about the violent consequence of steam meeting the cooling water in the pipes, and the need to drain any water lest the pipes break, as they did recently in the Top Suite. As for the heat, if ever we feel that the apartment is consistently too hot or too cold, we should just give a call and he will ask Enrique to adjust the thermostat. By which time, I reflect, the weather may have changed.

The thermostat is perhaps the real enemy to peace, since it decides what the ideal temperature in the house should be and adjusts it one way or the other. Yes, in the whole house: the living room of our apartment dictates the ideal throughout, and of course opinions may – and will – vary in the other three. The problem about our opening a window to relieve the heat is that the thermostat will climb to compensate and then everyone in the house will boil.

## *Tuesday 28ᵗʰ January, 2014*

By next morning, however, there has been an exquisite refinement to the noise of the heating. Benjamin had implied that they like the heat upstairs, but it strikes me they don't need it, since, noisier than the radiators, there is a sex god up there and the ceiling is thin. Yes, that kind of noisier. Great rhythmic cries and heavings in two male registers flood through the economically insulated ceiling into our sedate lovenest, with short pauses seemingly featuring forced marches to and fro across the room, though I don't quite see – and don't like to think – how that fits in. The desolate feeling, regardless of your own circumstance, of listening as on the radio to the pleasure of others, is well-known of course. This time I imagine the bloodied fangs of a sexual Dracula, in a salon awash with candlelight and incense. I realise my imagination is straying into early Harold Pinter territory, where the person in the next room of the rooming house, or watching it from across the road, or waiting in the garden, develop a terrifying plausibility but no features – so that they can be confidently fashioned into revengers, unmotivated assailants and ill-wishers of every complexion.

The effect is oddly enhanced because of the switchless light in the stoney hall; it will remain on throughout our stay, framing an ill-fitting door in our second bedroom with a penumbra of light: looking across at it from the bed, you could be convinced that some perhaps celestial, perhaps devilish manifestation lies beyond it.

And so, stinking of Tea tree oil and Arnica, both too hot and too cold and with melting-snow feet, I go to the Duke, where for the first time the cast and the full staff meet, and Jeff Horowitz is hosting the party.

## JEFFREY HOROWITZ

Good morning. One humid summer's day in 1979, I was moving into a small apartment that had two rooms – one for cooking, eating and sleeping, and a bathroom. The only distinctive feature was a parquet floor which I sanded and varnished to bring out the wood's colour and grain. When the varnishing was complete, I stepped into the bathroom to shower. I had just taken off my shoes and socks when I heard a whoosh followed by a loud pop. I looked out the bathroom door and saw flames from the floors to the ceiling. There was no time. I had to get out. The only way was through fire and my bare feet got third-degree burns. I had surgery and spent six weeks in the hospital.

It turned out that the can of varnish had been mislabelled. It should have warned to turn off the pilot light, a permanent open flame within the kitchen stove, which had in fact ignited the highly flammable fumes of varnish which then ignited the wet floors. I sued and won. After lawyers and doctors were paid, I had an insurance settlement of $50,000.

I had trained as an actor at the London Academy of Music and Dramatic Art (LAMDA) from 1968 to 1971. It was in the UK that I first saw plays from the world repertoire alongside commercial theatre: Shakespeare, European and American authors, musicals, drama and comedies. I saw there was no one way of doing these plays. Some productions had actors who worked together over time in companies like the Royal Shakespeare Company; some were individual shows. I could attend the RSC for twelve shillings – only 60 cents. I climbed the stairs high up into the balcony to those seats. Though the actors were the size of postage stamps and I saw only the tops of their heads, I could enter the imaginations of great authors through their language. Like Thisbe in *A Midsummer Night's Dream*, my soul was in the sky. The seat was cheap but the experience priceless: for a few hours, I soared free, and when the play was over and I went back down, I was a different person from when I came in. I had also heard for the first time actors expressing the language of these authors as if the words were deeply personal to them. I wanted to be able to express great texts like this.

After LAMDA, I returned to America hoping to become part of a theatre company doing Shakespeare and other great plays. But I soon discovered there were very few companies like this in America and, in any event, I wasn't being hired by them. So I became an actor in search of a classical theatre. I acted occasionally and made ends meet by working on Broadway – as a waiter.

Nearly a decade after I had finished at LAMDA, I used my accident insurance money to begin TFANA. Inspired by the artists I saw in London, TFANA's mission then, as now, was to be a modern classical theatre dedicated to language and ideas. We would play to a diverse audience including students from NYC Public Schools. Tickets would be reasonably priced, and artists' development would be supported. The name, Theatre for a New Audience, was a mouthful, but the word "New" modified "Theatre" and "Audience" and referred to something freshly discovered. We wanted to reach audiences interested in the connection between Shakespeare and other major plays so TFANA has presented Euripides, Molière, Edward Bond and Harley Granville-Barker, and Americans such as Rinde Eckert, Adrienne Kennedy, Suzan-Lori Parks and Wallace Shawn. We have toured nationally and internationally, played once on Broadway, and produced in eighteen different Off-Broadway theatres in Manhattan. We have worked with remarkable artists such as F. Murray Abraham, Arin Arbus, Cicely Berry, Peter Brook, Bill Camp, Fiasco Theater, Peter Hall, Kathryn Hunter, Jefferson Mays, Kristine Nielsen, Michael Pennington, Mark Rylance, Bartlett Sher, Julie Taymor, John Douglas Thompson, Darko Tresnjak, John Turturro, Robert Neff Williams and Robert Woodruff.

However in 1996 it became clear that without a permanent home, TFANA wouldn't survive. Space for the arts in Manhattan was drying up, and it was becoming more and more difficult to rent Off-Broadway theatres (defined as having up to 499 seats, but ideally up to 299 since between the two figures issues arise with the unions and stage hands). Because TFANA played in different theatres, it didn't have roots in any one community, and so fundraising was very hard. And, if we had a successful production, we couldn't extend because the theatre was rented to another group. Above all we wanted to build a home in which the architecture supported the art.

The design of TFANA's main stage (named the Samuel H. Scripps after one of our main friends and benefactors) was inspired by the Cottesloe at the National Theatre in London. We asked the architect Hugh Hardy and his firm H3 Collaboration to work with us, along with two theatre consultants: Jean-Guy LeCat, who had collaborated for many years with Peter Brook, and Richard Pilbrow and his firm Theatre Projects, who worked on the original Cottesloe. This would be a uniquely flexible space for New York City with great acoustics. As did the Cottesloe, it would marry an Elizabethan courtyard space with a modern black box – and would have seven possible configurations. Artists could shape the relationship between the stage and the audience: as there would be no fixed architectural perspective, there was no one way of doing the plays. I want to say that this dream would have been impossible without the support and deep friendship of Ted Rogers, the Chairman of TFANA from 1992 to 2011.

After years of looking for and failing to find a space in Manhattan, we learned that Harvey Lichtenstein, who had led the Brooklyn Academy of Music so brilliantly, was developing an arts district in downtown Brooklyn adjacent to BAM. Harvey asked us to consider building our theatre there: the City of New York would be our partner. Many were sceptical, but Ted, Sam, Hugh and myself believed it was possible and accepted his offer.

This was 2000. Our new home was completed in 2013. Twice the site was changed as we completed our designs. The third and final site was on a parking lot on which was once the Granada, a luxury hotel where teams playing against the Brooklyn Dodgers stayed. It then became a welfare hotel so infamous that the city tore it down. Jake, my son, pointed out that the theater is located on Ashland Place – the place of ashes. I got to pick the number of the address. It had to begin with 26 and I could choose the final digit. I chose 2 – 262 Ashland Place, as 2+6+2 adds up to 10 and $10 million was how much we had to raise by the building's opening if we were to pay for its running. I wanted to keep staring at that number to remind us to keep trying.

However by January 2013 we had not raised the $10 million, and opening was only ten months away. One day, Julie Taymor, a friend and colleague, sent me an email invitation to a party at the public television station WNET that she couldn't attend: it was planned to celebrate a Series on Shakespeare that WNET was broadcasting. The party was being underwritten by Howard Milstein, a philanthropist I wanted to meet, and I noticed that Trevor Nunn was being flown over to host it. I asked Michael Pennington, who knew Trevor, if he would ask him to introduce me to Milstein.

Trevor agreed and I went to the party. Trevor introduced me and Milstein listened for a minute and then said to write him. By a series of improbable events it turned out that Milstein himself was not interested, but it led to my introduction to an extraordinary philanthropist, Dr. Leonard Polonsky, who has a Charitable Foundation that, as much as the arts, supports medical and scientific research and international developments in higher education. In March 2013, he gave $10 million to TFANA, and in recognition of the gift we named the building the Polonsky Shakespeare Center. I wouldn't have got this money if Michael Pennington had not persuaded Trevor Nunn to introduce me to Howard Milstein.

And so, after thirty-three years of an itinerant life and mostly playing around Manhattan, TFANA opened its first permanent home in October, the first theatre built for classic drama in New York City since the Vivian Beaumont at the Lincoln Center in 1965. Our inaugural season has opened with *A Midsummer Night's Dream*, directed by Julie Taymor with music by Elliot Goldenthal; now *King Lear*, directed by Arin Arbus and featuring Michael Pennington, is our second show.

In this cast of twenty-two, twelve of the actors, the stage managers, all of the designers, the composer, the fight director, dramaturge, casting director and voice director, as well as many of the staff, have worked with Theatre for a New Audience before. So there is already a kind of family with shared values. In 1991, before 42$^{nd}$ Street was spruced up, we produced *Romeo and Juliet* at an unrenovated movie theatre called the Victory, the first Shakespeare on 42$^{nd}$ Street in sixty years. Mark Dold, who is now Oswald in *Lear*, played Tybalt and killed Tim Stickney (now Kent) who was Mercutio; now Tim and Mark will once again assault each other. Forty years ago, Chris McCann and I were summer apprentices at the New Jersey Shakespeare Festival: in acting class Chris, now Gloucester in our *Lear*, played Edgar to my Gloucester. Robert Langdon Lloyd, who is graciously playing several small roles in *Lear*, was Edgar in Peter Brook's film opposite Paul Scofield. This is a group which has discovered the depth and power of Shakespeare: there is enormous experience and talent here.

Why is TFANA doing the play? We're not consciously trying to do *Lear* differently from the six other major productions of it that are or will be playing in the U.S., Canada or Britain. This inaugural season is called *Words, Words, Words*, and has a Shakespeare comedy, tragedy and a modern play by Ionesco from the Theatre of the Absurd. What unites these three plays is that in all of them, there is no one fixed objective reality. In all of them, characters struggle to figure out what is true.

At this moment Michael Pennington has played leading roles in twenty-two of Shakespeare's plays; Theatre for a New Audience has produced thirty-two, but never *King Lear*. I asked him why he wanted to do it, and with Arin.

## MICHAEL PENNINGTON

I'd been asked to do Lear before in the UK – if you've played Hamlet, Macbeth, Richard II and the others, people expect you'll be getting ready for Lear – but you have to be careful and not do it just because it's there, only when it really sets your blood running. You probably also need to be the right age, and, to be sure, physically strong enough to deal with the part. The great and very eccentric English actor Ralph Richardson once said that you can be wandering along quite content, the sun is out and the daffodils are blooming and the birds are singing, and nothing is wrong and – ah! You get your foot caught in a Lear.

Well, I got my foot caught in this particular bramble at breakfast one day about six years ago, when I was playing Richard Strauss the composer. I suddenly realised out of the blue how much I wanted to do Lear and that meant I was probably ready for it. In any case most decisions in theatre are based on hunches. As things developed, or rather jolted along amidst other ideas, I got an intuition that I wanted to work with Arin if she wanted to work with me; ever since our meeting in 2010, it was obvious to me that this young American woman and this English veteran felt the same way about many things.

## JEFFREY HOROWITZ

Over the four years I've been having this Lear conversation with Arin and Michael, I've also spoken to artists who have done the play. Peter Brook said it was like Beckett. For me, there is the same rawness and ferocity in *Lear* as in Greek drama: then again Cicely Berry says it is the greatest Marxist play ever written. As it was also because of Peter Brook that I met Michael who then met Arin, I want to read you a few words of his, from a speech he gave about the oldest theatre in Rome, the Teatro Valle, which the government had shut down and were going to turn into a supermarket. Artists occupied the theatre and won it back. Brook was asked to speak about this and he did, on YouTube. He begins by saying it's great you saved the theatre, and goes on to talk about this play:

> "In *King Lear*, one very extraordinary man's entire existence is concentrated into his last years and that in turn is concentrated into three and a half hours; the situations are real life situations but all the shit has been drained out of them. The genius of a great writer is taking away the inessential and making the essential appear. In this way in *King Lear* – the people, the situations – all the unnecessary is boiled away by Shakespeare and then you have the events which come one after another, each event leading directly to the next as it so rarely does in everyday life…. There isn't a year to wait or even a week or even perhaps half an hour before the next event. In a film or a play it has to be second by second, otherwise it becomes a bore. So you have these great elements of concentration which enable life – whether it is a human life, a social life, a political problem, a relationship of a man and a woman or a man and a man, fathers and sons, mothers and daughters – all those questions, on a small scale or a very large scale can be concentrated in time and space.

> I always feel that a theatre, particularly an indoor theatre, is like an image of the human brain. That is why we are particularly attached to the Bouffes du Nord, because the shape of the Bouffes – those high rising columns that lead to a domed ceiling which can gather

the whole audience into one circular glowing space – is like a brain, and within this brain there are not only thoughts, but also feelings and also actions. There are also silences. But above all there is a capacity to feel levels of finer and finer quality that give more and more sense and meaning to the human situation."

Finally I asked Arin why she wanted to do the play, and with Michael.

## ARIN ARBUS

I first saw him on stage in *Love is my Sin* and was knocked out by his sensitivity with and command of Shakespeare's language; it was also clear from his performance that he was able to create complex and vivid relationships onstage. But how do you create a hurricane on that stage? Or a war? How do you decide the right period in which to set a four-hundred-year-old play that refers back to Jupiter, Hecate, Merlin, but is as experimental and timely as anything written today? Should the story be situated in a specific world, or should we invent a world for it? Is there a particular time period which illuminates it? Should it be happening right now? The characters encounter the harshest physical realities, so which elements should we be reproducing in exact detail? Do we need blood? Dirt? Wind? Rain? What kinds of weapons should we use? Swords, guns? Both? What should the actors wear? Robes? Pumpkin breeches? Shirts and pants? What should the set look like and how should it function? Is there music in this world, and if so, what kind? Is it live or recorded?

These questions have stayed unresolved in me for the years leading up to these last few weeks. For me *King Lear* simply cuts to the heart of the matter, and my desire to do it is instinctive, personal and intangible. I've been thinking about it for five years, working on it every once in a while with actors and students, prisoners and laymen. I've seen probably ten productions on stage and film; I've read scholarly articles about the text and reviews of seminal productions. What I do know is that this play mercilessly depicts the simultaneous fracturing of the state, the family and the self.

Riccardo Hernandez has designed some two hundred productions all over the States, in Paris and Vienna, Oslo, Moscow, Dublin, Warsaw, in London and on Broadway. And he lectures at Princeton. Yet, like many set designers, he is modest and reserved. He presents his model, citing as his influences the Holocaust Museum, Didi Huberman's photographs from Auschwitz *Images In Spite of All* and Claude Lanzmann's film *Shoah*; the architecture of Daniel Liebeskind, Russian film in general, Hieronymus Bosch, Shostakovich and Caravaggio.

## RICCARDO HERNANDEZ

While we were working together on *Much Ado About Nothing* at TFANA in 2013, Arin Arbus and I discussed plays we were eager to do. She mentioned there was a possibility of her directing *King Lear* quite soon; we started talking about how we might tackle it.

The project once slated, we discussed how to create the right space for a drama both intimate and cosmic. We talked through the dynamics of the new Polonsky Theatre and which configuration would prove best: proscenium, long or short thrusts, or arena? We met at the theatre while it was still under construction. This was invaluable; we were able to see the space totally gutted, just a shell without the seating. One time Jeffrey Horowitz brought us a photograph of a nuclear rocket standing amidst its control panels inside a large hangar – not for us to represent in any way literally, but as a visual metaphor. How does one show absolute power, with its visceral thrust, disintegrating into the void – in a limited space? Can it be done without the ideas shrinking into sheer illustration? How do you present the almost unrepresentable?

First I started thinking of emblems of this power: flags, thrones, carved texts, monuments. But there was also something in that nuclear warhead, menacing and obscene, which led us to think that perhaps a totem or a monumental slab of steel could be a good point of departure. I began to make an elemental steel world, ancient and modern at the same time. I started looking at military hedgehogs, like the ones deployed on the Atlantic Wall on the beaches of Normandy during World War II. From them you get a sense of some prehistoric animal, sexual and menacing.

My first modelled ideas were based on these thoughts, but Arin felt they were too specific, not transformational enough for the wide arc of the play.

So I then thought about symmetry and order, geometric shapes that represent perfect equilibrium. A monolithic square slab of metal proudly anchored on a deep rectangle made out of the same steel. The slab to represent the state, a patriarchal, all-powerful society emblazoned with archaic symbols (perhaps commandments); a war machine, its surface oxidised by time, and, like Wotan's spear, scarred with the contracts his power derives from. As Lear divides his kingdom and the state is no longer intact, the slab begins to fall, until its inevitable collapse. The storm could be played on its surface.

The final act reveals a black room, a space where personal possessions are removed and final goodbyes are said.

It is in this nothingness that Lear meets Cordelia again.

All that remains at the end is a complete absence of humanity. We wanted nothing illustrative, just bodies left onstage atop the slab. The surrounding world is simply the audience silently witnessing another historic cataclysm within the black walls of the Polonsky Theatre itself.

I must say that after working on productions like this it's hard to go back.

## MICHAEL PENNINGTON

Tonight at home – having fixed the TV almost by accident, or perhaps by the law of averages during a great deal of thumbwork on the remote – we watch Barack Obama on the podium in the House of Representatives giving the State of the Union address. A Democrat, his Vice-President Joe Biden, sits behind him on his right, while John Boehner, the Republican Speaker of the House on his left, offers a beady eye and very feeble handclaps to the proceedings. It's much the same staging as I tentatively imagine for Act One Scene One. There the resemblance of King Lear to Barack Obama ends, but maybe the passing thought has done its work as I think about this famously difficult scene. Imagine if the President suddenly burst out, went off script and played an embarrassing trick, requiring Malia Ann to declare how much she loved him and then attacking Sasha for refusing to participate? The darkest hinterland breaks into the room as, barely recognisable now, he invokes the sacred radiance of the sun, Hecate, the orbs, Apollo and Jupiter. Horror! Of just the kind we want.

For three days now we will sit at a long table, fourteen principals and a further group of eight male actors nominated as the ensemble – there primarily to play Lear's riotous knights, servants and messengers. These eight are not members of American Equity. This is not quite the same as in English practice, where despite the disabling of Equity's closed shop in the 1980s, productions are generally mounted with paid-up members – and sometimes trained professionals who've abstained from membership (and are under pressure from the likes of me to join). On occasion you might also have local amateurs, there to swell the crowd, as the townspeople of Canterbury do in *Murder in the Cathedral*. Meanwhile the RSC's recent innovation of mounting an entire touring production of *A Midsummer Night's Dream* in which amateurs in each town play the Mechanicals (the BBC are making a series about it jovially called *The Best Bottoms in the Land*) is a response to increasing insistence from the Arts Council that producing theatres must have a policy towards amateur actors. Several years ago I attended a meeting between the Artistic Director of West Yorkshire Playhouse and the Arts Council, in which, although prepared to defend himself against any number of things, he was quite unready for this looping ball of a question and was castigated for not having a response. Now the policy is almost mandatory. Whether you think this admirable or ridiculous, and whether you think the RSC is wise to assume that the amateur actors in the *Dream* should be played by amateur actors because they're famously and comically not so good – it's definitely here to stay.

The rules in the US are that if you have a minimum of eleven Equity members in a cast you can go ahead and hire, more cheaply, a limited number of non-Equity members too: if you have more than eleven you can hire as many as you like. *King Lear* has by the best reckoning fourteen principals, so in addition we could have had as many unruly knights (even a hundred as in the text) to attend on Lear. Naturally they must be identified in the programme and on posters, and of course be fit for purpose.

For us, Benjamin Cole was perhaps Lear's most unruly Knight.

## BENJAMIN COLE

This production was to be a very positive experience for me. I cannot really say whether the relationship between the Equity and Non-Equity members was standard or not, as I have only been in one other show that featured a non-Equity ensemble. But it didn't strike me as unusual in any way: the level of interaction between the two groups seemed to be based more on personality than anything else. Lilly Englert (Cordelia) and Jake Horowitz (the Fool) both spent a fair amount of time with us non-Equity folks due to similarity in age, while Rachel Pickup (Goneril), Mark Dold (Oswald), and Chandler Williams (Edmund) – who had become a bit of trio over the course of the show – spent a lot of time with us because for a great deal of it they were in the downstairs lounge area, near our dressing room. The true adopted son of the non-Equity fellas was Bob Langdon Lloyd (the Doctor). He was the only member of the Equity cast to join in on the after-show party that one of us threw at his loft in Bushwick. Bob had at least a good forty years on everyone else there but you would be amazed at just how well he fitted in.

Most importantly though, I thought the Equity members treated us Non-Equity members with respect. I loved it that Arin allowed for us to come and observe the read-throughs and table work if we wished and I loved that we were universally treated as valuable members of the production. However, one negative thing that I will say is that while no one goes into theatre for the money, in New York City it is incredibly difficult to live on the salary given the fact that even the cheapest of apartments charges at least $600 for rent.

## MICHAEL PENNINGTON

As we sat around the table, the fourteen and the eight, there was indeed no distinction as to who had the right to speak: many of the non-Equity actors had done as much preparation and had as much to say as the others. On the other hand the Equity representative who visited the company, whom you might have expected to be briefed and also to be recruiting, also had much to say but admitted she didn't even know what the production was, and certainly wasn't aware that there was any kind of temporary interloper such as myself present. She asked me when my annual subscription was due for renewal, why I was unaware of Equity's plans and programmes currently under discussion, and why they hadn't had a certain form back from me.

Arin hunched in a chair as if to protect herself, while bit by bit we read every line of the script. Everybody came to understand every word. Naturally this shaded into some tentative discussion of character and motive, as it did so explosively in the 2012 workshop, but really these were all gestures. To anyone outside the room, this process is essentially uninteresting, like clearing the ground, piling up the bricks, assembling the tools and measuring up. Like many ceremonies in the theatre it has a secondary purpose, of getting a disparate group of people to begin talking to and listening to each other, with the play, their nominal subject, as a decoy. It's a sort of small talk. Of course actors fundamentally understand each other; but this is where they really lock onto the sensibilities around them. Today I note some shyness towards me; an insistent checking (these actors are far from passive) that the director sees their part pretty much as they already do, since otherwise it could be a tough few weeks; a bit of actorishness in some of the vocal stylings, probably due to nervousness. I deal with the apprehensions as I generally do – by plunging right into the practicalities – how this and where that. This is probably a form of self-protection, an evasion of perfectly constructive discussion, but then I find too much analysis to be a sort of evasion.

What there's no shortage of is friendliness, and I soon stop imagining that everyone in the room is wondering about the stranger in their midst and how he'll shape up. Or that some of them may have a friend who could have played Lear, or feel that they could themselves, or soon will do, or are unresolved about how much they like the English way, if there is such a thing, and whether it should be imported. Still, I know the curiosity is there, and there is much apologetic sympathy about noisy radiators. And, as the week goes by, quite a bit of obligatory decrying of the Frank Langella Lear, which will still be playing at BAM when we arrive at the Polonsky next week. Some of this may be sincere, and I simper, demurringly. On the whole the women are, as women will be, more forthright: Bianca Amato (Regan) is in tears already in Act Four, and Rachel Pickup has immediately become like the friend her father Ronnie has always been to me. But when the first lunch break comes it is the loyal Earl of Kent (Timothy Stickney) and the treacherous Edmund (Chandler Williams) who sweep me up and take me to a short-order Korean restaurant. Chandler is something of an anglophile, having played in the Sam Mendes/ Kevin Spacey *Richard III* and in Michael Grandage's *Mary Stuart*, while Tim has been up and down the East Coast for some years playing Shakespeare – which I think somewhat eases his frustration, as a strong and good-looking actor, that he hasn't at the moment done much film – a thing that matters to him both as an actor and as an African American.

Peter Brook is in New York, speaking tonight at BAM after a screening of his film, *The Tightrope*. I want to see him, not least because one of the things that got me Equity approval was an extraordinary endorsement from him.

Peter is viewed either with embarrassing idolatry or, increasingly as time goes by, as an object of nostalgia. The film, directed by his son Simon, shows several workshop sessions he did in Paris. Like most such exposés, it runs some risk of gaucheness, despite his overwhelming charisma. The talk that follows, in which he is essentially interviewed by Simon, reminds me what a compact he has with his audience, part of which is to dispel any sense of the guru. He's always simpler than they expect; his warmth and humour completely disarm them. His stage coups are often achieved with the utmost economy, by a turn of the light, a sound or a shift in someone's performance; in himself too he always speaks simply, and won't rise to a query he can't do justice to or which he senses could lead him into mockability. This ducking of big questions becomes collusive: we rightly see him as a practical and instinctive man, not a magus who has always provoked a slightly messianic vocabulary in the press, where he has sometimes been described as "alighting" or "pausing" in London or New York, say, rather than just changing planes.

There are many ways of being with Peter Brook; I am a friend who views his shtick with affection. That is not, of course, to denigrate a very great artist, only to say we all have our favourite memories of a genius of theatre, and the personal ones may be pleasant to hear. I first met him in 1966, when I took part in a staged reading of Peter Weiss's *The Investigation*, in which I played a Nazi and he wisely advised me to come across as likeable. I met him again in 1978 when I worked with his wife Natasha Parry in Euripides' *Hippolytus* at Stratford. Giving himself a new role, Peter was the perfect camp follower – encouraging, open and loyal. When, seven or eight years later, I was founding my own English Shakespeare Company with Michael Bogdanov, he made a spirited and shameless attempt to seduce me from my own newborn with an offer to play in the English version of *The Mahabharata*, of which like most people I was a great admirer. Having worked this seam in our conversations as long as we both had patience for, he instead invited me to help him with the English auditions for it. I would read in, we would chit-chat in between sessions, sometimes about the actors, sometimes not. Afterwards he said how pleasant it had all been to "work" with me; it certainly was for me. I met him for suppers in Paris and London, sometimes with Natasha and sometimes not, and he came to see Otway's *Venice Preserv'd* at the National, which he had directed with Gielgud and Scofield, and which I was now doing with Ian McKellen. When my father died, he was among the very first to commiserate.

Anecdotally best of all: he once walked me and my son Mark through the woods at Rambouillet, his and Natasha's country home, and suddenly stopped to draw our attention to a rusty tin stuck in its course down a rapid, tinkling stream. We stood looking at it for quite some time. When Mark and I had got as much as we could out of it, we ventured to look to see how it was that Peter was still inspired by it. We found that the stream was not the only tinkle: Peter was solemnly and unabashedly urinating into the river. It was my funniest moment with him, a final antidote to all the alighting and the pausing.

When he directed me in *Love is my Sin* he gave me, with great affection, the toughest time – repeating, repeating, wondering why he could not exactly read what I was thinking during the single moment of breath between one word and another, on either side of one comma, between one line and the next. He was in much sciatic pain, and his sight was so poor that he didn't always recognise me at a couple of feet's distance, but he was still able to tell from the centre of the stalls in quite a large theatre – that is, at a distance of some twenty metres – that I was doing something unadvisable with my gesturing arm. This visual unpredictability is one of the features of macular degeneration; in his case it suggested to me that he had arranged for his visual acuity to be adjusted to concentrate above all on seeing actors on a stage.

During that time together he encouraged me with reflections on his time with Paul Scofield in *Lear*, very much in the manner of the three of us being equal partners across time and space. He was by then nearly eighty-five. Sometimes he and Natasha (whom I was playing opposite once more) and I would start the subway ride home after the show from 42$^{nd}$ Street to 56$^{th}$ Street, and these two quite frail old parties would leap up at about 47$^{th}$ or 48$^{th}$, quite a rumbustious area, because they suddenly felt peckish; they would wander the streets in search of a hamburger, or at least have a pleasant walk of several blocks home.

The whole experience was worth waiting fifty-four years for. And now Peter is ninety. I heard him on the radio recently in a reunion documentary with survivors (literally) from his legendary *Dream*. Asked at one point about the effect of ageing on his work, he said with the utmost calm that one keeps going, one continues and of course one day it will all have to stop, and there an end. It was as if, having given adequate thought to the matter, he had decided the time of his own dying. A few weeks later his beloved Natasha was dead.

My testimony is one of thousands, and no more partial and incomplete than any other. It is of course a privilege to know him and to feel the renewed rush of enthusiasm, of love for the job, appetite for work and good fellowship, that he always brings into the room with him, together with his Puckish, pragmatic and worldly air. And now I see him coming towards me down the stairs at BAM, with a little help. Nevertheless, when I greet him he looks up immediately, sees me and, as if in mid sentence, adds an elegant greeting to the seamless arc that he's described for years. This presence of mind is entirely typical, and he also of course remembers Prue, whom he has only met on two brief occasions in the past.

### Sunday, 2$^{nd}$ February.

In Café Angelique in the West Village Prue asks me over a necessary hot chocolate why actors want to play King Lear when he is so unsympathetic. I understand the question well. Why should you care about this terrible old man?

I would say Lear is another example of Shakespeare pulling off the near-impossible, manoeuvring the audience from dislike to deep sympathy – as he does, for instance, with Macbeth and Richard II. Invariably, the trick is in the monosyllables –

> You do me wrong to take me out of the grave…

and in the humble, quite homely tone of voice:

> Why, this would make a man a man of salt
> To use his eyes for garden waterpots
> Ay, and for laying autumn's dust.

As he and his syllables shrink, Lear comes into focus as someone like ourselves. An inner life we didn't expect peers out, a sense of humour, a willingness to clown to make his point, even the features not of a tyrant but of some great big baby. This is why to present Lear (or Macbeth) as an eastern European dictator closes the play down: it becomes some kind of political anecdote. Who, after all, cares about what Ceauşescu or Stalin suffered? But Prue's question wakes me up – we must let the sunlight in wherever we can, find any moments when Lear shines, before the storm batters into him. We must account too for his extreme popularity amongst his own generation.

The chocolate is necessary because the cold this first free Sunday, though liberating, is vicious. It's also as if we were meeting afresh: Prue has staked out the Brooklyn Museum this week and revisited the site of 9/11 – real life and death. This morning we've walked down the High Line, my grumpiness quite gone now I'm no longer catching up with myself but inhabiting this new semi-familiar place. In some sense our walk is a homage to Jane Jacobs, the writer and activist who is a legend here – not only for the High Line, which she did much to godmother since she felt it would be a comfort for someone living in a skyscraper to have "eyes on the street", but for her resistance to the reckless urban renewal of the 1950s and 1960s which nearly destroyed Greenwich Village. Reviled by *The New York Times* but vigorously supported by the new *Village Voice*, her reward at one point was to be arrested and charged with disorderly conduct.

The High Line, planted ten years ago on the old El Line as an elevated urban park or "greenway", runs for a mile and a half down the west side of Manhattan from the Javits Convention Center on 34th Street through the Meatpacking District and Chelsea to Gansevoort Street at the top edge of the Village. It gets nearly five million visitors every year, who can rest at the 23rd Street Lawn and enjoy the seesaw-like benches at 11th Street, or others which make xylophone sounds when tapped. It all looks great to me this morning, although most detail is covered in thick snow.

Warmed by hot chocolate, we turn down Bleecker Street, which seems now to be mostly shoe shops and a Costa or two; I am elatedly dissolving it forty-five years to 1969, when I remember it as the hub of folk-singing New York:

> I'm standing on the corner of Bleecker and McDougall,
> Wondering which way to go...

In this reverie I'm again bustling down the street quite late in the evening (Nicol Williamson's *Hamlet*, in which I'm Laertes at the Lunt Fontanne Theatre, doesn't come down until 11pm). I'm heading for the Bitter End Club, in the hope of catching Tim Hardin sing his last set of the night – even though it was always a question whether he'd turn up because of an unreliability almost as great as his talent. Or he might be at the Café au Go Go across the road (where Lenny Bruce was arrested on obscenity charges in 1964 as he stepped off the stage by undercover police who'd been watching the show, perhaps with enjoyment). Fred Neil or Karen Dalton, forgotten names now but great singers of the time, might turn up, or I could prop up a bar with John Sebastian of the Lovin' Spoonful, and wait for Hardin, the Black Sheep Boy of his own song.

As for the *Hamlet*, such is the shakebag of memory that my stick now turns up a series of snapshots only. I can't remember at all how our show was adapted from the Round House in London where it had previously played. I've no memory at all of the flight to New York, or the one to California later. But I do remember the mad excitement of arriving in New York for the first time – and of working on Broadway, of course. I know that on the Press Night one of our producers left not a bottle of champagne on every actor's place but a bag of Acapulco Gold marijuana, which startled some of the company's older members. Almost the only ones of us still alive are Francesca Annis, myself and Anjelica Huston (then 18). Those of the English cast who stayed home after the London run have survived a bit better.

In the spirit of the times I tried to make a Rake's Progress of it all without an Ann Truelove at the end of my rainbow. All young men need a little hero-worship, or sometimes antihero-worship. So I was spending my evenings with Nicol, a master of passionate precision and the only actor I know of who could play Hamlet faultlessly on a bottle of wine, like a latter-day Edmund Kean. This was not so many years after I used to watch Paul Scofield, an inspiration innocent of pharmaceuticals, plucking new visions out of the air as Timon of Athens at Stratford. The improbable third party in my trilogy of influence was Hardin, by far and away the most moving singer-songwriter I ever heard (Bob Dylan thought him the best in America), despite or in some part because of a talent for self-harm that even by rock 'n' roll standards set the bar about as high as it would go. I suppose I wanted to inherit a trace of the improvisational freedom, the recklessness, the ability to conjure pictures that these three great artists had in common: I wanted my Laertes to be as precisely driven, as well as warm and humorous, as Nicol's Hamlet; to accomplish some of Scofield's kaleidoscopic tonal shifts effected within a technique that never let him down; and as emotionally candid, effortlessly springing from his core, as Hardin's singing.

Of the three, Scofield needs no introduction from me; Williamson a little bit more as time has been unkind to his reputation, while Tim Hardin is almost completely forgotten – except by those who remember him with great intensity. He needs all the posthumous help he can get and I'm glad to provide it, if only to say that he looked like a stevedore but sang like a nightingale, that apart from not always showing up he might break off during his set for some pharmaceutical adjustment from which he didn't return – though if he did his musicality was such that he could pick up a tune in midbar and perfectly pitched. Or that he might show up in a doubtful condition in which he could always sing, even though the intros might ramble a little and he might take offence at the audience. Shadowed all his life by the addiction that defaced his career publicly, I know that he played his first London concert at the Albert Hall not only on the wave of great expectation but of a speedball – a heroin and cocaine mix in which the latter wears off more quickly than the former and the euphoria that's left can seem like somnolence. All this fades next to his prodigious gift; he was well worth the risk, and as time went by I became, improbably, his friend. Having only an onlooker's interest in addiction I couldn't share everything with him, but we were oddly and intermittently close for a decade until he died in 1980. We almost wrote a song together – it had only one performance when he sang it to me in the middle of Wigmore Street, as far as he'd got with it. He died in the same week (Tim-timing) as John Lennon, so nobody much noticed, except that my memories of him poured into that evening's version of Alas Poor Yorick in the Hamlet I was now playing myself in Stratford.

Williamson admired Hardin and Hardin admired Scofield; Scofield's views on both are unknown or didn't exist. He was a fairly otherworldly man and would probably have been suspicious of Nicol's importunacy; and as for the junkie genius, Scofield would have seen coke as something he put on his fire and heroin as what he called an actress playing opposite him. But out of this eccentric trinity I think I was gathering a certain force myself, some mixture of technique and instinct and imagining, until the blessed moment in a career when you no longer need any role models.

Forty-five years later I'm wondering what connects *King Lear* with the Bitter End – or with the Village Gate, where I was a regular for Dizzy Gillespie and Thelonious Monk. Or with the Scene, where I had a pleasant talk with Jimi Hendrix (soft-spoken and courteous). Or with falling in with some hippies in Boston who invited me to go to a Festival they'd heard about the next day. After driving to Newport Rhode Island we found ourselves in an empty field: the Festival was in Newport, Orange County, California.

Now Prue and I take one of those great New York strolls, from Bleecker Street up to 68th Street, to see the Coen Brothers' brand-new *Inside Llewyn Davis*, a film so uncannily accurate to its time – the late 1950s of the folk movement, while it was still more Dave van Ronk than Phil Ochs – that I expected to see Tim Hardin coming on any moment. As we're doing this, Philip Seymour Hoffman – who very slightly resembled Hardin physically, as they both slightly resembled Orson Welles – is dying, at 46, of a heroin overdose, quickly: the syringe is, it will be reported, still in his arm in his apartment, a few minutes away from where we've just been. The inquest blamed "acute mixed drug intoxication, including heroin and cocaine" – the very speedball that got Tim Hardin through his Albert Hall concert.

The next day I talk to Chris McCann, our Gloucester, who worked with Hoffman on a film. He said that no, everything had not been as it should have been with Philip, and we agreed how sad that was. He would be on first call but not turn up until lunchtime, but then would be so good, so completely prepared but also at his spontaneous best, that he did the work that had been scheduled for a whole morning in half an hour – impeccably, one take each shot. We talk a little about the effect of heroin and the unlikely brilliance that can peer out from beyond it, at how unusual it is in our profession. I mention Tim Hardin, of how they found him dead one day just as he was on the mend because all the heroin supplied in LA that week was inadequately cut and therefore lethal. As I talk, Chris – actor of sixty, family man and gardener from Queens, lecturer at New York State University – is gaping at me with admiration: "You KNEW Tim Hardin?"

So, dear reader, I may fall on my face in Classon Avenue like some wasted junkie, but maybe I'm a minor legend too. And there's now a photograph of me on the wall of the Village Gate, where I used to listen to Thelonious Monk. Just thought I'd mention it.

# WEEK TWO

A man of some age comes on and prepares to take charge of proceedings. He may look frail, or arrogant. There are three women present who turn out to be his daughters. Being the one in control here, the man announces that he is standing down from his position. We have heard just before his arrival that he has divided his estate into three and is gifting a third to each of his daughters and their husbands, but he now seems to have a new criterion: whoever is able to improvise the best speech about their love for him will be the most richly rewarded. In their efforts, two of the daughters please him; the third refuses to participate and he throws her out of the room, as he also does a colleague who tries to dissuade him. Having disinherited her, he then splits the kingdom into two instead of three and leaves.

Next we are introduced to another family without a female parent: a father and two sons, one of whom is illegitimate and seems rather manly and ambitious but has no religious beliefs. We get little impression of the other, but later on he turns up gibbering like a wandering beggar.

We watch the progress of these characters. The old man goes mad at some length, though he sounds rather sensible when he does so; the inheriting sisters quarrel, the illegitimate son plots against his brother and his father. There is a scene of unspeakable cruelty halfway through when the father of the two sons has his eyes put out in front of us, but most people watching this have only a sketchy idea of what he has done to deserve it. He survives his ordeal and lasts longer than some of the other characters, in particular a professional entertainer who, despite being protected by the King, disappears halfway through the story. All but two of these people end up dead, unable to come to terms with their circumstances or to tolerate each other, except for the son who became a beggar and the surviving husband of one of the sisters, who are nominally left in charge.

It is fairly clear that a moral point is being made or at least aired: that virtue is in general not rewarded but cruelly castigated. Those who speak the truth are punished by banishment or dispossession or death, or by the cruelly public discomfort of the stocks. The blinded man pursues an articulate life beyond blinding, a large physiological improbability that lifts the play out of the range of realism. His legitimate son is condemned to the trials of Job before winning through in the end – though he has to kill two people on the way, so he has blood on his hands and is therefore an unlikely hero. The good are definitely punished; but then so are the bad.

These figures move like resolute ghosts across a remote slate-grey landscape into which as watchers we are hardly invited at all; they remind us of no-one we know, though we may be familiar with their names in general from going to the theatre or school. For this is *King Lear*, said to be the greatest of all tragedies, an Everest among plays, an unscaleable thing, one which Charles Lamb said could not be performed in the theatre since for an actor to represent Lear on the stage would be as hard as to personate the Satan of Milton or one of Michelangelo's terrible figures. Nevertheless actors have had great success in the part: Edith Sitwell wrote to the heroic Donald Wolfit that the cosmic grandeur of his performance left her unable to speak, and that all the imaginable fires of agony and light of redemption were there. Cosmic grandeur is now such an outdated idea that one wonders whether this was a compliment or an affectation; we can only imagine what kind of noise Wolfit, now thought a little outdated himself, can have made to put the fires of agony into Sitwell's mind, and what whimpering was done to suggest the light of redemption, or from where that redemption was to come.

There is another version of the story, much closer to home. A father who has clearly had bad legal advice plans to give virtually all his estate to his three children before his death, even though he is still relatively healthy and able. This may remind us of some relative of ours, or even of ourselves. He is strong-willed and not inclined to listen to advice; once he has carried out his plan, he attempts to become a house guest at his two favourite daughters' homes, but is unwelcome because he travels with far too many advisors. Deeply upset at having to fend for himself, he develops some symptoms of dementia. In what is called his madness, he on the whole talks abundant good sense and shows a new curiosity about the world and the dilemmas of the people who depend on him. Occasionally he seems a little confused about his age and other things, but in fact he is rather entertaining and makes particularly acute analyses of politicians, jobsworthies, lickspittles and other corrupt functionaries.

In this version, despite various archaisms, everything about the play reminds us of our own lives and of the bad behaviour we are capable of as a species. It echoes what we see in the news, not only in terms of floods and natural disasters but of uncontrolled political power, of the grossest abuse of other people's rights, of moral degradation and unreasoning violence, everything that makes us wonder what on earth we have become. It fills us with a general pessimism about the future, and indeed the inadvisability of living too long. In this version what Edith Sitwell describes as cosmic grandeur sounds more like the familiar writhings of the human race in extremity. We may find the acute observation of Iris Murdoch (*Salvation by Words*, 1972) more congenial, when she says that all good tragedy is really anti-tragedy: that King Lear wants to enact the false tragic, the solemn, the complete, but Shakespeare forces him to enact the true tragic, the absurd and incomplete. Or prefer to be reminded by George Orwell (*Shooting an Elephant*, 1950) that *Lear* contains a strong element of social criticism, but that it's carefully veiled by being expressed by the Fool, or by Lear in his madness, or by Edgar in his disguise as Poor Tom, since in his sane moments Lear hardly ever makes an intelligent remark. Or Professor G. Wilson Knight's view that *Lear* is the most agonising of all tragedies to endure, but if we are to feel its agony, we must also sense its grim humour (*The Wheel of Fire*, 1949). On the other hand, if we approve the play's application to modern life, we may shy away from the patriarchal endorsement of Thomas Jefferson in a 1771 letter: "A lively and lasting sense of filial duty is more effectually impressed on the mind of a son or daughter by reading *King Lear* than by all the dry volumes of ethics, and divinity, that ever were written".

*Lear* is a play that has caused wise men and women to run as mad as its hero. Productions and central performances are faulted either for a lack of metaphysical grandeur or for not being true enough to life. One of the most damning criticisms of the central actor is that he has been not King Lear but merely Mister Lear, as if there was some bombastic peak he should have reached; another that he has failed to remind us of the newly-revealed pychopathology of Alzheimer's Disease. Of the opinions above, the most sympathetic would seem to be those of Orwell, Murdoch and Wilson Knight, in that they tend to view tragic scale as a fallacy compared to the quiet desperations of everyday life. And the fact is that when it comes to being moved rather than battered and horrified, most people prefer *Uncle Vanya*. In line with this, the excellent Michael Billington recently, to much disapproval in some quarters, left *Lear* out of his list of the 101 best plays in world drama on the basis that its tragic energy was engineered and its utter despair a shallow manipulation of its audience.

In some ways I rather agree with him, though it's not stopped me wanting to play the King. My conclusion too is that this is perhaps not Shakespeare's greatest play, though obviously one of unique power and authority. Like Billington, I wonder at the sadistic further punishment Shakespeare inflicts on his harrowed audience in the last scene. Watching actors carrying the dead Cordelia on, I can see why the vilified Nahum Tate, rewriter of Shakespeare's plays for the eighteenth century, let Cordelia live and marry Edgar. Or why, in the ancient play of *King Leir*, according to Geoffrey of Monmouth (a famous fantasist of early British history), Leir, his daughters Regau (sic) and Gonorilla (a name Shakespeare may have been particularly anxious to change) and Cordeilla (also sic, and married to the King of the Franks), rescue Britain and he lives happily for three years after. What kind of bloodymindedness is this in Shakespeare, who could have made *Lear* the first of his sequence of late romances (*The Winter's Tale*, *Cymbeline*) rather than the last of his gruelling tragedies (*Hamlet*, *Macbeth*, *Coriolanus*)? For four hundred years the end of *Lear* has taken audiences to the limit of their toleration and the actor to the edge of his resources – and therefore into nightly self-blame: lining up at St Peter's Gate is a procession of good actors still kicking themselves because they didn't quite get "Never, never, never, never, never…" to their own satisfaction.

When, as a student, I encountered *King Lear* as a text (where anomalies easily overlooked on the stage become obvious) I had already seen three productions and been duly impressed, though possibly not moved. But then teenage is not the time to be moved in the theatre – unless it is to side with Hamlet against his parents – but rather to be stirred by what it can do to your imagination. It is, after all, not long since you were quite unmoved by Tinkerbell being saved in *Peter Pan* and made a rush for the candy concessions in the interval while your parents stayed in their seats, blubbing. (The more recent *War Horse* may be an exception to this argument since it taps directly into children's love of animals.) My own grandchildren were happy to see me as King Lear, and it didn't occur to them to be disturbed by it. On the other hand, when he was eleven my friend Philip Franks was so upset by seeing the play that he couldn't go back to school for two days. By Eric Porter as Lear of course, but also by Michael Williams as the Fool, and by Alan Howard, racked with physical pain as Poor Tom. But this may not have been quite the same as being moved.

The unimpressed intellectual arrogance of the student is a mighty weapon of defence. Enjoy it while you can. Sure enough, trying to win some kind of English degree brought out the know-all in me. For all its loquacity, I insisted that the play didn't speak to me but remained a large taciturn thing. In my final exams (written, so there was no danger of having to defend my position in person) I chose to take the view that *King*

*Lear* was, if not a load of junk, somewhat overrated, for reasons I would endeavour to explain, though with more intuition than scholarship. I was finding that this sort of discreet heresy suited me well in examinations, for which I was rarely well prepared in any conventional sense.

In fact, to call *King Lear* a load of junk would probably have earned me a Third Class degree; to tip my hat to it in the conventional way would have got me a 2.2, and real insight might have put me in line for a First. I attribute my 2.1 to this air of cultivated outsiderism, a devil-may-care posture along the lines of some literary Edmund the Bastard. I don't now remember how I constructed my argument, but it will have had to do with the play's poor workmanship and faltering aim. I would have asked for clarification at the start as to who is or isn't in the know about the imminent division of the kingdom, and whether the decision really depends on the daughters' flattering speeches or has already been taken. I would have noted the improbability of the traffic in Acts Two and Three, when Lear, Goneril, Regan, Cornwall and Oswald bustle round the country, sometimes arriving at the same moment as others who've come half or double the distance. I'd have questioned (and still do) the dramatic value in Act Three Scene One of listening to a detailed description of the storm and Lear's behaviour in it from a Gentleman who can't possibly have been there, moments before you see Lear doing it, presumably for the first time. I'd have demanded clarification of who is fighting whom in Act Four – is it Regan v Goneril or Regan + Goneril v The King of France? In Act One Scene Four I'd have wondered how the request to Lear to reduce his attendants from a hundred to fifty and the decision to give him a fortnight in which to achieve it is supposed to take place during the mere four lines in which he is absent from the stage. And as a final *méchanterie* I would wonder what the point is of Edgar's being identified as Lear's godson when the only time they're seen together is when one of them is naked and chattering or the other seems stark mad.

Of course in asking these questions I was inventing a new form of pedantry. Now I know that most of them don't matter a damn in practice. At a slightly deeper level, I'd also have complained about an untypical failure to combine political and personal matters. At one time (*Henry IV*) Shakespeare would have done both, as indeed he would do afterwards (*Coriolanus*). Initially *Lear* looks to be a play about England, on whose fortunes the Duke of Burgundy and especially the King of France will impinge; so, a history play, at least in part. But Burgundy is sent packing after a couple of speeches and, unhelpfully, the King of France neither reappears nor is much mentioned again, though clearly he is meant to be significant since he and Cordelia – if you listen sharply – will lead an army to re-occupy England later in Lear's interests. But how can a state of the nation play contain only characters from two families – no incomers, no detached observers, no working men or women, no gardeners, virtually no servants? The three exceptions, Kent, the Fool and Oswald, are defined by their fierce attachment to one or the other clan, and deeply involved in its fortunes. Neither family has a female representative of the older generation.

Not much of a line-up for any kind of a political dialectic. The truth is that Shakespeare's overwhelming interest in the characters' extraordinary behaviour continually distracts us, while many narrative facts slip into second place. You might think that Regan and Goneril are fighting for control of the kingdom, but in fact they are taking on a common enemy. Much of Act IV – always the trickiest part of a Shakespeare play – is taken up with Edmund musing on whether he will sleep with Regan or Goneril or both; but his self-proclaimed outsiderliness is far less interesting than it was in the play's early stages, and we're now more interested in who's going to win the battle for England. Edgar's peregrinations with his blind father lead to the astonishing *coup de théâtre* when he convinces him that he is throwing himself off the cliffs at Dover when he is in fact on flat ground – and also features Edgar's magnificent description of the view – but what is its purpose, or indeed the purpose of Edgar's compulsive and entranced changes of character?

Fifty years later – of course – I know far more of what even the most good-natured people are capable of, and that horrible extremes can be reached by the simplest logic. People who commit dreadful crimes and follies may once have had the best intentions in their lives. In *Lear*, Shakespeare puts recognisable people into a sort of Plague Year in which they are drawn to the utmost malevolence and heedless destructiveness. The rare "good" character such as Albany becomes a stubborn eccentric. What is the reason? Shakespeare was always interested in what happens when a society falls in on itself – look at Ulysses's speech on order in *Troilus and Cressida*; in *Lear*, communal anxiety releases some virus of disinhibition and a latent need to transgress is indulged. Lear did not plan to become an intolerable old man out of touch with reality – in fact he may even have feared it – but that's what he became when he changed the structure of things. Regan was hardly born to pull people's eyes out, or a young man to guide his blind father painfully about the country without the mercy of telling him who he is. For all these people a point has been reached where such things are inevitable. *King Lear* is profoundly implicating, and we shouldn't be able to hold it at arm's length. Sooner or later and in one way or another, most good plays are saying This Could Happen to You.

The fact that Lear (a little like Antony and Coriolanus, his chronological contemporaries) has no soliloquies worthy of the name, and Edgar has ones of remarkable triteness, makes the empathy quite difficult; we're used to Shakespeare's protagonists turning to us for approval or to explain what they are up to. Here our only real accomplice is the existentialist Edmund the Bastard. He gives us notice at the start of how far he will go to realise his vision of the future, and is soon taking a knife to his own arm as a first step. He has no metaphysics, no assumed decency, no inherited restraint, but instead, a motive and some injuries to avenge – his father's dispatch of him for nine years out of the country and most recently, in the play's opening lines, his clubhouse jokes to a complete stranger about his bastardy. Edgar would seem to be the opposite: he says virtually nothing to anyone until he leaves home and becomes Tom o' Bedlam. His interpreters tend to take exactly opposite decisions as to how, fleetingly, to present his default mode. What is sure is that Edgar goes through far more extreme setbacks than Edmund and seems to relish them.

It seems to me that most interpretations of *King Lear* are either simplistic or not simple enough. The play is simplistic in the same way as a nursery fable – one that begins Once Upon a Time There Was a King with Three Daughters – and allows action and reaction to follow each other in a way that a child can understand. But this makes the play something much less relevant than it is. Unfortunately the opposite is also true: if it's imagined to be about any number of contemporary preoccupations – the danger of bad estate management without advice – that seems rather trivial. Or dementia: this makes an audience comfortable with the play's poignant application to their own aged, but again it shrinks as a result, much as the brain shrinks in that miserable condition. The idea also crops up sometimes that Goneril (but not Regan) or Regan (but not Goneril) – or both – have been sexually abused by the King, yes, definitely. I know of one Lear who thought that when Lear speaks outside the hovel of 'meeting the bear in the mouth', he is equating child abuse with the actions of the bear, rather than giving wise counsel to the Fool on the lesser of two evils, the edge of a cliff or a ravenous beast.

But what if the man giving all his money to his children before death has a mindset like a rock and a maniacal temper? What if the dementia-sufferer manages to put his condition aside for improbably long periods of articulacy? And what if the victims of abuse are capable of turning around at any moment and taking the most extreme revenge as if to the manner born?

And the fact is that most objections – mine in my Finals, theatregoers who find that though *Lear* has a loud voice it's not always a lucid one, and those of Michael Billington – are generally obliterated by the play's second half, which is marked by a sublimity – and supreme technique – in the writing. Whatever else, at this stage, *King Lear*'s assault on the heart is irresistible.

Imagine a space like the National Theatre's Cottesloe in London, if you knew it before it became the Dorfman, but with extra depth. The stage of TFANA's Polonsky is deeper than it is wide, and though generally defined as a thrust stage with the audience on three sides, has – at least for our production – two distinct areas. The upstage section has no audience alongside it. Where they might have been, the space is open right to the side walls of the building: on one side a jazz trio led by Michael Attias will be set (is this the first *Lear* to be accompanied by such a thing?), and on the other the sound mixer Nick Pope works, keeping the musicians in his eyeline. Despite their presence, this large, wide, high area, a little distant from the audience, was to seem a limitless, open space where you might well invoke the gods, survive a shipwreck, address the nation or be lost on a wild and stormy heath.

Downstage, where the audience starts, is what would be called a forestage but for the fact that it is probably no less deep than the upstage area, though narrower by virtue of three rows of seats on each side of it. It has the body of the audience at its front, some eight rows of them. There are three levels of seating on this pattern, of diminishing capacity as you go upstairs: the orchestra a little below the stage level, then the mezzanine, and then the gallery, which is occupied mainly by stage management but allows for about forty patrons as well. It's as if the audience has entered at one end and two sides of a large room, but not ventured into the further half of it.

If actors come from upstage to downstage the side sections seem to fill in on either side to enclose them; naturally this needs to be considered in the staging as these spectators are, increasingly, behind the actors as it happens. And the forestage will tend to carry the main business of our show, mildly suggesting a debating chamber where the lessons learned in the upstage expanse can be considered. Being so intimate, it allows me a rare opportunity: to make a big noise as needed upstage but also to come down and consult the audience as Hamlet might. Even without soliloquies, I had plenty of opportunities to open the dialogue up to the public while remaining within the scene.

A character arriving on the forestage will have come by one of five routes. Two are fairly long, from upstage left or right near the back wall. A further two are on diagonals through the auditorium, along pathways defined by miniature lights like a catwalk or a runway; these run from heavy doors at the auditorium corners which are used by both audience and actors. A third route cuts straight down the centre of the orchestra stalls from the back wall of the auditorium – where, however, there is no door: to approach by this route you must use one of the corner doors, visibly travelling behind the back row of the stalls (a passageway the width of one person only) before turning sharply to left or right to enter the central runway. Although not brightly lit here, it is possible to be seen approaching by the patrons on the side blocks of the audience if they care to look in that direction, or indeed by someone in the centre block craning to look over their shoulder. In practice, of course, they hardly ever do: they quickly get the idea, don't want to spoil the general illusion for themselves, and would only do so out of intense interest or mild curiosity – if, say, a character on the stage suddenly stared in that direction.

On the far, foyer side of each of these corner doors is a further door, and the space between the two is like a sort of airlock, or a well-carpeted decontamination chamber – well-carpeted because it is for the benefit of the patrons rather than the actors. However, sometimes the two constituencies meet or even collide here: actors preparing to make an entrance and members of the audience behind them arriving late (a latecomer once irately tried to fight her way through Lear's soldiers, who, well in character, bustled her away); or, a little later, spectators fleeing from the show at some unexpected moment. I was once followed off after completing the very first scene of *Lear* by a couple who had clearly had enough – or perhaps, I hoped, felt that nothing that ensued could possibly improve on it. Alternatively, I hoped they were leaving because of illness, but was punished for this unkind thought a few days later by the unmistakable victim of a heart attack being carried out by the same route after me: the show was suspended while the ambulance took an unconscionable time to arrive and he lay on a gurney in the foyer just where Lear's riotous (but now rather subdued) knights were inclined to hang out.

There is one further, complicating factor. Whereas the centre block of the stalls has the passageway behind it (as much for fire precaution as art), on the long two sides the back row of spectators is flat against the side wall but there is enough width in front of them for the actors – extended customers' legs allowing – to use in order to get to an upstage position. Or indeed backstage: the alternative route to do that is an unobserved journey through the theatre foyers, down the stairs to beneath the stage, along the depth of the building and up the other side (it takes about ninety seconds at speed). Part of the house style quickly becomes the willingness, if there's not that much time, to reach a new entrance by walking visibly through this part of the audience, sort of in character. Unless of course you have to achieve a change of costume en route; in that case, you must obviously go under the stage, adding the required time to the ninety-second scenic route. In practice it's just a matter of careful planning.

It is on this eloquent space that, this Monday morning, we converge to make a *King Lear* as new as the theatre. As I approach the Polonsky, I reflect on the miracle that the doors will in effect be closing behind us for the next six weeks, since the theatre has no performances during our rehearsal period. I also have a nosebleed, to go with my still purple knees, my scraped elbows and my complaining ribs. A paltry response to the cruelty and anguish of the play we are undertaking perhaps – and the nosebleed clears up pretty fast in the freezing cold – but still it is, again, not quite what I had in mind. With great kindness Prue has bought me a pair of Doc Marten ankle-boots which pleasantly remind me of the Eighties; but they're taking time to wear in so I now have severely chafed heels as well, causing me to hobble along like the blinded Gloucester.

The subway routes from Classon are numerous, but inconvenient practically. Sometimes, King Lear will come on the bus, but today, and more commonly, by foot, though he does have a childish love of buses. It's a thirty-minute walk. Meanwhile Graham Winton (Albany) approaches from Irvington in Westchester County, north of Manhattan (but not as far north as Albany):

> "I love living up there. It certainly eats up time in transit, but the train ride gives me time alone with no distractions, to work, or read, or just listen to music. So each morning I take a five-minute walk to the Metro North railroad there and get on a train for Grand Central Station – fifty minutes down the Hudson River and really lovely, especially in the fall with leaves in their full glory, and not bad even in January. From Grand Central I transfer to the No 4 or No 5 MTA Subway train for the thirty-minute trip to the Nevins Street stop in Brooklyn, a few minutes walk from the Polonsky. The whole thing can take around an hour and forty-five

minutes, depending on connections, and I hate to be late. There used to be a running joke when I worked at TFANA when it was in Manhattan, that in the evening shows you had to pick up your cues and be economical with your pauses because Graham had to make his damn train home."

Timothy D. Stickney is playing the Earl of Kent:

"I reckon I share the travelling honours with Graham. I use the New Jersey transit from where I live then New York's MTA: the connections are unpredictable, so I leave a two-and-a-half-hour window, and the day's travel time will be just short of five hours. I could drive but that presents its own challenges; there are cabs, but the meagre salary won't allow that. I'm not complaining. This work is a calling. I do it out of a selfish love for the material and the craft. Oh, and this is winter, so while the travel time once I'm at Times Square is fine, getting there is hard to guess: New Jersey gets, and initially holds onto, much more snow than New York City. Brooklyn gets a lot too, but Brooklyn's melts quicker."

I report all this not only because travel routes are what actors talk about compulsively before they know each other well (especially if they don't have the conversational fallback of last night's soccer match on TV), but because it was gratifying to note that the good guys in Lear's world – not only Kent and Albany, but Gloucester (juggling between the No 7, No 2 and No 3 from Queens) and Cordelia (the Upper East Side) loyally trekked from west, north and east to meet their King coming from the south. The doughty Kent, not risking being late; Albany, who, regretting ever having met Goneril, has dug himself in up country chopping wood and enjoying the mountains; the fidgety Earl of Gloucester, forever changing his methods, unsettled and anxious, uncertain which option to support; and my beloved Cordelia, who though gone to France, is within relatively easy call in Manhattan. Meanwhile the threats to my peace – Cornwall and Goneril and Edmund – lurk near Times Square, with Regan in Brooklyn Heights, ready to pounce from behind.

My half-hour walk, in spite of, or perhaps because of being alert to the slippery snow, allows me to talk to myself – a good preparation for rehearsal and not unusual in these streets anyway. Bitter cold does seem to wake up the Shakespeare braincells. On this stirring day, I've of course left far more time than I need. People are shovelling the snow from their porches, as in fact by law they are required to do, for the safety of callers. Prue's Doc Martens are soon full of slush because of the unexpected dips on the sidewalk's corners, now hidden, through which you can plunge shin-deep into the cambered road.

I splash down Fulton Street, past Buka the Nigerian restaurant, The Outpost Cafe, the 99 cent Store, the Junk Shop and the Hat Shop and two Laundromats. One thing segues into another with a little urban sense of struggle: a bookshop sits beside a parking lot, a wine store rubs up against two Health Centres. But in another sense, around Washington Avenue, where you move from the Bedford Stuyvesant neighbourhood into Fort Greene, I also travel into increasing greenness – the Greene Grape, a wholefood shop that could be in Camden Town, and the Greenlight Bookstore, which reminds me of the independent Primrose Hill Books on Regent's Park Road, likewise run by people who seem to have read every book in the store and have a refreshing opinion of it.

In fact my route takes me along the edge of three neighbourhoods. Brooklyn has sixty-odd of these and there's some vagueness about their borders, except perhaps in City Hall: nobody seems quite sure where Fort Greene shades into Clinton Hill into Downtown Brooklyn. This is of course not like some of Manhattan, where you can step off the kerb in Little Italy and mount the one opposite into Chinatown without the slightest doubt.

Although they're changing a bit, Brooklyn's neighbourhoods have always been as ethnically identified as anywhere else. Broadly speaking, Chinatown is in Sunset Heights, Little Poland in Greenpoint, and Little Pakistan in Coney Island; Brighton Beach is called Little Russia or Little Odessa depending on the current balance of Russians and Ukrainians. Bushwick is Hispanic, while Park Slope and Downtown Brooklyn have a Greek inflection. How would Nigel Farage pick the bones out of that? What you can still be sure of is that Bed/Stuy is 80% Afro-American and poor, as it has been since the Great Migration; both Fort Greene and Clinton Hill have been earmarked for the last century and a half for the middle class, who hope to save money by living outside Manhattan and are able to afford its Neo-Gothic brownstones. At one time they would have commuted by stagecoach and ferry; and now it's much faster by subway to midtown from here than it is from Upper Manhattan. On the other hand, property values are now nearly as high as in Manhattan. It's an obvious truism that this gentrification imposed on an existing poor community is uncomfortable and bespeaks an unevenness in underlying investment, even if *The New York Times* no longer complains unpleasantly of "filthy shanties and offensive smells" coming from the "inmates of these hovels" and their swine and cattle. In the 1980s Fort Greene typically fought poverty, crime and the crack epidemic: black artists and professionals have largely reclaimed the neighborhood, and it's now been approvingly described as a "rare racial mucous membrane".

My friend Avi Sharon is a former professor of Classics and a prize-winning translator from ancient and modern Greek. Nowadays he works in finance and travels each day to Manhattan. He says of the mucous membrane:

> "Brooklyn really is still a jigsaw of distinct neighborhoods, some still clinging to their ethnic tradition, but most experiencing so much change now that any ethnic singularity is hard to find – outside of the orthodox Jewishness of Williamsburg I suppose. (I, also Jewish, ran the Marathon last month, my first one ever, and this sense of Brooklyn being really a mishmash of demographic groups was brought home: the crowd was fantastic, loud, and pervasive, except for that Jewish section, where the streets were deserted.) In our area, Prospect Heights, the corner diner, owned by a Greek former neighbor of mine, was an Irish-dominated soda joint back in 1936, but the neighborhood rapidly became a home for the many emigrés from the West Indies, who own many of the homes still. That too is changing, as younger, wealthier, family-oriented (and yes, white) buyers like us move in. This wave of change is just one of many since the place turned from farmland into townhomes in the late 1800s, though the transition is painful for some."

Avi and his wife and two kids have been here for a dozen years, having moved from the West Village, which he regards as the most habitable part of Manhattan. But he is happy to champion Brooklyn, his enthusiasm sometimes shadowed by apprehension:

> "sustainable, locavore-tilted restaurants, superbly designed drinking establishments with the most recondite craft beers on tap… the Brooklyn we've known since 2001 (just post 9/11) has become cherished home turf. It's a lower-energy, simpler and greener life than one can typically find in Manhattan. We love that our boys, now 8 and 10, can run in the back and toss a ball when they go stir-crazy inside. I love that we can go out for breakfast, lunch, drinks, or dinner to joints that are actually good and interesting, within 3-4 blocks, by foot. We have the luxury of Prospect Park and several other great institutions (the

Brooklyn Museum, Botanic Gardens, Central Public Library) just
steps away, which makes a car unnecessary, and even a burden.
Highly curated Brooklyn haunts salute the young (rock climbing,
fencing, even shuffle board), and are all located around Gowanus
Canal – a Superfund Site attracting funds to clear up pollution,
and now a construction area for high-end condos and boutique
ice cream shops and southern barbecues. These are all signs of
healthy urban "renewal" but also upwardly sloping property
valuations. So we lose the vernacular, the local, the ethnic. But at
least here in Brooklyn you still feel as if you're not diminished by
the surroundings. You can still see the horizon, for the most part,
and that gives you the feeling that the dominant measure is still
human. In Manhattan you look and feel like an ant or worse amid
the scale of those buildings."

Nevertheless, because of its outrageous interest, Manhattan is still fixed
in many minds as what New York actually is: if it adopted a new clock
everyone else would have to fall in. But in many ways Brooklyn speaks more
clearly to the struggles of the city, the histories of families and migration,
the whole effort to haul "the broken land" into prestige and prosperity.
Red Hook (the setting of Elia Kazan's *On The Waterfront*) lies at much the
same distance from Ellis Island and a little closer to the Statue of Liberty
than does Battery Park at the tip of Manhattan. Brooklyn's literary pedigree
surprises those who thought there couldn't be one; its cultural quarter,
though patchy as a neighbourhood – there are plenty of gaps between the
teeth – are cause enough for the fourth biggest city population in the US
(behind the combined other boroughs of New York City, Los Angeles,
and Chicago) to boast commensurately. The Williamsburgh Savings Bank
Tower, just by the theatre, is one of New York's favourite skyscrapers. Some
people downgraded their expressions of wonder that I'd played Lear in
New York when they realised it was in Brooklyn. Old contempts run deep:
theatrically, the Great White Way remains the rather stale cherry on the cake
despite the fact that its theatres are unfriendly and the work not particularly
better and quite often worse than anywhere else. Downtown Brooklyners
can point not only to the Polonsky, but to the Brooklyn Academy of Music,
which is really a district rather than a location, with its opera house, concert
hall, Harvey Theatre and cinemas, and its smaller studio and performance
spaces. The Mark Morris Dance Center is here as well.

In four months here I often felt, like the hero of Thomas Wolfe's short
story *Only the Dead Know Brooklyn*, that "it'd take a guy a lifetime to know
Brooklyn t'roo an' t'roo". But then for the most part we were only moving to

and fro across the very top section of the city – its lid, so to speak, described by some Brooklyners as no more than South Queens. Hanging like a great belly to our south lay both the grandest (Prospect Park) and perhaps the most intriguing (Brighton Beach). Compared to the north-south-east-west angularities of Manhattan, Brooklyn seems more a streetscape of converging diagonals, though in fact there is a faltering grid system of a hundred and one streets and twenty-eight avenues here: sometimes the streets run north to south and the avenues east to west. Overall, the grid runs due south and north by the compass; it is Manhattan's that is skewed, south to northeast.

Now seen as an 'area of cultural expansion', Downtown Brooklyn is only just that, depending on what you call expansion and depending on what you call culture. My destination today being its heart, you might expect a plaza like that at the Lincoln Centre, glass and walkways plus community vibrancy of all kinds. In fact there's still a ramshackle air here, though not when it comes to the Polonsky on Ashland Place, a handsome state of the art building that, though perfectly traditional in structure, manages not to remind you of any other theatre. It seems to have shot up since I saw its footprint on my hard-hat visit in 2010 and was shown over it with some excitement by the foreman, who was genuinely fascinated by what the quite subtle artistic imperatives – involving material and acoustic patterns – needed to be in such a project (would there were more of him). Also sprung up now is a forty-two storey apartment block immediately behind the Polonsky – it hadn't even been started then. At least it's residential – lots of potential patrons a few moments away. Still awaiting transformation is the somewhat desperate-looking parking lot opposite the front. There is a real possibility that within a few years the Polonsky will be surrounded by high buildings, business and residential, and it will be hard to isolate it in a photograph. Meanwhile the Harvey and the Polonsky theatres, both of them as interested in the European repertoire as in the American, both of them inclined to import artists too, wink or glare at each other across Fulton Street. If Frank Langella stood on his roof and I on mine we could exchange some gossip, but he doesn't seem to want to exchange anything much.

I'm sometimes appalled at how little I did those sixteen weeks apart from going to work and coming back again, until I remember this was Lear and my job, which made me blind, deaf and dumb to most other things. Prue presents the human face of our stay. Sitting down to supper (she cooks the old boy's favourite dishes) I learned about real life again, before being tested on my lines. A couple of glasses of wine were helpful here rather than otherwise, since if I could be dead-letter perfect under those circumstances then I really knew them; I would be mortified to be thought to have made a mistake because of tipsiness.

This morning, as I stumped and muttered down Fulton Street making assumptions about the neighbourhoods, Prue branched a couple of blocks northwards, on her way to the highest point of Fort Greene Park, a cherished public space secured by Walt Whitman as Washington Park when he was editor of the *Brooklyn Daily Eagle.* The Prison Ship Martyrs' Monument stands on its rather barren ground – a single 45-metre Doric column, crowned by an eight-ton bronze brazier and funeral urn and itself atop a 30 metre-wide staircase. Specifically this is a memorial to British uncertainty going on callousness in the War of Independence as to what to do with the surviving revolutionary soldiers and civilians once New York was occupied in 1776; because of their perceived Britishness they seemed not so much prisoners of war as traitors worthy of the noose. Fearing that publicly stringing them up would inhibit the political settlement that would eventually be needed, we gave them a lingering end, stored in unsailable hulks sitting in the East River. When they finally succumbed to starvation and abuse the bodies were thrown overboard. Over the years these were found and pieced together and some ten thousand victims lie in a crypt under the Monument, which can only be visited by their descendants. Aptly, the memorial sits within the park as near as possible to Wallabout Bay (now the Brooklyn Navy Yard), where the most notorious of these hulks, the *HMS Jersey*, was docked.

In its way Fort Greene Park continues to be a monument to protest. A year on, one night in 2015, three artists dressed as park workers would glue a 40-pound statue of Edward Snowden, the National Security Agency leaker, onto one of the four columns standing at the edge of the Martyrs' Monument. Interestingly, the penalty for the installers (whose anonymity was respected) was a mere $50 fine for being in the Park at night-time, and they got their statue back the next day. Now there's talk of legally exhibiting it in the City's Art in the Parks programme.

## PRUE SKENE

I'd worked all my life and suddenly, by choice, there was nothing to do. Well, I had a book to finish writing but that couldn't take all of every day. I'd been to New York about half a dozen times before but never for much longer than a week. The first time was in 1970, as part of a trans-American journey back from living in Australia for two years. In fact it was the second part of a world trip that had started with a ten-week overland passage to India, on through South East Asia and a flight to Sydney where I earned the money for the journey back.

I still remember the excitement of booking a Broadway show for the first time; of Elaine Stritch belting out *Ladies Who Lunch* in the opening season of *Company* and the smoky café where *Jacques Brel is Alive and Well* was performed. In the late 70s, I was Executive Director of Ballet Rambert and tried to interest the mighty Nederlander Theatre empire in a New York season of our version of *The Tempest,* choreographed by Glen Tetley. Everything seemed to be going swimmingly until the final meeting with Jimmie Nederlander himself: his opening gambit was "What do you want to do Shakespeare for?", and I knew his staff's enthusiasm was not shared by the boss.

Otherwise there had been holidays and always the feeling of being plugged into an electric socket. Now I had four months to enjoy that current and the unexpected freedom of few immediate possessions: our apartment was pretty basic and I'd only brought with me what a large suitcase could hold. What I will always remember is a glorious sense of liberation. Before we left London Michael had given me *Secret New York*, a splendid compilation of interesting and largely unnoticed sites listed by district. New York was lying out there, ready to discover. Or re-discover.

## MICHAEL PENNINGTON

While Prue stood in the cold in a wintry park reflecting on a monument to English disgrace, I've spent the day with new American colleagues – any martyrs' descendants I wonder? At the Polonsky we start with a further meet-and-greet – the company in the stalls, TFANA represented by my friend Theresa von Klug, its General Manager. She extends a welcome as warm as Jeffrey's last week, but inevitably there are more prosaic rules to remember. I hug myself with pleasure at the familiarity of this traditional meeting of actors and management, known in England as Parish Notices. At every hint of a You May Not, the actors' eyes swivel around to each other, trying to establish whether we should be offended or not. Are we being ripped off here? Or patronised? Is this reasonable? Is this for our own good? This readiness to be aggrieved is a tribal link from Beijing to Santiago, from Reykjavik to Johannesburg. It makes me feel very comfortable, and no longer a visitor.

On Friday Bianca Amato would say she was particularly inspired by this first week's rehearsals in the theatre: "Every time I watched Lear's reunion with Cordelia, I thought 'this time I'm NOT going to cry' and lo, my heart was broken." I'm boasting here, but there's a point. This second week (the first on your feet) can be a bit banal. Having sat round the table, you now have to stand up (i.e, express something with your legs) with script in hand or not far away, and sort-of-act, sort-of-commit to something, if only so that that commitment can be changed. I hadn't worked it out in advance, but I sensed right away that the only way I could rehearse Lear was flat out. I often went and watched from the Stage Management box way up at the top of the house and even from that crow's nest got a surge of what our *Lear* might become, its extraordinary potential in this space. Why waste such an invitation to go straight into performance mode?

There's a slightly false memory in the TFANA company about this. Mark H. Dold, playing Oswald, insists that I "never ever" carried a script in my hand, and this made such an impression on him that when he later came to play Alan Turing in *Breaking the Code* – a Lear-length part – his model was the *sang-froid* of his recent English colleague who already knew all his lines, was never nervous and recklessly leaped into Lear. (You can see why I like working with these American actors: you know you're doing well when people misremember the early days in your favour.) The fact is that I did carry the script for a while, made the usual number of mistakes, and of course was anxious. But I was full out even when we were marking out moves or experimenting with ideas. Heretically, I began to feel that the part was quite simple. While it's true that the language, especially early on, needs tackling – it's contorted, full of double adjectives and abstracts – much of the time you must simply line yourself up with the target (that is, the feelings at any given moment) and let the writing affect you. Then you're only passing on to Bianca, like an echo, what Shakespeare has done to you, and she is duly moved.

In a sense this is like what happens every night in a play's run, but with less sense of responsibility. The run of a play is like re-cooking a favourite dish night after night – you know the ingredients and roughly how it should all turn out, but sometimes you're disappointed with the result. Nothing wrong with the seasonings or the raw materials – you could call them up in your sleep; maybe the temperature in the room is different, or the time of day, or the nature of the people to be fed. In rehearsal however, if ever the movement inside the lines or their emotional pitch – or your physical position – escapes you, you can stop, approach them from another angle and see what happens. Of course. The whole point is to stop and try again. And again.

Arin Arbus says she's at her worst in this blocking stage: it's the thing she likes least in the job. This is an exaggeration, but a reassuring one: there isn't going to be any self-conscious straining for stage pictures. In some ways *Lear* seems to be a play in which instinct is best followed by late selection; at the same time there are plenty of set pieces that need choreographing. This is a stage only Lilly Englert (Cordelia) and Jake Horowitz, who were in the *Dream,* have worked on before, and not without its difficulties. The forestage is so deep relative to its width that it tends to throw the action further forward, but of course that puts more people behind the speaker. I tell Arin she's monkeying with me by running herself down: I don't believe in this alleged incompetence of hers, and in fact I suspect the opposite. I know what she's up to – waiting to see what comes off the actors' instincts which she can then mould. She then does something I've never seen a director do before: she turns a cartwheel, right there in front of me, and runs off to the other side of the room. You don't see Trevor Nunn doing that. Perhaps it's a disguised note: am I doing enough inspired cartwheels of the mind?

In fact, come dress rehearsals, she will be like a demon of physical precision. We ended up with some remarkable, sparely eloquent images: the single figure of Edgar standing in the huge space, like Hamlet turning to the audience and saying 'Now I Am Alone' (one of the most thrilling moments in Shakespeare) – and, most hauntingly of all to me, when Lear turned back to look at the court after leaving the first scene, now dissolved apart from his three daughters, they were placed with instinctive care, the depth of the stage creating distance between them but its width keeping them visible. Cordelia and Regan were looking after me while Goneril stared across at them, all on different latitudes. All three were utterly isolated physically but umbilically tied together; desolate figures looking for different answers, none of them entirely trusting but all dependent on each other. It was something like an Edward Hopper, and also had the benefit of Marcus Doshi's lighting, which sharply defined them without anything as crude as a spotlight. In its bleak beauty it even made you feel sorry for Goneril and Regan, so lost were they, winners of the recent battle but less certain of their futures than the disgraced Cordelia. The human scale combined with light and depth was suggestive and perfect.

In fact Arin has unusual and beguiling strengths. She's completely unabashed by even a shade of testosterone when an actor disagrees with her; she's also an extremely funny mimic of bad acting, especially of the mock-heroic kind. We've agreed to do no more than 4 – 6 hours with the actors at a single stretch (except for a quick coffee – as if there was such a thing in the theatre as a quick coffee, without gossip) but we end up doing 10am – 6pm, perhaps because we legally can: in New York rehearsals, stage management rather than the director has supremacy in those decisions.

And of course none of us know each other very well, or whether we have shared assumptions. And if I want to bring an electric storm into the room from the start, no better chance than the notoriously difficult first scene. I attack it with savagery, spilling it out on the floor; Kent and the sisters respond in ample kind. And then again. And again, for a couple of hours. I have in the best way to give everyone a fright. If I glance at anyone, even just a flick, they should begin at least to drop to their knees. Later I will become very fond of these people and they of me. But though courtesy to one and all is important, this is called staking out the territory and needs to be done without quarter. I'm a little surprised by my vocal stamina but also by my compensating levity between takes, which slightly surprises my new colleagues, who tend to go on being serious when they've been acting seriously. At one point the Duke of Cornwall is worried that he ought to be reacting in some bigger way because it looks as if I'm going to cut his head off. I leave the answer to Arin, but I know it already: he only ought if he feels it. I don't discuss whether to fly at Cordelia, I just do it and see if she gives ground, afraid of a punch. Later she will argue that she's a person who stands her ground come what may, which is true. Well, then I'll fly at her and then change my mind at the last moment, not able to go through with the punch. That's just as good. There's lots to discover, but I already think there may be a sort of grim destabilising humour in the way Lear says he's going to "crawl toward death", given that he's a man who would imagine himself marching proudly towards it. He's not someone who sees himself as crawling anywhere. If Lear makes what might or might not be a joke, what happens? Nobody dares quite to laugh, only to simper a little.

These are all controlled experiments: this stage is all about impulse, all to be reviewed. We have a discussion about the crown. I'm not sure about it, and I'd rather avoid a throne. When the crown turns up a couple of weeks later it is, very untypically of TFANA, like something out of a cracker – gold-painted cardboard. This is the land of the free after all, not good old ceremonial England, and perhaps there's not much call for crowns. I end up with a simple rusty gold band, and every night will almost forget to wear it.

Jeff Horowitz is on the phone one morning. He's working on a press release. He says I mustn't be too chaste about my credits and threatens to replace Timon of Athens with Moff Jerjerrod in *Star Wars*, a piece of work I'm thoroughly ashamed of but which of course is a calling-card of sorts. I tell him if he does that I'll sue him, or perhaps afflict him in some more personal way – what it shall be I know not, but it will be the terror of the earth. He laughs, but a little uneasily, as if King Lear had made a joke. Maybe I'm beginning to think like Lear. In part, but not only for that reason, by the end of the week I can feel a hum in the company like static, like a current. As you can probably tell, I feel quite pleased with myself. Rachel Pickup is the best kind of youthful mother hen; she wants to know if we need help to get into Broadway shows via an agency that holds tickets for Equity members at a price that allows them not to bankrupt themselves seeing their colleagues' work. She is specially worried about the radiators at Classon Avenue and our relative lack of sleep. Bianca continues moved, and though I tease her, believe me, I appreciate it. Why are the women always so much more forthcoming than the men, who are polite but a little wary? Edgar isn't here much yet as Jacob Fishel is playing Orlando for the Two Rivers Theatre in Red Bank in New Jersey, and indeed has damaged his wrist in the wrestling scene. His absence just as I've got everybody's names straight (it does take a week or two) gives him an absentee's glamour. Edmund sees me as an English ally – he longs to come back to London, and he also invites me and Prue to his house in Maine. Robert Lloyd, whom I've known though rarely seen for fifty years, grips my arm eloquently at the end of most rehearsals.

But there are some worries. To finish the week the English fight director B.H Barry arrives to see if I can carry Cordelia. B.H looks like a raffish retired brigadier (when I told him later I was writing this book, he advised me to "take no prisoners"), or perhaps Jimmy Edwards, until he opens his mouth and unprintable theatre gossip comes out. This carrying is a choreographic extension of his work as fight designer, and an important as well as legendary matter: the one thing everyone seems to be curious about. This is really the fault of Ronald Harwood, who gives us, in his play *The Dresser*, a scene where the theatre company peers through the keyhole of the actor-manager's dressing room, to which he has summoned a young stage manager. They witness a recklessly passionate embrace all right, but in fact he is only lifting her up to assess whether she is light enough to be a possible Cordelia. Now in the public domain, this is perhaps the easiest question to ask your actor about this daunting play. With luck an anecdote or eight may follow.

The answer is that for the time being I can't lift Lilly, not at all. We lie her on the raised stage and from the auditorium floor, three feet below, I try to lift her. This way I don't have to plié or bend. I can hold her for a few seconds only. B.H sounds unworried but looks the opposite. But as I go home I wonder if I'm ever going to be strong enough to do this. As if she knew that the need for protein might arise, Prue has cooked sausage and beans as if we were in Toulouse. Like an aspiring Lear herself, seeking out the eye of nature's storm, she has today splashed to Wooster Street in the West Village, to find, in a cobbled street full of tasteful boutiques, New York's Earth Room: 2,500 square feet of earth two foot deep in a room within a Renaissance Revival Building. The earth has been there since 1977. The curator (how lonely a job is that?) worries that it might be losing its thirty-seven year odour; so he rakes and waters, careful to pluck out any green shoots that might compromise the mass of soil. Where it all comes from is a secret: the most you will learn is somewhere in Pennsylvania. The artist, Walter de Maria, also has 400 stainless steel poles planted in the New Mexico desert, like Anthony Gormley's men at Crosby Sands. I wonder how did they get it all in and what did it weigh? But then, on this elemental day – the thaw has begun too, shish slush slush – my mind is running on weight and mass and wading through solid earth.

There's also a very funny email from Roger Rees – well, funny to me. Like B.H he advises me "to take nary a prisoner". In it he's doing a favourite shtick, as if he were a nineteenth century barnstormer, maybe Edmund Kean:

> "Stap me vitals! I can't imagine a more <u>wonderful</u> idea than you
> playing this part for America, for all time and – for <u>you!</u> Enjoy it
> so *very* much, me dear! Why, you've essayed the role of Mercutio
> 'gainst my Benvolio – this little outing is whistling 'Dixie'
> compared to that."

It's really silly, and gives me so many laughs that it prevents me doing my stretches. We watch *The Bourne Conspiracy*. Matt Damon is really good – *really* good. Meanwhile our landlord has written again. He is sorry the radiators are still keeping us up! (his exclamation mark, not mine). He says he wants to replace the small hole in the valve of each radiator with a smaller one. This is where the air is expelled as hot steam takes its place. This results in a hissing noise, which in our case always happens at three in the morning. He points out that most New Yorkers are habituated to this and sleep right through it. Limey, I hear him think. If this doesn't work he'll give us extra covers "or even electric heaters" for the night.

This evening I decide to go upstairs to beard the slavering Lothario about his night revels. He turns out to be a shy, slightly owlish medical student from Denver with an exceptionally quiet and on this occasion reticent friend; he would seem to be barely twenty and already a little rotund in a harmless, big-helping, four-cheese, coca-cola sort of way. Needless to say, I talk about something else.

I had been dismayed at the thought of not rehearsing tomorrow just because it's a Saturday: I would dearly like to get something sketched in for the storm, specially musically. Do I want to rehearse, Arin asks. Well yes, I say, but you're the boss, you have the masterplan. No, she says, it's as I like, do I want to? So we did, just for the morning. Then while Prue goes to see a matinee of Brecht's rarely performed *A Man's a Man* at the Classic Stage Company, I slide off to the Museum of the City of New York to look at film of Hurricane Sandy in which people are buffeted by phenomenal winds. But without a wind-machine it will be difficult by pure acting to do what I see, not only because of the hair but the pulling effect on the skin, and the distortion of the breathing as well.

At the end of this week, we've roughly sketched in half of Lear's scenes. Act One Scene One already has bite and crackle, but for the moment we've left open the question of whether it's set up as a public or private occasion, congenial or highly formal in prospect, expected or a surprise. Probably public and formal. The content of Act One Scene Four, when Lear and his retinue arrive at Goneril's and he storms out cursing her, is obvious enough, but the steepness of Lear's gradient into the curse is still to be found. Some of the scene has unexpected comedy though, and in one way the curse comes horribly easily. It's also complicated to stage because of the number of people, and we need a longer session on it on Monday. For one thing, the question of how many knights Lear is travelling with and what becomes of them arises unavoidably, because of some carelessness, I would say, in the writing. The same staging challenges arise in Act Two Scene Four (after the relatively simple Act One Scene Five as Lear and the Fool wait for their horses) when Goneril and Regan conspire to send him out into the storm; I'm also trying to find the funny side of their trading off of how many servants I need and the pitiful negotiations which lead to the great central speech that begins 'O Reason Not the Need'. This is not, I hope, as daft as it sounds: the emotions are obvious in outline, and grim clowning could be part of them, so I overdo it, mopping and mowing, kneeling (uncomfortable for both Lear and me) and bowing like a restoration dandy: Lear fooling to save his life. I think Bianca and Rachel are surprised at this further evidence of Lear's 'unseemly tricks', but they serve as an anti-earnestness pill, since it's good to see the absurd in a tragic situation, and they handle them with appropriate irritation. I've also noticed that once Lear is out in the storm he never sees Goneril or Regan, or they him, alive again.

We're nowhere with the Storm, Act Three Scene Two, but we'll see on Monday.

In the meantime I'm beginning to wonder what is really going on in the minds of these people, not only of Lear, but everyone who has their own motives, their secrets, their ways of presenting themselves to the world. What if we could hear a sound track of their thoughts…?

## ACT ONE SCENE ONE:
## THE DIVISION OF THE KINGDOM

KING LEAR: It seems obvious to me. I'm of an age to retire, and probably should. I feel out of step with the time, I'm stuck in archaisms and formalities; lately I've found myself using two or three clattering words when one plain one would have done. Or reaching for others that I only just find in time: words with an uncertain ring which doesn't please me. But you can't keep correcting yourself when you're the King making a speech. You have to keep going.

As I approach the platform, I notice how familiar I've become with the top of my male subjects' heads: I could tell you the precise development of their various baldnesses. As they kneel, their heads go down as if they expect me to execute them – or massage their scalps. The women do the exact opposite; also kneeling, they look up at me hopefully, like birds, as if no act of domination or favour from me would be unwelcome, oh no, they would happily perform any kind of debasing service. I despise them for this. But if it were otherwise, if they didn't do this small dance, I know my temper would flare and hateful words of punishment would come out of my mouth. There seems to be no third way for me, between silent contempt and large affront. It's a form of nerves, I suppose. I used to have the natural touch, but now only an old man's vehemence, cranky and faltering. My temper looms and presses in on my good cheer like a tumour, ready to blow.

When I now turn to address what passes for the public, as I must this morning, my kneeling court are gathered behind me on the platform: it's as if I were giving the State of the Union address, both a friend and an enemy behind me. When I turn my back on them, I no longer know what their faces might be expressing. I need their guarantee and a measure of approval, but they are in perfect knifing position, their eyes trained on my back.

The sea of faces in front of me I can't altogether read either – what they think of me, whether I can count on them, whether they take me for scornful granted. Perhaps this is the reason I use all these multiple adjectives, as if I were trying anxious variations on the same thought. The end effect is hot with effort but without much warmth.

For all this, I'm pleased with my plan:

> Meantime we shall express our darker purpose.

At one time I thought of holding this meeting in private, away from the cameras. But then it could have been misreported, have leaked out through crevices in the court – crevices like the Earl of Gloucester, say. Resolved to seem open and transparent, I also thought of bringing out the big map and spreading it on the floor for all to see. But I may need some freedom to manoeuvre, depending on how things go.

I must say that dividing the kingdom into three (much better than two) is smart, in my old way. Divide and rule, and sub-divide too, distract with special cases and exceptions. But which bit definitely goes to whom depends a little on... what? A little test has occurred to me on my way here, one that nobody expects, one that will settle matters. How will my daughters compare if I set them this question:

Which of you shall we say doth love us most?

I must wait and see. After all, England needs to know their answer as well as me. This will be a humorous caprice to get at a desperate truth. It came to me in a flash: make them bid for what in fact I've already earmarked.

Not having a son has caused some difficulties, no doubt about it. I don't really see these three girls collaborating, and one of their husbands, the Duke of Cornwall, I don't like much; so if Regan performs well, we'll most likely make his and her portion a long squashed thing from his home duchy all across the country to the east coast south of the Thames. The Duke of Albany and Goneril can have the north, the high mountains and lakes: they can nag and bore each to death up there and no-one will know. That part of the landscape will need a bit of talking up: I shall imply that they're getting all sorts of shadowy forests and rich champains, plenteous rivers and wide-skirted meads – the northern heartlands, we'll call them. It's a permissible fudge, and nobody in this audience is near enough to check it on the map – any more than they'll see if I change my mind after I've heard who makes the best speech.

The rich centre of England meanwhile – its orchards, its forests and rolling wheatfields, our trading heart – I hope can go to my favourite youngest daughter, our last but certainly not our least, who I think will marry the King of France and be inheriting there as well. She'll come off best, and good luck to her. Compared to her sisters', Cordelia's voice is soft and low; her nature, though stubborn, is principled in a way I recognise, and I think that toughness of hers is affectionate.

Impertinent people say that she's more like me than her sisters are, though I don't quite see that.

My wife is dead. And now all this means saying goodbye to my girls. I dread it, abandoning them to these men. But I have in mind a rota of visits, to each in turn, a month at a time – from their point of view, that's one month on, two months off, from my company. In Cordelia's case, it may mean going to France, so I'll need people around me that I know, for the journey, and maybe to keep my routine familiar once I'm there. I wouldn't admit it, but I'm not sure how welcome I will always be.

I make my announcement. It takes so very little time compared to its preparation. But as I approach the point, I keep thinking: do they love me as much as I do them? I mean, really? In parting, how much? Have I done well by them without a mother or not? I wish someone could give me the answer. Meanwhile, as at an auction, they must compete in their love for me:

> That we our largest bounty may extend
> Where nature doth with merit challenge...

There I go again: what do I mean by that last phrase? It's just not succinct; you can work out what "nature" and "merit" stand for if you try, but you have to work at it. I mean nature as instinct and merit as learned intelligence, of course, but am I being understood? I used to do this sort of thing better. But I must show no doubt. Three hundred eyes are watching me, and the question hangs in the air.

THE EARL OF GLOUCESTER: What is the King up to – and is he really up to what I think he's up to? What is he thinking? He's become so capricious, not as forthcoming as he was. These last days have been dreadful, filled with foreboding – the skies have not been at peace. Now, today, comes this division of the kingdom. I'm afraid. Why such secrecy before, and why such a public event now?

I've seen the map, though I wasn't supposed to. The Earl of Kent has as well. The country divided into three, with the most fruitful portion to be given to whoever wins Cordelia's hand. No-one knows yet who that will be: the King of France is here, but so is the Duke of Burgundy. Whoever it is will get a third of our country as a dowry – will this sharpen divisions or slacken them? The French might want to protect themselves by establishing an army inside England: French troops on the fields of Albion? This won't sit well with Cornwall or the mild, thoughtful Albany. Poor good-natured Albany. He has to work hard to soothe his Goneril's undeclared desires. I have the feeling she expresses her ambitions by means of sexual largesse and her disappointments by sudden chastity. I've tried to talk to the King about all this: so has the Earl of Kent. We both hope that Albany – favoured by Lear, less fretful than Cornwall (and husband to the first-born, after all) – will end up holding the balance of power.

In the middle of all this, my bastard son Edmund (God love him, there was such good sport at his making) has returned to court after the nine years I sent him away for. He's excited, he wants to make an impression, to observe our inner workings. I got him admission to the session today from the King himself, who remembers how, in a clear-eyed moment, he cleared the scandal up for me – and then later, the nine years away was his idea. Ah Lear, you showed such kindness then. Be clear-eyed now!

Instead of which, he sends me away. This day I so fear I'm not even to witness: what is the first thing he says, as soon as he arrives?

Attend the lords of France and Burgundy, Gloucester.

I have to go, entertain the visitors, look after them until their turn comes. What is he thinking of?

EDMUND: Today is my formal introduction to the court – a public acknowledgement from my father at last, nine years after he sent me away. Nine years, as if I was being punished. Nine years, until his sins, not mine, were forgotten.

And I was always diligent, loving to him in spite of being always at his arm's length. I grew up alongside my legitimate brother Edgar and loved him – quite – though less was made of my accomplishments than of his. I bore it. And even in those nine years I dedicated myself to building credit, being neither a borrower or a lender and all that, but in the end I have a bastard's credit only, humiliated, made light of, pushed to the sidelines again. Then today, my father says to a stranger that away I shall again. News to me.

And here is the King in action, sending my father away and letting me stay. I'm intrigued. But what I do know is that life is draining out of these old concepts of sovereignty and society. As for me, my sins are my strengths. I hug them close; they're mine.

KING LEAR: So far so good. Goneril has moved me very much. She spoke first of course, as the eldest. I am dearer than eyesight, space or liberty to her. So, a little hyperbole, some affectionate complicity: she understands what I need at this moment. She knows and I know this is not a matter of strict literal truth but of a proper reassurance. And close enough to the fact, I dare say: if she was blind or imprisoned in a tiny cell, the fact that I was still alive would be some comfort to her:

Above all manner of so much I love you…

So I give her the plenteous rivers in perpetuity, almost wishing I'd decided on Cordelia's heartlands for her. How can Cordelia improve on that?

Regan has been another matter. There's always been a guile in her, some unyielding thing, perhaps mocking even, something I don't like in her speech, though I can't put my finger on it: something a child withholds from you and laughs at you for looking for. Essentially she just says that she feels as her elder sister does, but even more so. It lacks a little in inventiveness. Just the dull fact of it, no imagination, nothing that could ease or stir a man. And she generalises – speaks of:

> all other joys
> Which the most precious square of sense professes

without troubling to list what they are – unlike Goneril's eyesight, space or liberty. She could definitely have done better, and I find myself giving her back her own medicine: like her praise, everything she gets will be just the same as her sister's:

> No less in space, validity and pleasure
> Than that conferred on Goneril

– and there we are, that's all there is to it, I'll make no more effort than you have or spend further time on you. On to my beloved Cordelia.

CORDELIA: I love my father deeply, but I know you cannot quantify such a thing. Soon I am to be married, and must support and care for whoever it is to be. I challenge my sisters to explain how they could love our father "all" when they have husbands as well. I don't hate the two of them but I know them for what they are. And I believe in bonds, both legal and emotional. I want my father to understand my truth, to listen to a new idea. I am not driven simply by emotion, I have my own way of seeing the world and I am strong. I tell the truth. I have a sense of who I am. I think I may be a revolutionary.

KING LEAR: I knew this, I knew she'd do this. She thinks she is a revolutionary. She would never sing for us when she was little, never oblige for our visitors. She wasn't warmed up, she'd say, she thought all music was a fraud, a massaging of the emotions. As I led her to the rostrum today I enveloped her with love, but she was stiff as a board, stiff and quite sweaty. When I look at her I see myself, but also some obscure reproach to myself.

Nothing, my lord. Even by her standards this was her most unobliging moment. I have all this land ready for her, as well as what she may get across the channel with Burgundy or France. And "Nothing" comes back. Absolute zero. Well, there is going to be much ado about this no thing. My clothes tighten on me, my crown presses in on my temples. What does that writer say? I am lost in nothing, in the sound of the two syllables as well as in the nothingness, lost and drifting, and dread begins to seep in. The word keeps ringing in my ears, a kind of annihilation.

I must try her again, and reason with her, find out what can she mean: I can hear a wave like a wave of the sea approaching, but I must hold it back. Perhaps I misunderstood. She is certainly making a tactical mistake:

> Mend your speech a little
> Lest you may mar your fortunes.

Now she says she loves me as much as she's supposed to. No more than that. She says it and I hear it, but nothing seems to touch me. And she is – of all things – sarcastic; she asks what point husbands are if you love your father best. So sarcastic that I heard some of the people laugh discreetly. What a comparison to make, in front of everybody. These are different kinds of love, entirely: everyone knows that. What husband could object to her loving her old father best?

She seems to have finished, to have said all she has to say. Signing off:

So young my lord and true.

Suddenly it's as if someone had shone a light straight into my face, too bright for me to see. It's as if I was looking straight into a fire. I'm blinded with light more surely than by darkness. I hear a roaring: is that me?

So young and so untender?

What are these words?

For by the sacred radiance of the sun,
The mysteries of Hecate and the night...

Who forms such words? I accelerate:

Here I disclaim all my paternal care,
Propinquity and property of blood,
And as a stranger to my heart and me
Hold thee from this for ever.

I regret the bit about the barbarous Scythian, though, who eats his children, but it's said now.

And I have recovered myself, my brain is working again: I find the fluency I thought I'd lost, and it's to do with planning, the sort I was always good at, the linking of one thing with another, the proposal and the guarantee of safety that goes with it, for me especially. Get France and Burgundy in, fast, and wrap this up. One idea slips in under another. Cornwall and Albany must share her part of the kingdom, but at the same time the question of how I will live myself, whom will I be with, becomes urgent. I will visit them, with a good retinue. It all fits together perfectly. This is the knack I used to have, and thought I'd lost: to find a solution, to make all well, to make the line of my argument clean and elegant and easy to follow. This horrible experience has made me myself again. I can even make a joke, that I shall still be the king, but more like a president:

they do the work and take the decisions, they are the executive, while I am comfortable, sitting in my great chair in the corner of their rooms. I shall have the name and all the additions. Three linked decisions in one. It's terrific.

But now the Earl of Kent is calling me a mad old man. Majesty stoops to folly? Hideous rashness? See better, Lear? Thou dost evil? You may think me mad, my lord the Earl, but you could be dead. To call a King a mad old man, and in front of an audience? Oh yes, you could be dead. Instead, you must go away. Now, right away.

I shall miss him, but in fact it is the Kent he used to be that I'll miss: this wasn't tolerable.

What else before I go?

CORDELIA: Leaving my father, and even my sisters, is extremely painful. I am banished and my bond with them is to be broken. But at least when he rushed at me, his fist upraised, I didn't back away.

My sisters tell me nothing, they just tell me off.

> Prescribe not us our duty...
>                          Let your study
> Be to content your lord, who hath received you
> At fortune's alms, you have obedience scanted
> And well are worth the want that you have wanted.

The King of France had to rescue me, he rescued me from their force field.

KING LEAR: I was like a fire, now I have turned to stone. I've done a good day's work. I have recovered myself. I found I could even make another joke, or enjoy a comparison. I asked the Duke of Burgundy to take her on when it's perfectly obvious to both of us he should do no such thing. I like the Duke of Burgundy. I like him in fact just because he turns me down and treats Cordelia, whose dowry I've now withdrawn, like the piece of disposable income she is. He's right to deny me since she is worth no money, and no intelligent leader would accept such terms. This is manly in him, it shows the right respect for his office and his people. Compared to him, I think the King of France is wet behind the ears, he thinks it a romantic thing to take a poor orphan princess for his Queen. These French sentimentalists – he sounds like François Villon or someone. Did they not understand – I invited Burgundy to take her for nothing, and urged France not to take her at all. But still France did take her and insulted me too. I went off for a drink with the Duke of Burgundy – he is a man after my own heart.

# WEEK THREE

## ACT ONE SCENE TWO: THE GODDESS NATURE

EDMUND: I was thinking on the way home: what is this huge performance I've witnessed, this mad scene? While I let myself into our house – in all its gloom and staidness, its stillness – my father was backstage at the court, fussing around I suppose, making himself nice to everybody, cracking jokes to his friends about his bastard son coming home. In fact I was left alone in that council chamber for a time after the King left, but no one noticed me. I stared at his great chair, it looked as if it was still hot and breathing. I touched it with my hand but didn't sit on it – an alarm might have gone off, or that crazy old man come back and curse me as well by Hecate and the night.

They think in metaphors, these people, they compare themselves all the time to people in the classics. They're full of precedents, full of their own importance, all the excellent foppery of their world, they think there's a mystical reason for everything, that it's all a matter of the weather, or the gods, they blame the world for their own stupidity and their failure to look after their business. But the gods don't care, they'd kill us for their sport. And what gods?

Now, I need do none of this; well, I'll never be part of it anyway, not from my side of the blanket, I'm the result of my father waking in the dark, in the warm part of the night, after some dream of sex, and finding some woman – who was she? – next to him. That's how my life happened, that time of the month, that time of the moon, that time of the morning. I owe everything to that waking dream of his and the surrounding heat and her half-asleep. Phut. I owe to none, I owe nothing:

> Thou, Nature, art my goddess, to thy law
> My services are bound.

The house is empty, apart from my walking rebuke of a legitimate brother, about whom I understand nothing at all, except that he's as credulous as our father and – I'm beginning to hope – as easily led. Does he read? Does he think? Does he drink, has he the lustfulness of our father? He's a mystery I can't fathom, not yet, nor care to. He's so understanding to me, so kind, he's so fucking kind to me, I could kill him, just to get that considerate look off his face. He's a fop's child, tired in the making one dull dawn, not like the heat of me, he was just a matter of the morning routine. But my father I know because I'm like him. He knows, with that jolt that turned out to be me, that he was passing on the composition and fierce quality that he had then, before he became this old woman of a man, diddling about – when he could once take a young woman without a second thought. We've no mother now, either of us, no-one to watch us but the old fool.

Bastard. Bastard. Bastard. It's all I ever hear. Base baseness bastardy base base. All for being twelve months the younger. And now my father says I must away again – he never told me that when I arrived, bad news, it leaves me little time to work in. But I have him on the hip with this letter. I've made it as if it came from Edgar to me, complaining that a man could wait until he were dead before inheriting, because nowadays the old just won't die. It's what I think myself in fact, but I can't say. Here's the phrase I like best:

> The policy and reverence of age makes the world
> bitter to the best of our times [meaning you and me]...

Father's always going on about The Best of our Times. It's the sort of stuff he'll understand. But I also like this that I've put in Edgar's mouth, a summing-up that will work for me too:

> If my father should sleep until I waked him, you should enjoy half his revenue for ever, and live the beloved of your brother Edgar...

What I know is that fortune blesses the brave, the one who does for himself. Aren't I my own masterpiece, my life a testament to brain and strength?

I know this having a letter and seeming to hide it in a hurry is like something in an old play. But he likes old melodramas and he'll want to see it then, paranoid old fool. I'm gambling he won't know his Edgar's writing, that he doesn't know his own son even that well. The idea of Edgar plotting with me is ridiculous, really, least of all for some new legislation whereby the children control the estate of a living father. I wonder if the King would support that, for all his splitting in three his kingdom – which I doubt, knowing human nature, is going to end well, but everyone else seems happy about it.

It may work. It just may work.

GLOUCESTER: Kent gone, France gone, Cordelia gone and the King himself: he's gone too, listening to voices lodged deep inside his skull. I hear them sometimes myself; they frighten me, and then it's difficult for me to regain my balance. The night-time skies seem to be full of these sometimes-voices; aligned in fury, dead-set against composure and peace. It's because of the eclipses. They're the reason love freezes, friends fall out now, brothers make war. It's because of…. Well, and what is this, this letter, this letter Edmund won't show me, is everything secret? Is nothing clear and level? It's from Edgar to him, he says. I whimper to hear it, then I rage. My fuse is short I know, as short as Lear's, it seems, was with Cordelia. Oh if only his mother was here, how can I handle all of this? But her absence is one of the eclipses, and this letter proves it. Everything is upside down; nobody knows anyone.

EDMUND: And of course it worked, he believed that Edgar put this nonsense under my door. That's how he trusts his own son. Listen to his language, right off the bat:

> O villain, villain!

What's the matter with him? Beneath all that geniality, he's ready for hatred; lucky it's not of me. And then the dumbest philosophy to explain himself to me, the wrong son:

> These late eclipses of the sun and moon portend
> no good to us...

Mind, I know my astrology too. The Dragon's Tail and Ursa Major – the wickedest planets – are the ones you can trust to make a man like me.

EDGAR: I think I should say at the outset that I've never quite known how to speak to my half-brother. I was always careful to welcome him, not to make him feel outside our family group, now that I know the whole story, especially now my mother's not alive to be hurt by the sight of him. I always greet him and call him brother, I'm amused by him and rather impressed. There's something of the showman about Edmund, I think – today I found him looking like The Great Thinker, and could only tease him for studying the stars like some sectary astronomical – more my field than his, I'd have thought. He's talking about unnaturalness between the child and parent, death, dearth, dissolution of ancient amities, and all because of this eclipse he talks of. I've heard about it too but I'm a rationalist, I don't hold with such thinking.

At the same time I'm a little nervous of him – he's a man of action and maybe something like my father when he was young. My father isn't easy to know, not at all, he's preoccupied at all the wrong moments for me and there's something brutal in him – the whole history of Edmund, for instance, suppressed for so long. He's weakening too now, and I don't know what goes on inside that brooding head, the same brooding head as Edmund's, so I tuck myself away and keep mine down.

But now my father's angry, it seems, God knows why or how, and Edmund's offering me protection, I can stay in his rooms and wait until the wind passes through. It all seems a bit theatrical, really, a little nonsensical, but I'll do it.

EDMUND: Really this is too simple. I might as well fall off a log. They're two of a kind. What fools, father and son. Fool and son. The rest is theatricals. Edgar's ready to believe anything, so I advise him to keep out of the way. I tell him I am his. Well, his lands will be. I grow, I prosper.

# A PAIR OF EDGARS

## MICHAEL PENNINGTON

In terms of length Edgar is the second lead in *King Lear*, and sometimes, because of the eccentricity of the part, it lingers in the mind as long as Lear himself. The title page of the First Quarto (1608) reads:

M. William Shak-speare:
*HIS*
True Chronicle Historie of the life and
death of King LEAR and his three
Daughters.
*With the vnfortunate life of* Edgar, *sonne*
and heire to the Earle of Gloster, and his
sullen and assumed humor of
TOM of Bedlam:

This is good billing for Edgar: Poor Tom as the main attraction, though I'm not sure sullenness plays very well; better, a frenzied inventiveness. I did it for the RSC in 1976 with Donald Sinden (a fine Lear, even if he often felt the best position for Poor Tom would be well downstage of him and over to the side – an opinion he would always give up with great charm if I challenged it). As a possible warm-up for Hamlet in an actor's career, Edgar is certainly a treat: you can join the debate, shrug at the inconsistencies, accept that you will not be deemed finally to have resolved them, and still get to exercise some new muscles.

Certainly, I went on to Hamlet and Richard II, and I can see Jacob Fishel, now arrived, will too if there's any justice – and Cyrano de Bergerac into the bargain; a highly intelligent and charismatic young actor with a wicked sense of humour, especially as a mimic.

## JACOB FISHEL

Edgar's one of the most challenging roles I've attempted. At first, it seems impossible to follow his journey through the play: he's only faintly sketched in the first two Acts, and hides behind several disguises for most of the rest, so what's his true identity? He lends himself to many interpretations.

## MICHAEL PENNINGTON

Five disguises if you include the masked hero who arrives in the fifth Act – six if you consider his own person eventually becoming a kind of disguise.

## JACOB FISHEL

I felt I should make him proactive throughout: I was suspicious of the idea that he was a victim of circumstance, passively taking blow after blow, his suffering bringing him closer to sainthood.

## MICHAEL PENNINGTON

Well, he's certainly not saintly: he becomes an angel of revenge, a killer. He disposes of Oswald and is a sort of half-fratricide in the end; and, you might say, a torturer of his father, depending on how you view it.

## JACOB FISHEL

Well, my hunch was that he's capable of taking full advantage of the breaks that come his way – an opportunist in fact.

## MICHAEL PENNINGTON

Not that one would wish those sorts of breaks on anyone: running for his life from Gloucester without knowing what he's accused of, hunted across the landscape…

## JACOB FISHEL

In rehearsal I found the part quite treacherous: if all these assumed characters become too interesting in themselves, they really distract. I wanted to deceive the other characters, but still be enough of Edgar that the audience could sense what he was doing, rather than getting too involved in *how*. When I went too far, Arin would remind me that Edgar might not be as accomplished an actor as I am, which was a generous way of encouraging me not to make the mask the main objective, but always to assume it is a tactic, a subtle but essential shift.

## MICHAEL PENNINGTON

I totally agree. The disguises became very interesting to me, an opportunity to demonstrate an actorly range, to do an inspired series of impersonations, and lo, I kept finding I'd lost my way. You have to be sort of holding hands with the audience without anyone on stage seeing you. It's a temptation for any actor who's physically unafraid,  who aspires to be a shape-shifter. We were rehearsing in Stratford in a bleak autumn, and I used to go running through the Warwickshire countryside – Tom's text is packed with its landscape and folklore – yelling 'Poor Tom's A-Cold' at the empty air. And

I insisted on a painful necklace of sharp hawthorn in my nakedness to emphasise his self-punishment.

## JACOB FISHEL

Sometimes he's thinking so hard of what he's doing that he jeopardises the disguises. I couldn't completely keep my cover while I was preoccupied with one objective or another, so I sometimes had to improvise my way out of trouble.

## MICHAEL PENNINGTON

Like with a special display of pyrotechnics to divert attention when you're being looked at too closely. There's the moment when he comes face to face with his father in the storm; and then hears him say

> Our flesh and blood, my lord, is grown so vile
> That it doth hate what gets it.

And Edgar spits back at him (I think he does)

> Poor Tom's a-cold

And again a few moments later; Gloucester says

> I had a son,
> Now outlawed from my blood: he sought my life
> But lately, very late. I loved him, friend,
> No father his son dearer….

And again Edgar cries:

> Tom's a-cold.

He's stripped down to nothing, shaking and hungry and hurting, in the middle of the night in the middle of the storm, and then he hears this from his father. What does he imagine has happened to turn him against him so? He'll never find out.

## JACOB FISHEL

I needed a perfect disguise to feel in control and safe – Edgar was in constant jeopardy. So I approached each scene as though I was juggling one more ball than I felt comfortable with, where a single mistake would bring everything crashing down.

How easily Edmund fools Edgar in Acts I and II! It's led critics to say he's naïve and simple-minded and that's encouraged performances of a bespectacled and bookish young man. That might be OK in the first two scenes, but it creates great problems for the rest of the play: after all, he becomes the chorus/philosopher in Act III and the merciless revenger in Acts IV and V.

## MICHAEL PENNINGTON

I think I did that somewhat – a bookish man inside whom a genius of invention and wild improvisation and fantasy was lurking, waiting for its cue.

## JACOB FISHEL

But it does call into question why such an eligible, obedient young man would have been absent from the court in the opening scene. Edgar's privilege as Gloucester's legitimate heir, indeed with the King as his godfather, should give him security in a crumbling world. It's this very privilege that blinds Edgar, not a diminished intellect. His confessions, through Poor Tom, of having lived a lavish, licentious life:

> Wine loved I deeply, dice dearly, and in woman out-paramoured the Turk

– coupled with Regan's accusations of keeping company with Lear's 'riotous knights', might, I thought, shed light on Edgar before he appears. The picture begins to resemble something like Prince Hal at the Boar's Head Inn, a paradoxical wild boy rather than some blinkered student. With this in mind, I made my first entrance a little tipsy and smelling of some lady's perfume: well groomed, but fashionably dishevelled. It's Edmund, not Edgar, who's in deep contemplation of his books: Edgar has the self-confidence to abandon his studies. Another element I added was an impulse to go deal directly with Gloucester, to disabuse him:

> Some villain hath done me wrong.

## MICHAEL PENNINGTON

Yes, I see that you're doing that.

*(Above)* The Samuel H. Scripps Mainstage at Polonsky Shakespeare Center [DS/ESTO];
*(Below)* The Hoyt Street Subway – King Lear Checks His Billing [PS]

*(Above)* Arin Arbus (Director), Michael Pennington (Lear) [GG];
*(Below)* Jacob Fishel (Edgar), Chandler Williams (Edmund) [GG]

*(Above)* Meeting and Greeting – The Company [GG];
*(Below)* Jeffrey Horowitz (Founding Artistic Director), Robert Langdon Lloyd (The Doctor) [GG]

(*Above*) Arin Arbus, the Set Model, Riccardo Hernandez (Designer) [GG]
(*Below*) Arin Arbus, Michael Attias (Composer) [GG]

*(Above)* Lear's Daughters: Rachel Pickup (Goneril), Bianca Amato (Regan), Lilly Englert (Cordelia) [GG]
*(Below)* Mark H. Dold (Oswald), Jeffrey Horowitz [GG]

*(Above)* Christopher McCann (Gloucester) [CR];
*(Below)* Timothy D. Stickney (Kent) [GG]

*(Above)* Rehearsals: Mark H. Dold, Rachel Pickup [GG]; *(Below)* Jake Horowitz (The Fool) [GG]

*(Above)* Jacob Fishel [GG]; *(Below)* Chandler Williams, Bianca Amato [CR]

## JACOB FISHEL

Throughout, the choice is to play Edgar either as the play's force for good, Granville-Barker's 'very Christian gentleman', or a cruel fratricidal moraliser, but I would argue that Shakespeare was more interested in raising complex questions than giving us simple answers. Edgar is the embodiment of all the conflicted forces at work in the play. In him we see reflections of Lear, Gloucester and Edmund.

And as for the crux of Gloucester taking Edmund at his word when he maligns Edgar, it's not so hard to believe: there's absolutely no evidence that Edmund has ever done anything to be mistrusted for, either by Edgar or Gloucester. So there's no reason for his father not to believe him. For him, Edmund has been entirely trustworthy: it is only the audience that knows of his utter duplicity.

## CHANDLER WILLIAMS (EDMUND) INTERVENES:

The irony of the trap I set with the forged letter is that it relies on Gloucester springing it because of his own suspicion. He's ready to deceive himself. Springes to catch woodcocks, you could say.

Edmund always has to achieve his aims through cruelty, but his consciousness and introspection keep him from being an unmitigated villain. His past makes his actions understandable. He was hurt to be sent away from home for nine years at the suggestion of his father (maybe it was to the military, by the way) but he dedicated himself to overachieving – only to be presented with a bastard's shield. At that time the standard mark of illegitimacy in heraldry was a wavy line across the family crest. A bastard was immediately known to other knights: the fact was clearly emblazoned on his shield. But when Edmund comes back, the invitation to join a conversation with Kent and Gloucester fills him with pride and hope. He plans to stay close to Kent, but then Kent gets banished too. Allegiances change so quickly that by the time he soliloquises Edmund has realised the uselessness of following anyone – Nature and his own might must be his way.

Coleridge describes what takes over next:

> "the ever trickling flow of wormwood and gall into the wounds of
> pride, the corrosive virus which inoculates pride with a venom not
> its own, with pangs of shame personally undeserved and therefore
> felt as wrongs, and a blind ferment of vindictive workings towards

occasions and causes, especially towards a brother whose stainless
birth and lawful honors are the constant remembrancers of my
debasement".

For a moment later, having "saved" him from the treacherous Edgar, he
will bask in the renewed love of his father – he feels like an only child at
last. But when Gloucester's support of Lear threatens to deprive him of
his status with Cornwall, Edmund betrays him and moves upwards for
betterment. Now the old are in his way. From then on his loyalty must lie
with Cornwall. His castle becomes Edmund's territory. He is his vassal.
And that loyalty transfers to Regan upon Cornwall's untimely death. He
has committed no treasons, remember.

As you watch how bad Goneril and Regan and Edmund are going to
be, you realise Shakespeare has also been building up our sympathies for
them. At the end, "Yet Edmund was beloved" reminds us how intensely we
can feel dramatic sympathy where we don't necessarily feel moral sympathy.
The more human you make any monster the more interesting they are.
Every man has his reasons. It isn't Edmund we hate really, it's his method.
And part of Shakespeare's genius is not to have Edmund and Lear address
even a single word to each other. Then you'd probably turn against Edmund
completely.

Meantime, his initial impact on the audience comes from his energy,
humour and self-command – he knows himself, and he is physically strong.
In fact he moves you because he speaks from intelligence, not anger. And
you miss him when he's offstage. He is action, comedy, exciting conspiracy!
He represents the 'new man' in an emergent capitalist society, where
commodity, appetite and authority are key mechanisms. But he's also
descended from Vice in the morality plays:

> Humanity must perforce prey on itself
> Like monsters of the deep.

Edmund knows that the natural state of man is not to be found in a
political community, but in an anarchic condition, a war of all against all.
Even when two men are not fighting, they must constantly be on guard
against one another.

As for the ladies, it isn't that he likes either Goneril or Regan particularly
– it wouldn't occur to him to like someone while using them. And once
that's done, it would clearly be absurd to start liking them. The unconcealed
eagerness of both women indicates he hasn't consummated with either, yet.

When I was cast I went up to my house in Maine for the holidays and that's when it really sunk in. I'd seen quite a few productions of *Lear* – it's one of my favourite Shakespeares – so have had my private thoughts gestating. But ideas are just that until you actively breathe life into them in the sweat and dirt of being on your feet with other actors. Still, I read and reread the play: it really does hold that with Shakespeare you need nothing else. Emerson says "Shakespeare is the only biographer of Shakespeare; and even he can tell nothing, except to the Shakespeare in us." When questions arise like "what the hell does that mean or why do I do that?" you continue reading the scene and he's figured it out for you. The best supplementary reading is more Shakespeare: you'll find Edmund's ancestry is Aaron the Moor in *Titus Andronicus*, Richard III and Iago. And above all Falconbridge in *King John*:

> And I am I, howe'er I was begot.

Then you jump off into it with all that you've got: the past productions you've seen, the actors you've admired, the similarities that touch privately upon your own life and the fresh work you've done with your fellow-actors. When Lear says, "When the rain came once, and the wind to make me chatter, when the thunder would not peace at my bidding, there I found 'em, there I smelt 'em out", each audience member privately recalls their own cold, wet, thunderous nights too, what fear tasted like.

So – just do it! And imagine there's a fire in the dressing room, so don't slow down and luxuriate in the language. Getting out of your own way is the lifelong task for an actor. But as for these early rehearsals, I think table work, sitting round talking, often feels more like something to be borne than truly useful, a democratic hoodwink that everyone's opinion matters. You're sometimes at the mercy of actors with plenty of background but not a hell of a lot going on in the foreground.


## MICHAEL PENNINGTON

Okay, we'll stop then!


## CHANDLER WILLIAMS

And by the way, did you know that in Sidney's *Arcadia*, the bastard gouged out his father's eyes himself?!

## ACT ONE SCENE THREE: THE SECOND CURSE

GONERIL: I still can't believe it. A throw of the dice and I came off best, I was the one who convinced him, difficult old party that he is, of my unlimited devotion, better than eyesight, better than liberty. Well, I've known him longer than my sisters, of course. I know what plays well with him, and then I could see he didn't like Regan's hyperbole, all grunt and effort. And then by some ghastly logic he turned on the fool Cordelia: it's almost part of a pattern, the older the favourite, the youngest cursed. Ha! For her complete neglect of duty, her duty to praise and indulge. And what a curse it was.

And then the little shit felt she could turn on us. What was that? I know you what you are, she said, I'm loath to call your faults as they are named. Little punctilious shit, who doesn't see how lucky she is. Hooked up with the French King – it's a worry, he may be more powerful than Albany and me and Regan and her Cornwall put together.

And of course everything changed for the worse at that moment, on that day that had dawned so well. Since that very night he's been with us with his hundred knights. Christ. We've always talked of this, my sister and I, his failure to understand, his obsession with Cordelia, his wilfulness. Only trouble is that Regan hesitates, she keeps hedging, she thinks again, she takes her time, and we've none of that to spare. I have to take the lead in this. I'm the eldest. I warned her as soon as it happened, as soon as the little shit turned her back with her Frenchman. I told her we must talk, but we haven't, not really. The reasons for all this, she has to understand, are clear: he loved Cordelia better than he loved us, so he's turned on her the most viciously. His pride is hurt. And all so quick: one moment we're called to a meeting and made to make a kind of love to him; the very next, he leaves home with a private army and knocks on our door. Changeable, sudden, rash, at his best still impossibly impulsive. And worse and worse with age, the unruly waywardness that infirm and choleric years bring with them.

But my sister could do with a bit more choler and waywardness herself. We'll further think on it, she said. Who says? No, not think on it, darling, and talk again, we have to act, now, in the heat – because here we are in it, and he's coming our way. And no sooner was he here than he hit somebody. One of my men says something slighting about that idiot boy he runs around with, that Fool, though he seems to have disappeared for a bit, thank God, he makes my father look like a child. Father, hearing this as a huge criticism of his darling self, slapped my man down. How dare he. And then it goes on, every hour a fucking insult. Now he's out hunting – I can hear the din from here, across the fields. But I'll prepare no welcome home, Oswald must cover for me, and that way I'll bring this to a point.

The answer is, we must be seen to make no effort, then if he dislikes it he must go to Regan, this idle old man. Old fools are babes again, so naturally they must not be indulged. And my staff must – pointedly – do him no favours; that'll bring him to a point and then I can confront him. But my Oswald – I don't trust him either. He goes all formal on me. I keep telling him to show a weary negligence, and all he says is Ay Madam, He's coming Madam, Well Madam. It is as if he was counting the odds. Between whom? Regan and me? Whom can I trust in all this? Not my fucking husband, that's for sure. Actually, non-fucking.

## MARK H DOLD (OSWALD)

Oddly, I've loved Oswald ever since my drama school days. In my first year of Yale Drama, Thomas McCarthy was playing Oswald, and look what happened to him – he went on to write and direct *The Station Agent*, *The Visitor*, *Win Win*, and now *Spotlight* starring Michael Keaton.

Shakespeare's writing career is more than two-thirds over. By this point he's a master craftsman. Audiences have experienced *Hamlet* and *Othello* with *Macbeth* just around the corner. He doesn't "waste" writing or character development. Oswald's arc is so specific in *King Lear*, it would seem short-sighted to ignore it. Why would this master writer do a character whose sole function is to "serve" when dramaturgically he's placed in the text more consistently than most of the principal players? Oswald's presence is felt throughout the first four Acts. Why was he given a name? Couldn't he have as easily been called "Steward"? Yes, the name does come from "stïg weard" which loosely means house guard or hall keeper, but why then does Shakespeare have him interact with every major character but one? He shares scenes with Lear, the Fool, Goneril, Regan, Cornwall, Albany, Gloucester, Kent, Edgar, and Edmund. The only principal he's not seen with is Cordelia. Why does Shakespeare write him a death scene, for goodness sake?

What's always fascinated me about Oswald is the arc. I saw him as a man who imagined himself as the power behind the throne one day. Maybe today he was the keeper of the house, but tomorrow....?! I could never get Malvolio's words out of my head: "Some are born great, some achieve greatness, and some have greatness thrust upon them." I believe Oswald is doing his best to achieve greatness and at several moments in the play almost does have it thrust upon him. Under the rules of primogeniture he imagined Goneril would rule Britain after Lear's death. By serving her – her Chief-of-Staff, her Secretary-of-State, her Aide de Camp – he would be one of the most powerful men in the world. But Lear's division of the land puts an end to that. However, Oswald is still certain that Goneril's wit and craftiness will get them there, and his own keep him on track even when her prospects begin to fade.

I saw him as a doer and a thinker. He uses his brain, his body, his sexuality, his friends – and simultaneously his enemies – to climb upwards. So he's the perfect metaphor for the world the play takes place in. The old order is out and the new order is in. Or is it? The ground is opening up around these people. No one knows which way is up. Anyone can become King. Anyone can lead an army. Anyone can have or lose land and wealth.

Father betrays daughter. Brother turns against brother. All of the bets are off. It's the perfect opportunity for a clever man to rise up, almost sight unseen.

By the way, I shared all of this with Arin in the audition. Fortunately she was willing to hear it, and fortunately she agreed. Therefore we had our Oswald play on the sexual frustrations of the duelling daughters, on the ageing of the monarch and all the other male egos. Does that make Oswald a sociopath? Maybe. I think it makes him a realist, an opportunist. Anyway I had a ball.

## ACT ONE SCENE FOUR: THE KENT BUSINESS

THE EARL OF KENT: I am an honest man pledged to dishonesty. I must make amends: it must have been something in me that made him send me away. In any case, I couldn't leave. And now I deny myself entirely – if anybody spots me, I'm dead: my disguise must be permanent and impermeable. For two nights I've laid low, my beard is growing, I've slept in ditches. Hardly enough time has passed, but I'll risk this. The King's just started his first visit, as he promised, to his eldest daughter. I dare not think of him among them. And I might, just might, get away with this.

When Lear cursed me and Cordelia, I thought my world was at an end. Banished, after a consuming life in service. When I was thirteen, my father the Earl sent me to the Court. For a recruit, the formal structures of the life were daunting, but I was used to discipline – my father was a very stern man who brooked no disagreement, for him there was only one way. But he was also good and loyal. With such a training, I thrived.

Lear seemed to mistrust me the moment he saw me. I was to replace some bedridden squire for one day's hunting. Perhaps he was upset because I was not his regular man, perhaps I was too confident in my abilities, perhaps I was just taller: I dared to meet his gaze when he asked who had saddled his horse. "Do you squinny at me, boy?" "No Highness. I meant no offence." "And yet you offend." And then he laughed. As if the whole thing had been his joke. This is what he's like.

We went on like that for some time, his humour disconcerting then reassuring me. It was quite tiring, to be honest. But eventually he saw that my loyalty didn't waver, and released more warmth. Then my father died and I became the Earl: Lear and I had a bond. Of war, of blood and the bottle, truth to tell.

Now I must tell you I am a private man, a reticent man. There are things about me that nobody here knows. For instance, as it happened Lear and I enjoyed a brief wedded bliss at the same time, he with his queen and their girls and I with the love of my life, a rare woman who tended to notice not so much the King but the man standing at his right hand. I retreated from the court. But when the French began murmuring war and again I was called to my King's side night and day, my wife was heavy with our son. She and I parted with harsh words for the first time: but duty and honour is a cruel mistress.

Goneril and Regan were young teenagers and Cordelia was beginning her lessons when I arrived. I all but lived at court: I barely saw my own child. I never speak of these things, now or then. But Lear's daughters always saw me as blood, as an older brother or a young uncle, as they matured. But then as young women they became hot-tempered, sharp-tongued like their parents; they made cruel jokes about my now-dead wife. Well, I'm a man of honest dealing and direct speech, and the ways of women have long confused me, and my loss apparently made me an irresistible target. Cordelia, much younger and more gently disposed, would console this flustered uncle with wild flowers and herbs from the gardens. I love my King and his girls but Cordelia's kindness most of all. The passing of their mother the Queen hardened the elder girls further and put a tension into the family – and the court – that's hard to describe. There was little softness, no more adornment; art and beauty fell away; there was only duty, honour and a readiness for war.

What has been done to Cordelia now is terrible, terrible. When Lear flew at me I spoke in a way I never had before. In fact it was a day when nobody spoke as they had before, except Cordelia perhaps. I'm told she married the King of France. But by that time I was gone, in the twinkling of an eye after all those years, with five days' grace to tie up my affairs.

And now I intercept him. You can hear the pack of them a mile away, returning from the hunt with him, as I used to. I know these men, but they don't know me well: they were a special cadre, and used to camp in the King's forests, like a private army around his fire. They could be troublesome, always pushing boundaries if they felt the King wanted it, or reining themselves in when he was keeping his distance; they were like a barometer of his moods. Essentially these are made men, but they must take care not to make a mistake. Now they're on the road with him, to Goneril's for a month, then Regan's, then back again – and their hosts have to pay for them, their every expense, their food and lodging. I noticed that the King, even in his rage, gave them his "rents and revenues" so he has nothing left, only the name of King. It's a worry, though – he's very expensive, the King, very high maintenance, let alone a hundred knights.

They don't know me well enough to see through me. If I could recommend myself – some jests, as if I were his second-best Fool – then I could bide my time and serve. The real Fool, he's the one I fear here – nothing gets past him – but I hear he's disappeared since Cordelia was banished, so I have an opening as the King's new entertainer. I'll start by not knowing who he is.

His eyes are fixed on mine.

They're as sharp as ever, and I see immediately how it is with him. He's hoping for something. He's enjoying himself, but there's a worry in him, as if he'd waited for this freedom and now doesn't quite know how to be. He asks me who I am.

KING LEAR: Today began so well. This new life suits me. I hunted with my team and we brought down a boar, speared him and brought him back. My men sang. Everything is new.

Now a stranger is standing in front of me. A familiar type – I seem to have seen him before. A new kind of Fool, perhaps: certainly he's funny – and unafraid, which I like as long as the man is funny as well. When I asked him who he was he said:

   A man, sir.

When I asked him to elaborate on this statement, he said many courtly things, about being what he seems, loving wise and honest men, only fighting when he can't avoid it, la la la, but above all, he said he chose:

   To eat no fish.

So he riddles like my Fool, and he's also very blunt. I asked him what he wanted, and he said to serve me; I asked him if he knew me (perhaps I no longer look like the King) and he said I have something about me, some air, an authority that he wanted to call master. That's right, the perfect answer, not just because I am the King. I think he's found me at the right time, giving me what Cordelia should have offered. Then he became like my Fool again: he's too old to admire a woman for her singing but not too old to dote on her, he says.

And as for my Fool, where is he? They say he's sick since Cordelia went away. I don't like this at all. Why can't I get an answer to this question? They just swirl around me, both Goneril's people and my own. Hers hardly answer, mine worry me, the word is we're not respected here. It's true, I've noted it, though at first I thought it might be my own fault, my nerves which have taken such a battering. And I know my own temper.

So this stranger wants to join my team. My instincts are good about such things and I take him on, on a hunch. The next thing he does is he trips up my daughter's insufferable manservant – Osric is his name, or Oswald? Something. He described me only as My Lady's father, he So Please You'd without breaking his stride, and my new man – I shall call him Caius, a noble Roman name like Caius Julius Caesar – tripped him up and floored him as he stalked away.

I think the world's asleep, but this is my man.

Because it's true: there's something bothering here, something humming beneath the surface of things. I no longer think of Cordelia, no, except a little about when she was small perhaps, or of Kent who defied me; but there's something with my oldest daughter that has changed. She said she loved me dearer than eyesight, health or liberty, but now she's critical, askance, haughty. Her husband doesn't control her is the problem. Albany, too mild, too complaisant. What it adds up to is that while I may have the name still, it is an idle thing without all that comes with it. We've been here a day only, and I sense a showdown coming. And now her man is more impertinent than ever. But then my Fool has arrived from nowhere, as if he knew it, here he is.

I know how he operates, my boy. He initiates everything. He makes a proposition that makes no sense then talks his way out of it. Sometimes he fails in this, in which case he moves on to a song. Or a snatch of song, either some old tune or something he makes up for the occasion. He will take an egg and split it in two. Today he's onto me right from the off, riddling about coxcombs as if I were the Fool, asking me questions that are all to do with my daughters, my resignation.

> This fellow has banished two on's daughters,
> and did the third a blessing against his will...

Well, he is not altogether Fool, as Caius says. But he calls me one, he says it's the only title I'm left with after giving the rest away. We understand one another, and I would never hurt him, though sometimes he chills my blood:

> Thou has pared thy wit on both sides and
> left nothing in the middle.

He always means something: he warns me, he chides me, he fears for me, above all he makes me laugh. Today he is a bitter Fool, and I have trouble concentrating on him, pleased as I am to have him back. I hear each fourth or fifth word through the din in my head.

Now he wants to sing me a song:

THE FOOL: Keep your hands on your wealth
Keep your thoughts to yourself
Only lend what you've got
Let your horse only trot
Lay out your stall
Keep your own counsel
Keep your stake small

Leave the wine and the whores
Don't go out of doors
And you'll find you've done better
Than any jetsetter.

KING LEAR: But what has this to do with me? Caius?

KENT: This is nothing, sir.

FOOL: Now there's a word I've heard before.

The fools are out of favour
Due to wise men's mad behaviour

KING LEAR: I still only hear some of the words. They keep ringing in my ears: Fool... Coxcomb... Nothing... He says his own name, Fool, directly to me. He says it's my only attire... I have pared my wit on both sides.... I am transported from myself... then here she is... and I think I heard her:

> Be then desired
> By her that else will take the thing she begs
> A little to disquantity your train...

Everyone has changed but me. They know I reserved a hundred knights, that was no secret, they should have said at the time if that would be a difficulty. So: I have a hundred knights.

GONERIL: These men laugh at me behind their hands. But I am First Lady now. We've a partnership of course, my sister and I, we each won half, but what if something were to happen to the King? Someone would have to be Queen, and their husband the consort. But these men, what use are they? They're just an anagram of the semen.

I become very fluent under pressure, I've noticed. I don't splutter, instead I feel a chill in me, like being about to faint or vomit. It happened when father put me under the spotlight first, as if he was lifting the oldest little daughter onto a table in front of all the party guests, isn't she sweet, isn't she charming. Now again, with all these men's eyes on me, I find long smooth sentences spooling out of me:

> Not only this sir, your all licens'd fool,
> But other of your insolent retinue
> Do hourly carp and quarrel, breaking forth
> In rank and not to be endured riots...

Such smoothness, when all I'm really thinking is you shits, you stupid old man, you terrible father, you fucking nightmare and your idiot knights. And then, maybe because it fell out of me, or maybe because I knew I'd only so much space before he started roaring again, I did a sentence two or three times longer than that so nobody could interrupt, something like this:

> "I thought it would be enough to tell you when it started, but now I see you've decided to ignore me, you protect this course, it's all approved in spite of what I said, in which case you must be corrected, you must even be punished a little, which looks bad for you, but your feelings are not so important as running a government, it would be shameful for you but only a sort of discretion for the enforcers."

How did I do that, the words just came, seventy-nine of them? Except they didn't come out of me like that, all stuttering with anger, but in a great flow, and I found I'd only to take a breath a couple of times when nobody was attending. I feel I've washed him in contempt, not hammered him with insults.

I've also shut him up.

All his Fool can do is make up a rhyme about a cuckoo. Father absorbs it, gathers his forces, but then all he manages is:

> Are you our daughter?

So the Fool has to make another joke, something about loving a jug.

Father obviously thinks monosyllables are the way to reply, a great stack of them. Then he asks me my name, like an idiot, and it triggers me again. I give him another sixteen lines, more practical this time, with breaks in them. He keeps a hundred knights – which is unthinkable, corrupting of our people; you'd think it was a speakeasy here, or a whorehouse. I ask him to do a cull, to reduce the numbers, I leave it to him how many, except he should have contemporaries, people who've known him, like that Kent did, or Gloucester, people to make allowances for him instead of riding on his back.

He makes to leave. He calls me a bastard. He'll go to Regan. I must act fast. I must warn her. And then suddenly he paralyses me.

KING LEAR: Immediately I think of Regan, I see her in my mind, then of Cordelia. They give me strength to deal with Goneril. But what is this I'm saying?

> Hear, Nature, hear: dear Goddess, hear.
> Suspend thy purpose if thou didst intend
> To make this creature fruitful...

But that wasn't enough for me:

> Into her womb convey sterility
> Dry up in her the organs of increase
> And from her derogate body never spring
> A babe to honour her. If she must teem,
> Create her child of spleen, that it may live
> And be a thwart disnatured torment to her.
> Let it stamp wrinkles in her brow of youth
> With cadent tears fret channels in her cheeks,
> Turn all her mother's pains and benefits
> To laughter and contempt, that she may feel
> How sharper than a serpent's tooth it is
> To have a thankless child.

What have I done now? Who was that? It seems all I'm left with is ingenuity. I think I'm damned.

GONERIL: I'm speechless. He'll pay for this.

KING LEAR: I should apologise. But how can I? Now I learn she wants me to send half my fellows home. On two weeks' notice. She couldn't even say it herself, but now I've found out, I've heard it. I've heard the words. And I'd been sorry for a minute, but now I'm not. She'll pay for this. Only I must stop crying. Or cry with anger. She must understand it's anger. I tell her – I have another daughter, she'll have me and all my hundred. And what's more she'll come up to you and scratch your eyes out of your face, flay your beautiful skin; you'll be barren and skinned all in one day. And I'll have my lands back from you. You'll see.

GONERIL: He'll pay. And my fool husband too who avoids my gaze, who spouts meaningless proverbs. He cannot be so partial, he says. I must take charge of this.

## ACT ONE SCENE FIVE: LEAR AT THE BUS STOP

KING LEAR: I've written a letter to Regan and Caius will carry it. But he must not, MUST not tell her how Goneril has behaved, I don't know why.

Where are my horses?

The Fool is fooling. A joke about my brain being in my feet and so I might get bunions. But where are the horses? We had horses when we arrived. Now we have none. I call for them, this way and that. Nobody replies. The Fool goes on fooling: I dread his next joke. He says it will be ok, then that it won't. I'm thinking of Regan and Cordelia again.

He's telling me my daughters are as like each other as two apples. It's not true. Regan is kind and comfortable. Now he makes a joke about a nose having to be in the middle of your face, but in fact a wind is blowing in my face – Cordelia. I've thought of her so little until now. Until the moment when Goneril said that thing... I was wrong. I was wrong. Wrong, wrong. It's suddenly so clear to me that when the Fool asks me now why the seven stars are only seven I have the answer – because they aren't eight. Not much of a joke, but my own joke. I would make a good Fool, after all I am a fool already.

This has taken so much time and now it's so quiet out here.

I made a mistake back there. I should have left when I told her How sharper than a serpent's tooth it was to have a thankless child. But as soon as I was out of the room I stopped as hard as if I'd hit a brick wall beyond it. I had to go back to the scene of the crime. And I cursed her again, well, began to, but then broke down, like a fond old man. But I think I managed to pass this off as rage, I shouted my way through it to the other side, and away I went. And in fact I think perhaps I pulled it all out of the fire. I saved the day. I warned her that Regan would punish her for this, and I was going there now. I think I pulled things back to true.

And now I'm outside, alone with my Fool, with Kent gone on ahead to Regan with my plea for hearth and home and help.

Where are the horses?

## JAKE HOROWITZ

There are so many facets of Lear's Fool which fascinate me. The first is that he is usually talking about several things at once. Take his first line, 'Let me hire him too. Here's my coxcomb'. In this one gesture, offering his fool's cap to the disguised Kent, the Fool is addressing – consciously or not – two ideas. First and foremost, he is removing his hat, and this is a jab at Lear for what he has so carelessly done a couple of days earlier – remove his king's hat; secondly, he's calling Kent a fool for following Lear, who has put himself out of favour. The Fool is saying any man who wants to follow this crazy old would-be-king-of-the-world is a fool, so you might as well wear the hat! And this first thing he does is take off the very thing that makes him who he is. I imagine a factory worker or a fast food attendant throwing their apron or visor cap on the ground and yelling "I quit!" Later in the scene the Fool declares "I had rather be any kind of thing than a Fool." So it seems he is extremely discontented with the current state of Lear's kingdom.

Disrobing and rediscovering oneself is a constant theme in the play. One way the Fool's journey could be seen is as a rediscovery of what it means to be a Fool. What it means to try and walk this tightrope of making a man laugh and telling him the ugly truth. Finally he discovers he can no longer bear it, and he abandons Lear.

*Lear* is, amongst other things, about paradoxes. The play is laden with them: a King with no sons for his lineage, honesty seen as deceit, becoming naked in order to conceal oneself, a man who cannot see until he is blinded, etc. Another is age: the old King and his young wise Fool. The King looks like a wise man but acts like a fool, the Fool looks like a boy but speaks like a wise man. They're not what they seem to be.

What's taking me a long time to discover is the Fool's physical existence. Who is this character? Where does he come from? So much of him is left open to interpretation. Men and women of all ages, shapes and sizes have played the Fool, with a multitude of takes on his physicality. So we've started from square one: I am a young man, and we've decided to have me clean-shaven and looking as – well, young – as possible.

But there's more to be found. Yes I look very young, but something isn't quite right yet: the questions of "Who is the Fool?" and "Where does he come from?" are still unanswered. I appear to be separate from the world around me, as to some extent the Fool is, but in fact it doesn't seem as if I am even from the same planet as these people. Ours is a gritty and dirty land. I believe the Fool was not born into his practice. Rather, he grew up outside the thick bubble of majesty, which gives him some insight into the disturbing way the real world works. In my imagination, the Fool had brutally abusive parents, and one day he ran away from home. For some time, he was homeless, then one day Lear, out hunting, came across this sickly-looking boy by the side of the road who probably said some crazy thing like "up isn't down if down is up, but I'll sing for you to give good luck, if luck is good or bad who knows, but hither and thither it goes and goes." And Lear, strangely touched by the boy, replies, "Well isn't that the truth, come along with us, lad." To support this idea we'll make a few adjustments: I'll shave my head, making me completely bald, and maybe every night we'll have our brilliant make-up artist paint two deep gashes on my left cheek, draw red around my eyes (as if I hadn't slept well in a while), and paint my teeth brown. Here is a boy who has certainly not grown up in a palace.

What is essential to the story of Lear and his Fool is its emotional value. It's a love story. I find it very interesting that the Fool is not present in the first scene. Whatever he knows, he has heard from somebody second hand. Why is this? I think the King has purposefully not invited the Fool, made sure he doesn't know about the meeting. Maybe he unplugged the Fool's wake-up alarm… If the Fool were present in the first scene, I think he would sing and dance and fly in the face of all threats and danger until he were whipped to death in order to stop Lear from doing what he does. And Lear, maybe, deep down, knows this.

Shakespeare writes beautiful details which point to the idea that he is heartbroken after hearing what Lear has done. The first comes in his first scene, Act One Scene Four, in the conversation between Lear and his Knight:

> LEAR: But where's my fool? I have not seen him this two days.
> KNIGHT: Since my young lady's going into France, sir, the Fool hath much pined away.

Ever since the Fool hears what Lear has done to the kingdom and to Cordelia, he's holed himself in his room. What is he doing in his room for two days? We find out later in the scene:

> LEAR: When were you wont to be so full of songs, sirrah?
> FOOL: I have used it, nuncle, e'er since thou mad'st thy daughters thy mothers.

So the Fool has been singing. This, to me, is a sad, beautiful image. He cannot face the outside world yet. He is furious with Lear, but also devastated. And he deals with this by singing for a couple of days. The Fool knows that the end is near.

When he enters, he ignores Lear at first. He talks right to Kent, offering him his cap, and only after a few lines turns his attention to Lear. Now this could be seen in two lights, and is probably a bit of both. On the one hand the Fool is mocking Lear by ignoring him, biting his thumb at him. On the other hand, he cannot even bring himself to look at this poor, old fool who was once the most powerful man anybody had ever laid eyes on. The scene goes on and the Fool continues attempting to sing and make jokes about the truth, but it really isn't very funny. He is in an awful mood, and a bit ruthless with Lear, piercing him right where he knows it will hurt. He then arrives at one of my favorite songs in all the play:

> Then they for sudden joy did weep
> And I for sorrow sung
> That such a King should play bo-peep
> And go the fools among.

The pain underneath those words runs deep. The "they" is Regan and Goneril, feigning tears at Cordelia's banishment whilst being inwardly joyful of their own gains. The rest is remarkably clear in most of the Fool's words. He often ties the truth into a complex and intricate knot, or plants it behind a little joke (as he will do at length in the following scene), but here he drives it straight home. He has been singing, full of sorrow, because the king is playing games with his own livelihood. It's as if he is saying, "Now you're a fool too, well join the party, you idiot."

### Tuesday, 11<sup>th</sup> February, 2014

Now Jake Horowitz, Fool-like, takes my arm and says he'll show me the best lunch, like Caliban offering to show Trinculo where the best berries are. Like a good Fool, he's sensed that I haven't really worked out what to do about this. The choices are all out of kilter – a hot dog shop just round the corner or a somewhat precious sandwich shop attached to BAM. Instead we walk up Fulton Street, it seems to me about half way home, until we find The Greene Grape. Jake tells me that he's worried that as Jeffrey's son there's going to be comment about him now being cast as the Fool. I tell him he has absolutely no need to worry, and I mean it (I was wrong).

We talk about the questions we ask in England about the Fool. Such as, should Lear's Fool be old or young? Unsurprisingly: as we have really no connection with the idea of a King's Fool, except that most monarchs had them, we have carte blanche. There is a history of fine old Fools in my memory – Frank Middlemass, Michael Bryant, Michael Williams, who played him as an Archie Rice among Fools – who completed Lear's world as part of an intensely loyal old guard that also includes Kent and Gloucester. A young Fool on the other hand suggests love of the King from another age group, some mystery about how they met, and even the possibility of some orphaned child Lear has unofficially adopted.

As we step off the kerb to cross Ashland Avenue on the way back, a car swings round the corner and quite close past us, en route to the car park opposite the front of the theatre. I think, what if I and my Fool were run over after two weeks' rehearsal in front of our own Front of House display? A little later in the day I get an email from Jake's father:

> Nice to see you and Jake crossing the street and hanging out.
> Sweet. I miss you, Jeff.

Well, Jeff, you only just missed us.

# WEEK FOUR

## PRUE SKENE

I recently had an ominous birthday ending in '0' and Michael had asked me to keep this evening free. It's also Valentine's Day, and I was touched to find he'd organised a visit to the Metropolitan Opera to see Borodin's rarely performed *Prince Igor* – with enough notice so that I could get suitably dressed. What a treat. He'd also sorted out dinner first at Café Fiorello, an Italian restaurant which is something of an institution just across the road from the Met – if a restaurant can be an institution. Like the Ivy perhaps in that way.

The Met is amazing, and would deeply appeal to those Tory ministers back home who think the arts should depend only on flamboyant philanthropy: almost every surface carries a donor's name, and the amount given each year by Board members seems to stretch into millions. On the other hand the audience itself isn't as dressed up as they might be in London – no European snobbishness in the land of the free – but the feeling of being around money was palpable. Someone told me – and the donor plaques confirmed it – that the annual subscription necessary to get onto the Met Board was $250,000 – no talk of the balancing of skills and diversity here of the kind also, conflictingly, urged by those same Tories at home. It would be interesting to know how much this blatant purchase of influence affects the artistic programme.

The opera was wonderful, and although its four-hour length initially might have seemed daunting the evening passed too quickly. This opera needs an authentic feel and the Russian voices of the principals, specially the tremendous bass of Ildar Abdrazakov as Igor, certainly delivered, backed up by the full resources of the Met chorus on stage, the Americans convincingly becoming Russian courtiers and peasants under Dmitri Tcherniakov's direction. The only disappointment was the famous Polovtsian dance sequences which took place in a field of poppies so you couldn't see the dancers' legs and feet.

The next evening we see *Outside Mullingar*, with a jolly Broadway drink with one of its stars, Dearbhla Molloy, afterwards. An insight into the Broadway jungle: she tells harrowing tales of the replacement of a cast member just before the first preview, and also illuminates us as to what happens when the star of a certain Broadway show "gets God" in rehearsals and invokes Him as a reason for sacking his co-star.

## MICHAEL PENNINGTON

We sit with Dearbhla, feeling as the three of us always do when we sit in a bar in any part of the world. A member of her cast comes by and looks expectantly at me: I thought he was great but didn't recognise him out of context so couldn't give him what he (or I in the same place) would have wanted – the recognition that lays to rest an evening's hard work. His transformation had been too complete.

Dearbhla's been a friend of mine since we did *Shadow of a Gunman* at the RSC in 1980, when we hardly got on at all. Then, when it was done, with equal suddenness we became the best of friends. She's terrific in the play which is by Patrick Shanley (*Doubt*, *Moonstruck*). One character is so painfully unable to deal with women that he convinces himself he is a bee in order finally to admit his passion: the joke of Irish sexual hesitancy rather than English embarrassment. I'd forgotten how shallow the foyers of these old Broadway theatres are, and how wide and flat the auditoria. We were among what seemed like an out-of-town audience determined to have a good time and let everyone know they have Irish roots; the play is funny but not that funny, not in that way. Unkindly, I decide this was their cue for showing off, and sure enough, as well as lots of good stuff, the play has plenty of calculated blarney for them to work with.

## PRUE SKENE

Next day we see Ian McKellen and Patrick Stewart in *No Man's Land*. Ian's invited us back to his apartment afterwards: large limos await and we get into the back while he and Patrick do their duty signing autographs. Jonathan Hyde (who played Ian's Kent in *King Lear*) and his wife, the terrific Scottish soprano Isobel Buchanan, are squashed in with us and as we eventually travel down from Midtown to Tribeca, I find myself gently sliding to the floor, leaving half of one buttock still attached to the seat.

It seems Ian's rented apartment has just been bought by singer Taylor Swift for $18 million. It's rather gloomy in its panelled vastness and, surprisingly for something so grand, it has no porter's desk and is reached via a lift clad in builders' felt. A vital feature of such New York homes is a special gun cupboard, and Ian's aide shows me this one, lurking amongst the empty shelves in the library. With typical generosity, Ian has asked his car to wait to drive us home to Brooklyn – plenty of room this time.

## MICHAEL PENNINGTON

*No Man's Land* with these two actors is an affectionate War of the Roses, Patrick being from the West Riding and Ian from Burnley, now at the top of their games on Broadway in perhaps Harold Pinter's finest work. Patrick is as excellent as you would expect and falls on my neck afterwards saying it's urgent we meet up as if he's been waiting impatiently for the chance to say so. Meanwhile I think Spooner is the best thing I've seen Ian do, but I don't tell him so, because I know this always sounds like a double-edged compliment, begging the question of whether the speaker has seen enough of the rest, or might be hinting that the rest has somehow not been quite up to the mark. It reminded me of what a great clown he is: physical virtuosity is combined with all his other gifts. Give him a breakfast tray with champagne glasses, coffee, orange juice and toast, and a bottle to open and pour and refill across the table while delivering one of Pinter's most hilarious riffs about the upper class women they have or haven't known, and he's unbeatable:

> May I further remind you that Muriel Blackwood and Doreen Busby have never recovered from your insane and corrosive sexual absolutism? May I further remind you that your friendship with and corruption of Geoffrey Ramsden at Oxford was the talk of Balliol and Christchurch Cathedral?

(Note how Pinter goes with the rhythm rather than the sense in the last sentence: it was hardly the talk of the Cathedral.) It's theatre heaven, just as the challenge of lighting cigarettes and having a pee with a withered arm was in his *Richard III*. As is the sheer speed of response with which, when asked if he's slept with one of the women, Spooner snaps back Yes, as if it were the stupidest of questions.

The Tribeca apartment rather resembles the huge anonymity of the set for *No Man's Land* – dark wood and deep recesses. Ian sits hunched in it like Hirst, dwarfed for once by his surroundings: in fact his two aides remind me of Briggs and Foster in the play. He is about to move, which I think is a good idea. He tells me he does nothing else in the day but the show. He is tired, extremely hospitable and affectionate, and goes on to throw a Sunday party and undertake two pieces of major publicity with me – in *The New Yorker* and in a video – which as a recent Lear himself I take to be an act of generosity. We've known each other for over forty years, and I bask in the pleasure we now take in the fact. In the 1970s we worked as Romeo and Mercutio, a little uneasily perhaps, then, still watchful, in the 1980s as the two men in Otway's *Venice Preserv'd*, and latterly with delight in Eduardo de Filippo's *The Syndicate*. Now we're of an age when we exchange health checks on meeting and I count him a very good friend. I have an abiding memory of both of us standing more or less up against the stage side of the curtain at the Haymarket Theatre during the interval of a charity show, he practising his Leontes in *The Winter's Tale*, me trying to convince myself that my tap routine for Archie Rice in *The Entertainer* would be OK on the unexpected stage rake. We were, like many of us much of the time, closer at such moments than over a cup of coffee.

> All sorts of people have taken different views of King Lear,
> as of all the other great Shakespearian roles, and if you
> play them up to the hilt you can be as interesting in one
> way as you can in another.
>
> John Gielgud, *An Actor and His Time.*

I didn't see Ian's McKellen's Lear but being in New York with him makes me think a degree more than I would anyway of the Lears that I have. When we started the readthrough at TFANA and I thought suddenly of my Mum, it was because, at the outset of her long anxiety about and ultimately pleasure in my choice of career, she had, between February 1955 and when I started proudly going on my own, seen rather a lot of Shakespeare. Including, at twelve and during my first few months as a Shakespeare junkie, my first *King Lear*, a prospect at which she may have trembled and would have trembled more had she known that the Lear would look like an Emmental cheese.

As for me, I already adored the Old Vic, loved Stratford only a little less, and suddenly found myself disconcertingly in the West End watching John Gielgud playing the part for the fourth time, even though he'd only just turned fifty. From one point of view, his embrace of this notorious "Japanese" *Lear* was his professional equivalent of a delightful personal tendency to put his foot in his mouth, in that it stimulates both admiration and compassion. The production was laughed to scorn by almost everyone ('not a damp eye in the house'), but was clearly driven by an experimental impulse entirely typical of the actor, who'd been much impressed by the work of Martha Graham on a trip to New York and had now hired her designer Isamu Noguchi to do the set and costumes for him. It may be that both men were about fifty years ahead of their time: nowadays we might like the set, an abstract design untied to any time or place of startling egg-shaped and triangular abstracts floating above the actors' heads. And presumably Gielgud's bold self-transformation into a character actor, abandoning his typical vocal music for a Stanislavskian portrait of a wheedling, whining old man who had only himself to blame, would be much approved – it would have come into the same canon of "character" work as he showed in his Spooner, as triumphant as Ian's, in *No Man's Land*. Gielgud was so sure he wanted to achieve this characterisation that he gave himself a fright: a slip in the programme asked that patrons should not smoke (!) during the performance as it was bad for his voice.

We would also most likely admire the soundscape designed by the avant-garde Catalan composer Roberto Gerhard: the first electronic score ever done for the British stage. The trouble was the costumes, which Noguchi was less experienced in. They were intended to reflect both the essence of each character and the decline in its fortunes – in most cases, bits dropped off as the going got rougher and Gielgud's great cloak developed ever-bigger holes as he descended into madness, as if huge moths had been at it. All this sat oddly beside Noguchi's professed intention to step aside and allow the mythic story to come through as directly as possible in the words.

Well, if only. The costumes and wigs shouted for attention at the expense of almost everything else. One of his knights had a Wellington boot on one leg and a hockey-pad on the other. Gielgud's face was haloed by white horsehair so crude that it hardly seemed meant to be taken seriously either in human or metaphorical terms. He was described as looking like a Henry Moore sculpture, a piece of artistic strangeness then but nowadays popular enough to be considered a compliment. All this took place under the eye of the very British (albeit revolutionary) director George Devine, mastermind of the Royal Court.

And so on: if I go on I'll begin to sound like one of the gleeful critics who butchered the show. Inspired to great satirical heights, they chopped, stripped and gutted, vying with each other in joyous references not without an element of xenophobia – *The Mikado* was slightingly mentioned. And as is the way of these things, there were a couple of rebel reviewers, now forgotten, raving complimentarily in the wilderness.

Even then I think I had an instinct to despise the critics when they were in this frame of mind; nevertheless, at age twelve, I could see I was witnessing something eccentric. What I now know is that history has been kinder than they were to Gielgud's progressive instincts, which were very much stronger than those of many of his contemporaries. Interestingly, Laurence Olivier was extremely supportive – which he wasn't always of Gielgud – as I think any intelligent professional would have been. Gielgud later told me he passionately believed in the production, which he felt his symbolic mentor Harley Granville-Barker would have loved, though his eyes shot heavenward at the memory of his costumes. However he was quite amused (much time having passed) to have been described as looking like both the Wizard of Oz and "Gypsy Rose Lear" in the part. Peggy Ashcroft, playing Cordelia, confirmed that without the Noguchi costumes the production would have been a triumph; and in fact Peter Brook acknowledged a debt to it when he came to do the play with Paul Scofield. At the time, not imagining I would have the benefit of their opinions one day, let alone play the part myself except in my back garden (where I already fancied myself as Hamlet and Richard II, and for some reason Lucio in *Measure for Measure*), I didn't really know what to think. I may have been bored, or perhaps rejoiced in the middle of the life-changing summer I was having with Shakespeare that I had the mature judgment not to like absolutely everything I saw.

Obviously I remember the externals of this first *Lear* clearly, and I have a mental snapshot of Gielgud standing there looking remarkably like himself inside this startling garb and perhaps not enjoying it – but then Lear doesn't enjoy himself very much. And in fact I'm baffled at how little I remember about many of the dozen or so *Lear*s I've seen – the earliest ones least of all of course: I can hardly offer more than a sentence or two about most of them. I may have been right to say earlier that there may be something uninteresting to the young about the afflictions of the aged. At any rate, I have a sense in general of having travelled alongside the play rather than becoming involved with it, at least until I came to be in it for the first time as Edgar.

I know that after Gielgud, I hoped to see some noisier, blood-and-thunder Old Vic production, since all good things began for me there. I had a loyalty to the building which had neatly replaced an early devotion to Tottenham Hotspur. I got it for sure in 1958 when Paul Rogers, whom I'd admired inordinately as Macbeth, was felt to have unaccountably stumbled as Lear. (It was the first time I'd heard the critical damning of an actor as merely Mr Lear.) Rogers was only 41 and beneath his bald pate (probably shaved, as bald wigs were extremely unconvincing at that time) he wore a huge white beard. The actor was a Devonian, vocally warm, sinuous and sensual, a dead ringer for Claudius (which you can hear on record with Gielgud as Hamlet); his Macbeth that I'd so admired was described by Kenneth Tynan, better than I could, as a performance of "bellicose ecstasy". Maybe the sheer starkness of Lear's speech was too near the edge of his range, though he'd certainly have been willing to enter his psychological hell: he had trained just before the War at the Theatre Studio run at Dartington Hall by Michael Chekhov. Chekhov was a fascinating figure who, quite apart from being the son of the great playwright's dissolute brother Alexander, and apart from marrying the niece of Olga, Anton's widow, had been Stanislavsky's favourite pupil until he broke away after the Revolution to pursue his own Method. He moved to Germany and then the States, where he influenced both Marilyn Monroe and Elia Kazan with his theory of the "psychological gesture" – whereby the actor develops a comprehensive physical action to summarise the needs of his character, then internalises it until it becomes a guiding attitude. In fact you might well do "bellicose ecstasy" that way, and much else that Paul Rogers, an extremely expressive performer, could do. At the time I didn't quite know what the significance of Michael Chekhov was, but it seemed to chime with a fact reported by his biographer that for Macbeth, Rogers had cut his nails short so that his hands seemed bulkier.

I remember incidental things from this *Lear*, but surprisingly little about my hero. This being a time when you had two intervals (a thing much feared today) it was possible for Edmund to stand alone like a malign Prospero at the opening of the first and second Acts, and for Edgar, the (more or less) good guy to perform a similar overture before the third. This kind of directorial intervention (by Douglas Seale) was rather untypical of the time: mostly at the Old Vic they just got on with it. It's also not the kind of intervention you'd see now: you'd more likely start with some kind of video, or with a famous speech from the play in another mouth or transferred to prologue position, rather than with a single posed figure standing there in silence. I also remember Paul Daneman's Fool, a sort of beatnik intellectual and satirist, not far from Thersites in *Troilus*. It was an entirely original reading of Lear's "boy" from a remarkable and versatile actor who moved readily between panto, musical comedy, revue and the Old Vic: he played Richard III a couple of times, and Henry VI and Justice Shallow, and he was the original Vladimir in *Waiting for Godot* for Peter Hall.

❖

I shall fail, of course… The further you get into that play, the more you feel that never, never will you, or any other damned actor, be able to act it fully. From all that I have read of the past, no actor has succeeded, and I am not vain enough to think that I will.

Charles Laughton

My Lear is the greatest because I'm the first to play it on a rising graph after the storm.

Ibid

Laughton's 1959 Lear was part of Stratford's hundredth season, and Glen Byam Shaw's last production there before yielding place to Peter Hall. Laughton was at least about the right age. I learned later that Gielgud had been asked first (it would have been his fifth time – those were the days), but he knew Laughton wanted to come back to England to play Shakespeare after twenty-five years in Hollywood and was obsessed with the part, so he personally suggested him (those were the days as well).

I was there of course but I remember virtually nothing of it except the impression of a tubby and rather avuncular man with a snowy halo of hair who spoke rather quietly, with Ian Holm cowering under his cloak as the Fool. It was a prehistoric *Lear*, of a kind favoured by Donald Wolfit but largely discredited now – though I would be curious to see one such production again, just to see if huge distance helps us to see the play any better. I learned later that after elaborate preparatory visits to Stonehenge, Beachy Head (to yell the storm scene at the sea) and the Rollright Stones near Chipping Norton, which date to about 3000 B.C and represent a King and his knights being turned into stone by a witch (Regan? Goneril?), Laughton was something of a pain in rehearsals, even trying to turn the cast against the director and claiming he was doing all the work. Also that he had difficulty projecting to the back of the house (where I would have been), and so took the option of playing the Storm Scene quietly, as Derek Jacobi did in his Donmar performance in 2010 (but as a choice, not a limitation). And that Peter Hall believed that in a more intimate theatre Laughton could have been a great Lear. Like many actors of the part, he was adjudged rather good in the later stages but less effective in the tyrannical early ones. It seems that at moments he transcended acting, and that he was good in some sections every night, but never in the same ones. He also had little interest in the company around him (Ian Holm, having been impressed by him in rehearsals, is unprintable on the subject of the performance – he would have felt strongly, being so close at hand – saying in effect that Laughton thought the part was all about Charles Laughton.)

Still, as a discontented student yet to be impressed by *Lear*, I'd at least got a sighting of some of the cruxes. Should there be real sound in the storm? What kind of madness is Lear's? How bad are the sisters? Or the knights? Peter Brook solved the storm sound in 1961 by having no music at all, just three visible rusty thunder sheets to be rattled at cues in the text. He also, unlike Laughton, saw the play as essentially an ensemble piece, requiring a high standard of acting from everyone and getting it.

And here with him comes Paul Scofield, once every actor's favourite actor (now, miserably, somewhat forgotten by a younger generation) playing Lear at forty and by his own account later having had 'no larger experience in the theatre'.

I have slight reservations about this legendary event, though directed and led by two supreme talents. I'm not sure how warmly we would nowadays take to Brook's insistence that you need to be shocked rather than moved by the play (I think empathy was just what I missed) – and I even wish that the influence of Beckett, especially in the grotesqueries of madness and blindness, had not been quite so insistent. Scofield certainly delivered a Lear battling on in the shadow of nuclear destruction – utterly unyielding, pig-headed in his cropped hair and beard, the voice like a lyrical foghorn. Harold Hobson rightly said he was a man capable of tramping twenty miles a day over sodden fields and arriving home at nightfall properly tired and in a filthy temper, insulting the servants and cursing his relations. Scofield, as I later came to see at close hand, was capable of genius on one night and just very good acting on the next: I'm not sure I saw him at his best as Lear, and slightly preferred his performance in the 1971 film. Here at least the inspired bits are there for keeps, like his superlative version of the Dover scene, as deep and confounding and inexplicable a piece of great acting as I have seen. On the stage I think he may have been a little too flinty, at least for me.

What's less well-known is that Brook had done the play before – in a manner of speaking. This was in 1953 on American TV, for PBS's *Omnibus*, with Orson Welles, and Natasha Parry as Cordelia. It was introduced by Alastair Cooke, who implies (without quite attributing it) that Brook felt that the film's running length of 73 minutes was the ideal length for the play, because otherwise you have to fall in with the tiresome Jacobean taste for long plays which therefore require from the author a whole unnecessary subplot. (An artistic decision then, nothing to do with the sponsors....) Well, the *Lear* subplot is at times vexatious and cumbersome, but from what we know of the attention span of King James's Court (where the play premiered) it is hard to imagine that a long entertainment was ever welcome. Equally extraordinary is the fact that only eight years later Brook was to deliver a production that changed our view of the play forever, and in which the Gloucester family was particularly well played.

There's one good idea in it – no, two. It's good to have Kent in the stocks being visited by a Gentleman, a covert Lear man able to carry letters between Kent and Cordelia in France (at last, a use for one of those tiresome Shakespearian Gentlemen). The other is to have Goneril kissing Oswald (not Edmund, who's entirely cut, together with the rest of the Gloucester family) in order to "raise him up": we did this in Brooklyn too. There are less happy touches: at the start Brook has Lear tear a sheet of flimsy paper into three to give the remnants to his daughters, as if the country were a little notepad. In an interview, Welles himself once said of the play that "Lear is not a star part like Hamlet is. It requires five star actors, not just a supporting cast. There are tremendous parts in it, you know, they have to be played marvellously. It's an intimate, domestic tragedy. The epic quality has to be in its poetry and the mind of the audience. I don't think people have the ear or the taste for the operatic approach. It must just be the actors, and that's all, absolutely all."

Well, with one exception he didn't get what he dreamed of. Micheál MacLiammóir does an odd double of the Duke of Albany and an anonymous character identifiable as Poor Tom but not as Edgar. Alan Badel, meanwhile, amidst all this fustian and ranting, is timeless as the Fool, and in quite a different class. (If you don't remember the work of this very great actor, catch his Count Fosco in BBC TV's 1982 *Woman in White*.) Welles's Lear, astonishingly for such a great actor, is a pop-eyed creation with a great deal of bouffoned hair and wearing one of those plates round his neck meant to set off the head in portraiture, which together with the women's frilly ruffs makes them all look like cakes. He's also quite approximate with his lines and quite often comes in too soon on his cues.

I've sometimes talked to Brook about his involvement with *Lear* and he's never mentioned this outing. I'm not altogether surprised: I don't suppose Welles felt it was his finest hour either. Looking at it, like listening to recordings of very early twentieth-century actors, is depressing rather than amusing. But you do get vast relief and satisfaction that we live now and not then, and that our acting is altogether better.

I'd come to man's estate and even done a stretch in bit parts at the RSC when I went back to Stratford in 1968 to see Eric Porter's first shot at Lear and Michael Williams's at the Fool. Eric Porter was a granite-like man, onstage at least, who like Scofield had no difficulty playing such a part at forty. I knew him because I used to dig him out of line trouble in *The Jew of Malta*, as young actors can sometimes be quick to do for older ones; now I sometimes depend on the same kindness of strangers. In return he did me a great kindness by saying that I had the same technical problem with verse as he had, of running out of breath just short of the last, clinching word of a Shakespearian sentence. I've never forgotten the thoughtfulness of this advice, with its implication of equality and good fellowship. But sadly I've forgotten his Lear except as an atmosphere and a presence, of which he had plenty. By some extraordinary chance I've just flipped on the TV and seen him do If My Friends Could See Me Now from *Sweet Charity* with Ernie and Eric.

Pete Postlethwaite's 2008 Lear arrived in London from Liverpool with a whiff of internal dissent, as indeed there had also been among the critics. It had been trounced and now it was eulogised: clearly many fences had been mended. I enjoyed it well enough: Pete was a terrific actor, even if he did take an odd decision, which he defended to the death, of wearing a patterned floral dress in the Dover Scene and masturbating into it; there certainly is a dire comedy is Lear's madness, but maybe not quite of this kind. Regan suctioned out Gloucester's eyes in a fellatistic gesture that was no more physically improbable than any other way. The Gloucester, and a great one, was my dear old friend John Shrapnel, and he went on to Lear himself for the Tobacco Factory in Bristol in 2012, directed by Andrew Hilton: a production that was admirably clear and uncluttered and in which John, whom I'd known since we'd left school some fifty years ago, fulfilled himself. He is tremendously powerful vocally: I have a recording of us all doing *Oedipus* at Cambridge University. It's rather impressive in that these still non-professional but determined young actors already showed very well, but John was miles ahead of us in vocal maturity. Most of us sounded like four-string guitars hoping to find a couple more some day – impassioned, intelligent, but a bit reedy; but John sounded as if he'd been working big theatres for twenty years. He was that rarity, a Lear who really could play both ends of the part: the power and intransigency and danger of the early scenes were there in spades, and when he came to do Lear's Howl, Howl, Howl with Cordelia in the classic position in his arms, it was a series of peremptory commands, instructions to his court from the other side of grief. It was extremely moving in that he knew no other way to assert himself.

In Bucharest in 2008 I saw, at the Romanian National Theatre, Lev Dodin's *Lear* which he had originated at the Maly Theatre in St Petersburg two years before. The Bucharest theatre has now mercifully been modernised under the directorship of Ion Caramitru, but then the ominous box in the centre of the dress circle where Ceauşescu might drop in was still there, gradually becoming purged of associations. Dodin is a great director, but this time his cast laboured through a sea of Russian clichés: mechanical pianos, a Fool with boots, braces and a top hat over a T-shirt, an enormous amount of not so much musical underscoring as overscoring. Meyerhold in other words (sort of), not Stanislavsky. I'm an enormous admirer of the general timbre of Russian actors, their extraordinary combination of physicality and lyricism; but in *Lear* they were just slow-motion hams. They all got naked in the storm but were carefully lit to keep their privates private, which rather spoils the point; the Lear seemed to be in terminal lethargy from the opening, making an exhausted and gloomy first entrance and remaining so. There were periods of such pitch darkness that we seemed to be watching the action through Gloucester's blind eyes, even if he wasn't on.

So my personal jury remained out on the Russians in this play. Some, but not much, of the gloomy slowness is still present in Grigori Kozintsev's 1971 film with the Estonian actor Jüri Järvet, whose Lear, though very good, often offers sadness where you would expect fury, and seems to fit into a certain tradition of melancholy Lears with the weight of Russian history bearing down on them. But it's worth anybody's while, as it will be ours tonight in Classon Avenue. Kozintsev had also filmed a superb *Hamlet* with Innokenti Smoktunovsky in 1964 which won the Special Jury Prize at the Venice Film Festival. Preceding the *Lear* he published an essay on the play in his *Shakespeare – Time and Conscience*, and the subsequent film was his last work, two years before he died. As with the *Hamlet*, the translation was by Boris Pasternak and the music by Dmitri Shostakovich, a composer Kozintsev admired for his ferocious hatred of cruelty and his fearless but somehow threatening goodness.

The essay is both fascinating and a curiosity and, like the film, unmistakably Russian in its sharp humour, its simultaneous grandiosity and detail. He illuminates the accidental nature of tragedy by pointing out that an avalanche can result from the slightest shift of a single stone; but the essay soon crumbles into fragmentary exclamations about the extremity of the play, repeatedly declaring that Edmund, Regan, Goneril and Cornwall are monstrous, totally and irredeemably without humanity, creatures rather than people, ruled by the counter-revolutionary Dame Avarice. This is a polarisation – obviously enough – rather typical of Soviet thinking; Kozintsev was a People's Artist who had filmed a propaganda essay about Maxim Gorky.

Andrew Dickson, in a recent article, definitively describes the prevailing climate: "Tarnished greys and flat, mute skies; shadowy hearths from which no warmth ever emanates. The seraphic eyes of Jüri Järvet… as always with Kozintsev, images of people – farmers on the heath, plunging spades into the sod; a torrent of peasants shambling towards Lear's castle, anxious of what the mad old King will do with their country. The text suited the play's clotted density and stony non-lyricism, its urgent muttered asides and sclerotic outbursts of poetry. It seems absolutely true to what the Jacobean Shakespeare, mindful of land enclosures, watchful of his new king, was writing about."

Tonight, I watch again the ragged procession of cripples and children in carts trailing through the landscape of grey stone and rock to converge on Lear's castle – whence, having divided the kingdom, he will gallop off for his first night in Goneril's house. The image is both Russian and universal: at the time I'm writing the travellers greatly resemble the wave of migrants arriving in Europe from Syria, even though there are fewer of them in the film and they are more passive.

In fact, Kozintsev's actors are drawn from the Baltic states, chosen perhaps for their chiselled features and magnetic eyes. Intriguingly, the Edmund and his half-brother Edgar look alike, as if their common father Gloucester rather than their two separate mothers dominated their genes. Jarvet, originally cast as Poor Tom – imagine, an actor who could equally play Lear as Edgar – ended up in the lead, with his fine, wasted, sorrowful face, its grief and delusion a little like an emaciated Paul Scofield. In *The Space of Tragedy*, Kozintsev reports that he was drawn to Jarvet's way of walking grandiosely, with a sort of clumsy ceremony, and to his sinewy body and enormous peasant's hands, which made him look simultaneously like everyone else and the first among men. Horses rear up in their stables at the start of the storm – as they breathtakingly did when they were the first to sense the approach of the Ghost in *Hamlet*. The hovel at first seems full of rats, but they're derelicts, as in some terrible Gorkian dosshouse, dozens of them in a stable, layered on top of each other, a Bosch drawing. When it comes to the mock trial in the hovel Lear therefore has plenty of witnesses eager to participate. Pilgrims continually criss-cross the huge empty terrain, Edgar and the blind Gloucester joining them.

These are all extremely arresting impulses, as is the first sight of Lear carrying the dead Cordelia. This is nearly as striking as the famous appearance of the Ghost on the skyline in *Hamlet*. (It was easy for Jarvet – he then put her in a chair rather than carrying her around for take after take). What's harder to explain is the way the camera retreats from Lear himself in the second part of the film, as if in distaste. It is a little as if Kozintsev had lost interest in him, disdaining such advanced suffering and encouraging us to look at the state of the nation instead – a Marxist inflection the play doesn't really support.

Throughout there are scenes the director visits rather than expressing, let alone allowing them to be moving. The Fool survives everything, playing a little recorder, and indeed closes the film. There is no scene at Dover with Gloucester and Lear, nor does Gloucester endure his attempted suicide on the edge of the cliff. Surprisingly – this is a movie and able to do such effects – you don't see the blinding of Gloucester, which is accomplished on a darkened screen; Regan shrinks from Cornwall as he dies, then hunts for Edmund in the castle and begins to tear his clothes off (this happens much later in the play if at all); then, to show how depraved she is (I suppose) she goes back to the dead Cornwall and kisses him too.

Kozintsev's interpretation is also faintly misogynistic. Pointedly, Goneril does not hear Lear's great curse on her fertility, which he instead mutters to himself as he climbs into his carriage after rather a quiet formal dinner with her. Therefore what might reasonably be seen as her justification for closing her heart to him is removed. Likewise, Reason Not the Need is murmured by Lear to himself, not to his possibly discomfited daughters, with occasional reference up to the gods. Instead of close-ups the second half is powered by the smoke of permanent battle, conflagration and marchings; the collapse of townships as by a tsunami is scored with a great deal more Shostakovich, particularly choral. Regan and Goneril are both quite mature, in the Russian manner. This doesn't compare at all with Susan Engel's wonderfully beautiful Regan in Peter Brook's film of the same year, weeping as she throws the blind Gloucester out of the house – not from repentance but from the sadness of fulfilment: a half-tone, you might say, that totally reveals Regan, and a much more complex observation of her character. In fact Brook's film is in every way, at least for Western audiences, very much more accessible and illuminating, and extremely imaginative. It certainly takes you, through the miracle of Paul Scofield, into Lear's head, though not with much sympathy.

However, there is a consensus beneath all the discrepancies. The curious fact is that these two projects, with their very different emphases and edits, come out at exactly the same length – they are precisely in step with each other. Lear goes into the storm after an hour and seven minutes in both, eighteen minutes later Gloucester is blinded and the overall running time of both is two hours and twelve minutes.

Jüri Järvet went on to star in Andrei Tarkovsky's *Solaris* the following year, as did Donatas Banionis, who played Albany. Graham Winton and I are awaiting an equivalent phone call.

## ACT TWO SCENE ONE: THE FLIGHT OF EDGAR

EDMUND: Wonderful news: my brother's still in the lumber room. I'm not quite sure what to do with him, but now I'm told we have visitors in the house, Regan and Cornwall no less, so I'll be cheek to cheek with maybe the two biggest shakers in this new world. Also I hear there's trouble between Cornwall and the milksop other husband Albany – which really means between Regan and Goneril: they look more like factions than sisters now the big dog's away, bitches on heat for a fight. I don't know yet what move to make, it's all half-thoughts, but what's for sure is that in disposing of Edgar, I become the family hero.

So now – Father's watching out for Edgar to reappear so he can pounce (Father? Pounce?!), but there's a risk, as he's quite malleable in the wrong hands. I need to get Edgar out of the house under the paternal nose – and fast: I must keep his head spinning. If he settles on one explanation of events for long, he'll see through me. Edgar's a rationalist but a political simpleton: I can jumble his mind with my father's bodyguards, Cornwall's faction, Albany's faction, all against each other, or rather against him:

> Intelligence is given where you are hid...
> Have you not spoken 'gainst the Duke of Cornwall?...
> He's coming hither now, i' th' night, i' th' haste,
> And Regan with him.

And keep it coming:

> Have you nothing said
> Upon his part against the Duke of Albany?
> Advise yourself.

I've noticed that intellectuals think slowly, oddly prone to overload. Edgar doesn't know what to think; now, while his vertigo lasts, I'll pretend I have to fight him:

> Draw! Seem to defend yourself! Now quit you
> well...
> (Fly, brother!) Torches, torches! (So farewell).

Trouble is, it's not much of a fight. I don't want him to wound me – and he won't, why would he? – and I don't want to wound him as it'll slow matters down. All I want is him out the door, over there on the left, all this stuff unprocessed in his brain. So not much clashing of swords, and mostly by me, I can smack and scrape mine on the floor and make a big noise to attract Father. And then he's gone, poor non-bastard.

EDGAR: I've armed myself. I'm willing to fight to preserve my life if need be. I'm the Earl of Gloucester's son, after all, I've been properly trained in the art of combat and I'm skilled. So now Edmund insists on a mock duel, I can do it. His heart seems not quite in it at first – well, he's my brother, why would it? Then he gets some stab of jealousy, maybe, that he can't control. Anyway, he makes an attack that surprises me – why, it's as if he really wanted to hurt me. I can defend myself but it is a tense moment between us. Then he demands that I flee and, one way and another, I'm convinced. But it's all so fast: from hiding in Edmund's room and being out on the street I had space for just one word.

EDMUND: All right, easy. He's gone one way and when the servants arrive I send them after him by the other. Who will believe I fought to keep him in the house and lost? I need to cut myself. Fuck. But the flowing blood makes my imagination run too.

I tell Father that Edgar was mumbling all kind of incantations, muttering to the moon to help him – he'll like that, this whoremaster fop of a father – and when I wouldn't oblige he charged at me and wounded my arm.

I'm amazed at what these people will believe. I warm to my task. I tell him Edgar called me an unpossessing bastard, and that whatever he did no-one would believe my word against his. Sounds like Edgar? I think not. But my father's such a fool, he now decides that Edgar's the bastard, and I'm the legitimate. I'll inherit.

It's been a good day's work. The pieces are moving fast around the board. And all because of being indispensable, always there.

GLOUCESTER: My Edmund has been injured fighting with my legitimate Edgar. It seems he found his half-brother mumbling wicked charms, conjuring the moon; it's the fault of the eclipse all right. Edgar wanted to murder me, but I mustn't think of that awful thing now, because Regan and Cornwall, whom I think of as my patrons – I'm not so sure of Albany and Goneril – have arrived.

REGAN: We need Gloucester on our side – and we need a place to stay away from home now that I've had this letter from Goneril – all our father's rioting at her house, the insults, the obscene cursing. I don't want that at home, so Gloucester's will do.

And his son is plotting against him, do I hear? Edgar? Surely the King named him as his godson (well, I think he may have done). I hit my best form here: I always find a nice warm atmosphere leads to inventiveness. And yes, wasn't Edgar on good terms with those riotous knights I've just had Goneril's report about? (I didn't think I'd get away with this, but Gloucester's such a credulous man.) He hasn't heard about that – obviously, it didn't happen – but Edmund hastens to confirm it, so I know he's our ally by instinct. So – we're suggesting the knights could have put Edgar up to the murder of the King so that they could make hay of his estate, such as it now is – well, we'd be in danger then too. I'm really cooking now: a complete invention, this military coup, but I can tell my husband's proud of me. He enlists Edmund – which could mean against Goneril and Albany as well, soon enough. We have him, and in a sense Gloucester too.

It's a good day's work. We'll get inside and lock the doors, as if a storm was coming. Well, it is. My father.

## ACT TWO SCENE TWO: THE STOCKS

KENT: No sooner do I arrive at Regan's with the King's letters about Goneril than I'm given not an answer but an order, to follow them immediately here to Gloucester's. I'd been leap-frogged – somehow – by that wretch I tripped up at Goneril's. He must have flown like a bird (although sweating like a greasy pig) and given Regan her sister's letters, which they read and immediately, without listening to me, told me to join their crazy ill-natured caravan. And here at Gloucester's I meet him again, this unnecessary zed, this base football player. He affects not to recognise me at all now – just as he pretended not to recognise the King – and now he takes me for a servant of Gloucester's and demands I take care of his horses. This time I have him alone, no-one can see us. So I tell him, Leave them in the pissmire ditch, because I know what he is:

> a knave, a rascal, an eater of broken meats, a base, proud, shallow, beggarly, three-suited, hundred pound, filthy worsted-stocking knave...

Sweet heaven, where did all that come from? I can feel something give way inside me, a door I'd been holding shut at Goneril's swinging open, and out that spills; I seem to have all the time in the world.

Because I'm a different man now, I have a different talent!

> A lily-livered, action-taking, whoreson, glass-gazing super-serviceable finical rogue, one trunk-inheriting slave... nothing but the composition of a knave, beggar, coward, pander, and the son and heir of a mongrel bitch.

It's true, this man is in one body all that enrages me now I've re-entered the world. I'm seeing all the worst of them now, all these placemen and careerists, these men who change their faces with the weather, the weather of their master's moods; these women too who'll say anything, do anything to keep their position strong.

There is only one Cordelia in this court, and she's gone, the one who won't oblige, God bless her. I've found a way of reaching her but I'll tell no-one of it, not even you onlookers. This new world is terrible, a place of utter falseness; I like the Fool, who won't dissemble, although he risks his neck each time he speaks. I'm impressed by his ability to clown, to improvise, all at a moment's notice.

I'm like the Fool now, or rather the Fool crossed with the Kent I used to be. As for this lickspittle, it's not a fair fight, it's a beating not a fight, I could take him apart in a second, but he bleats for help. I could never have talked like this when I was the Earl of Kent. Though I did call the King a mad old man in front of all the court, I told him to see better, that he was doing evil, invoking his stupid gods in vain. I was trying to make him see the simplest sense but I couldn't match his language. I'm not surprised he banished me and would have killed me.

When I think about these things I can't be stopped:

> You whoreson cullionly barber-monger...
> I'll carbonado your shanks.

CORNWALL: I have to put up with a lot. They call me a toff, but I have a temper and a brain: this servant of my father-in-law's (I don't think of him as any kind of king now), is a thing I recognise, one of those men who like being Honest Joe, who cannot flatter, he. He's here at the right time too: I need to show Regan that I have the balls to deal with such a man. There's a restlessness in her these days, she wants something new from me. I'm not sure of Goneril and Albany either, but the more we can make common cause the better.

OSWALD: My lord, I spared this fellow only because he was old, my lord, I was just doing my duty, my lord, I raised the alarm. And I'm clear about it: the King struck me at his provoking, and he made it worse by tripping me up and harassing me, attacking me, my lord, just for doing my job.

KENT: My adversary stands there, wagging his tail anxiously. I tell this Duke:

> I will tread this unbolted villain into mortar and
> daub the walls of a jakes with him.

I can't put it more squarely than that. But I should explain more patiently, in steady verse; this is the Duke, though I'm not sure he has a brain. So: my lord, these people are like rats, but rats who soothe their masters; they bite all right, but not their masters, rather they fan their masters' flames and cool their moods, they renege, affirm and turn their kingfisher beaks. Why don't I like him, you ask? Let me put it simply, I don't care for his face – no, my lord, don't laugh, I don't like yours either, come to that, or your lady wife's.

No, I shouldn't have said it, and I feel a noose curling round my neck, but it's too late to stop now:

Sir, in good faith and in sincere verity,
Under th' allowance of your great aspect
Whose influence like the wrath of radiant fire
On flickering Phoebus' front...

CORNWALL: I'm a bit of a philosopher as well as a swordsman, as well as an all-round alpha male. And now this man mimics me. A big mistake. I believe I'll put him in the stocks. I saw Gloucester had a pair, well, he probably needs them, he lives in the town, he has to deal with thieves and criminals, stock them until they die of exposure, their bare feet tickled by passers-by, insulted, kicked, spat on. And anyway they fascinate me, these ancient instruments. How long can a man last at this time of year? A cruel and unusual punishment for sure, but just within the limits of civilised standards.

KENT: I can bear the stocks. I can bear the pain and the sheer inconvenience. I can see the world turn, and now the sun is coming up. My King's sun, I hope, the very sun I can read this letter from Cordelia by. She's hoping to return the world to rights, she's somehow heard my story – but from whom? Who knows me now?

## ACT TWO SCENE THREE: ON THE RUN

EDGAR: I have no choice. I don't know what the charges against me are, I can only run and run. My execution lies behind me. Its cries are wild, inhuman. I even hid in a tree, like a wild thing myself. In the dirt, I welcome the dirt. It could be the saving of my life, it's my disguise. There's nothing else and no-one to confront. I flee and live or stay and die.

...Whiles I may 'scape,
I will preserve myself...
And with presented nakedness out-face
The winds and persecutions of the sky.

I've read about this, these Bethlehem beggars, half naked, frantic, pins in their flesh and their arms, they put themselves to this, to beg for their keep, they care not at all. They're as wild as the men behind me, my father's men. I feel myself falling off the edge of the known world, but then I am caught by a slipstream, something within me, and carried upwards:

Poor Turlygod! Poor Tom!

Not bad, not at all. That's something yet. But how did I think of Turlygod?

Edgar I nothing am.

## ACT TWO SCENE FOUR: THE END OF THE PAST

KING LEAR: It sits up in front of me like some animal in the middle of the road, its outline as sharp as a waking dream. Except that it lingers. I go to Regan's, but they've left without telling me and come to Gloucester's. Without a word. So I come here too, following like a dog. If they're worried about space at their house how are we going to stay, all of us, at Gloucester's? There's not nearly so much room, and what about their retinue, never mind mine? It was a sudden decision, the man there said, as if they were evading someone. Me?

And now the stocks, like a joke from an old folk tale: my loyal Caius has made the same journey and now he's sitting in a pair of stocks. It could be me. In the stocks, where I put the King's enemies, adulterers and thieves. Stocks, where your feet are higher than your buttocks. Stocks, in which you are pelted to near death. Like me.

Caius greets me, but really I'm staring into the eye of a beast. This sort of thing gets my Fool going, he immediately riffs on about cruel garters and wooden stockings. I wish he'd shut up for once. I just need facts, hard facts. Has something come free of its hinge? Does the world spin against itself? Is there something I'm missing here, something on my blind side, some new operation of events? My servant in the stocks – by whose word, by whose allowance? I feel my gorge rise, my head sing.

No-one who knows Caius, nobody who knows me, could do this. And then it comes, like concussion. Who did it? He is blunt – it was "your son and daughter", no more ceremony than that: Cornwall (no son of mine) and Regan. No they didn't, I insist. They would not, I half-plead. Yes. No. Yes. By Jupiter – will he help? No. For one thing they daren't, and anyway they couldn't: it's worse than murder. Explain it. And I learn that the idiot who serves Goneril, the "my lady's father" man, has complained to Regan about Caius.

This will stifle me, I can hardly breathe. But I must find this daughter of whom I hoped so much.

FOOL:
If your servant wants wealth
And follows for gain
It comes like a death
The wind and the rain...

KENT: He runs inside to them. I'm left with the Fool, a sitting target for sure: he must love a man in the stocks, looking like a fool. Think of the jests that are coming.

But he says nothing. He just watches. I ask the servant why the king has so many fewer men now. Maybe half what he had before, only fifty. Then the Fool joins in, making it nonsense: he gabbles about ants and schools and not working in the winter. I have no idea what he's talking about. Then he sings a song I can't make head nor tail of. I could never put up with this, that's the difference between me and the King – he and this Fool have some code no-one else can break. But I know there's always something swelling up behind what he says, something ominous and unclear. This time it's – what is it?

Let go thy hold when a great wheel runs down
a hill, lest it break thy neck with following.

Does this mean a great man falling who could take me down with him? Does he blame me for my loyalty? I can't be sure, I'm never sure. He makes up a rhyme about the difference between a knave and a Fool, rain and storm, a wise man flying, breaking his neck, a great man stinking. And all the time he has his eye trained on me – does he know who I am? He's the one who would, as a dissembler of sorts. My body is disguised, while he disguises his thoughts. He draws you out and then punishes you. I ask him where he learned his song, and he says:

Not in the stocks, fool.

I suppose that was a gift for him. I'm glad the King is back, angry as he is.

KING LEAR: They speak a language I've not learned. I need a compass. They deny to speak to me, but I asked them to speak with me, so how can they deny it? It makes no sense. They say they're tired, tired with travelling, and whose fault is that? I've asked to speak with them. The Duke of Cornwall has a fiery quality, Gloucester says. So? What does that have to do with me, this fiery quality? Even if he has a quality. There's too much talk here about daughters, fathers, qualities. Some things endure and I am the King. It's as if I were about to speak and he interrupted to say the sky is blue.

Now Gloucester says he's "informed" them of my wishes. What word is that? You "inform" a man of the road to the palace if he's lost his way, you "inform" someone of today's news, but I'm saying they are to come here to me. It's not a thing you "inform" someone of, after all.

I'd better explain to Gloucester. Are you listening to me? Cornwall is married to my daughter. My daughter Regan, whom I must speak to. Do I need to explain that this is an order? What is this "fiery" Duke? Is the weather too hot today? No, a light flashes: he might be unwell. This is, in present circumstances, a comfort. They've travelled a long way and I know what that's like. Sickness you can't argue with, I know it myself. Sometimes the afflicted body poisons the mind as well, making it long for rest.

But still, what is Caius doing there, his legs sticking forward out of holes, sitting upright in pain? This must be their doing. Why does the lackey Gloucester not resist them in his own house? All he says is that all in all he wants all to be well between us all. But they've immobilised my Caius and gone off for a fiery rest: he sits here and I stand here while they sleep. Or whatever they do. No, no, enough of this. They are slaves, tell them to be here in a heartbeat. Or... what? Or I'll... what? What, quite, will I do? Hammer at their bedroom door? I have a feeling they spend too much time in there anyway.

My heart is not good, it thunders, it rises in its seat, I can feel it in my throat. The Fool thinks I should beat it down like a piemaker, whacking down the eels in his pie as they poke their heads up to look around. Or like the man who put butter on the horses' hay, knowing horses hate butter. Why would he do that? What has it to do with me? I've taken little care of things like that.

Now, this is better. As soon as they arrive they set Caius free. That's better.

CORNWALL: I thought the first thing to do was to set the servant free, just as a gesture to the old man.

REGAN: I thought the first thing to do was to be nice to the old man, tell him how pleased I am he's here.

KING LEAR: It's Cornwall who greets me first, I notice, but still she says she's pleased to see me. I believe her, I should think she is. My blood flows back like a dam breaking. Of course she's glad, or she'd be no daughter and my wife would have been no true wife, and I'd divorce her even though she's dead.

Regan straightens my collar, which has ridden up, to spruce me up a little. This also puts me at a disadvantage.

REGAN: Well, it didn't last. Immediately he complains about my sister. What a fool he is; does he think he can please me, denouncing her? He always set one of us against the other, just as he did when he made us all make our speeches about him. And Cordelia always won anyway. Except that time. I am staunch. I point out it must have been his followers that made Goneril throw him out. Perhaps she wasn't candid enough with him, but I can be. He should take advice, he's too old for his own opinion to be enough, he should make amends. And – I'll chance it – he should say he's sorry.

KING LEAR: Sorry?!

I see we're entering a maze, some multiple thing. This is not going to be like firing at Goneril with all my guns. Regan was always more subtle, readier to shift around. I need no blunt weapons with her, I must tack around myself. Not lose my temper, for then I only hear one word in three. She must see Goneril with my eyes, in her depravity. But I don't like this measured response:

> I have hope
> You less know how to value her desert
> Than she to scant her duty.

Less/more, know/scant. How can I "less" know anything, I'm twice her age. Tick-tock. As if all human action was an equation, a reduction to one thing against another, and me flying up in the air in the other seat of a see-saw, because she thinks my grievance lighter than hers. She must say it again, and she does, at twice the length. For her, one thing follows from another: if her sister corrected my men they must have needed it. False, the wrong way round, but I must be quick, I know her tricks, though I must not be seen to calculate.

So Goneril is cursed. Damn her. Damn her. What does Regan say to that? That I am on the edge of my extinction, I should be ruled by younger hearts. I should go back and grovel. Does she know me? This is not Lear. Doth Lear speak thus?

I stumble to my knees in front of her, her husband, of Gloucester, Caius and my household. I only dare look at my Fool – he will be amused and proud of me, he's my audience:

> Dear daughter, I confess that I am old...

She's right, they're unsightly tricks, but whose fault is that? I tell it her again.

REGAN: I have to hand it to him in a way: he's some perverse diplomat, flicking sideways shots at me, circling me. He thinks I'll respond to my sister being damned to utter hell, this cursing of her bones. Oh, fie, fie, fie: may her beauty rot, may fire burn out her eyes, may fogs drop on her, their shit on her fine clothes? Is he mad, to think this will work? All I can think is, it'll be me next.

KING LEAR:

> No, Regan, thou shalt never have my curse...

I meant to say this, but I find it turning into a question in my mouth. So, a little flattery. Regan was always my favourite until Cordelia came along. She's never been unloving; she can be giddy, a little bit Daddy's girl, but I've probably encouraged her in that. But now she's firm, like a judge, and I'm edging towards something terrible:

O sir, you are old....

I don't think she ever called me Sir before. I'm fearful. Yet have I left a daughter. Don't I? I rear away – the stocks are still here, though Caius is free. I yell at her – WHO PUT HIM THERE? – and then, as if its brass harmonised with mine, I hear a trumpet sound. I can't quite take this in. It seems to mock me, a roaring trumpet.

She, the other one, is here, with her rudeness, her bare fists. As usual, in one sentence I hear only every few words. Dotage. Indiscretion. Worse, she's gone straight to Regan. They make a barrier of hands, like a cordon, outnumbering me. You shall not pass, they say. They will be each other's forever, long after I'm dead. Do they think my fifty men aren't strong enough for the two of them with their hands joined? Or my hundred?

I feel this crushing in my chest again. Is my head about to burst?

How came my man i'the stocks?

Stocks, stocks, stocks: it keeps repeating like a blow. Tock, tock, tock of the clock. Now I hear a new voice, I hardly know it, from nowhere. I swing this way and that. This is not Gloucester, apologising feebly as usual, but Regan's husband. It was he who did it, he who's not even my blood. I'm suddenly stronger than he could ever be:

You, did you?

Regan swivels her dial, to a soft sweet reason, even elegance. I'd be proud if I wasn't so ashamed of her. Lurking inside her words I heard mention of "half" my train. I'm stalked by three dogs now, one snapping gently, another taking great pieces out of me, one watching me in silence. Should 1 go back to Goneril with fifty men?

> No, rather I abjure all roofs and choose
> To wage against th' enmity of the air,
> To be a comrade with the wolf and owl.

I begin to hear chimes: a hundred. Fifty. Twenty-five. Ten. One. The wild air is beginning to call me.

Who would that be, that last one?

GONERIL: We're working together well. Well, sisters do; we sense each other like cats, like two instruments improvising together in time. It'll be a relief when it's over, of course.

KING LEAR: I've cursed her once, twice, three times. A disease of the flesh, like a sex disease, an outgrowth, a disfigurement that once you've seen it you can't take your eyes off. But enough. I'll not call the heavens to witness a second time. Let her mend, cure herself, as diseases do. I'll go to Regan, I and my hundred knights.

She picks up the cue. She's not ready, she says, she hasn't cleaned the place up. Of course not, she is here at Gloucester's.

REGAN: I make the same rhythm as before, over and over until he understands. I have to now, since he says he'll have no more to do with Goneril.

I'll fire the questions at him. Isn't fifty enough? Why more? What will they do? Why so many? There's a problem of focus. I have staff, you have staff, who will call the shots? Two private armies under the same roof, jockeying: impossible, absolutely impossible.

Still, I've galvanised my sister after that terrible attack. Her house is hers to command, mine is mine, and if he wants his own, let him stay at home. He still has a palace. And if our staff don't please him, he has my permission to correct them. Surely that's a concession, so much so that I'll reduce his number as a quid pro quo. Not fifty. Twenty-five.

Then he plays a strong card: simplicity. He gave us everything, well, yes he did, as far as he was able, and he was right to. Now the deal is, we look after him, take all the decisions, but he keeps his hundred bodyguards all the same. No, his twenty-five. It doesn't look good.

The trouble is, he's right. If he goes on like this, I'll be lost, for I know deep down we shouldn't be doing this: I hear my mother in my ear. But luckily he speaks to the heavens now, making a fool of himself just in time. He talks to the gods, thank God. As if there were any gods.

GONERIL: My sister's flagging, so I'll take a chance. Look: Why twenty-five more servants when we have fifty?

REGAN: Got it. What need of one?

LEAR: How have they done this? But now I'm calm. Yes, "need" is the word. If you've nothing you already have too much, it could be said. But what does that make life into? It makes a man an animal, a minimal design. Look at you, dressed to the nines, your colours and your hightailing. Even the coat that keeps you warm is more than you need.

What does a man need? Can't you see? Look at me, now I've given them all.

WHAT NEED?
WHAT NEED?
WHAT NEED?

Patience is what I need. The gods look down. They see me, reduced to a small thing, I'm old, I need patience, I'm abandoned by my children, utterly cast out. What can I do? Not bear it tamely. I will not weep. Make me angry. These monstrous women, I will have my revenge. I don't know what but I will have it, the worst you can imagine. I'll never weep, not if my heart breaks in my chest a thousand times. I know the cost will be my reason. If I can't weep, something worse will overtake me:

> O fool, I shall go mad.

REGAN: And he's gone. There is silence, a long one. I'm shaking like a leaf. Thank God he called on the heavens. Thank God he threatened vengeance. Thank God he couldn't weep and called us hags. I thought we were lost there for a moment, but he made himself a fool. I'm telling my sister why we did it:

> The house is little, the old man and his people
> Cannot be well bestowed.

Why am I telling her? She knows.

GONERIL: I keep telling my sister why we did it:

> His own blame hath put himself from rest
> And must needs taste his folly.

Why am I telling her? She knows. Now she's telling me again:

REGAN:

> For his particular, I'll receive him gladly.
> But not one follower.

GONERIL: Yes, I know. I know, you don't need to tell me. It's as if she was telling me her name and that she's my sister. But I'm doing the same thing to her.

REGAN: We've worked so well together and we've done it. So why are we telling each other we've done it, what our point of view is?

Gloucester keeps telling me it's a foul night: well, I know that too and I can't help it. Shut and lock the doors and go to bed. He may launch an attack. Shut it all up, pull up the drawbridge, lift the duckboards. There's going to be a storm, and he'll be in it. The old fucker.

# WEEK FIVE

---

## MICHAEL ATTIAS (COMPOSER)

...For once again, the fierce dispute
Betwixt damnation and impassion'd clay
Must I burn through...

– John Keats,
*On Sitting Down to Read King Lear Once Again.*

I remember, towards the end of the awful bargaining scene with Goneril and Regan that precedes Lear's expulsion into the wild, that first crack of thunder and the moment of silence that followed it. It was when Lear said:

> You think I'll weep;
> No, I'll not weep...

You could sense the whole company – actors, operators, stage managers and musicians – collectively brace their nerves, and draw breath for what was coming.

## MARCUS DOSHI (LIGHTING DESIGNER)

What is the storm in *King Lear*? And what does that mean for what comes before and what comes after it? For me and for director Arin Arbus these were the essential questions in the process of making the lighting for our production. The storm is a reflection of Lear's mental state, to be sure, but it is also real, as the Earl of Kent says:

> Such sheets of fire, such bursts of horrid thunder,
> Such groans of roaring wind and rain, I never
> Remember to have heard.

## MICHAEL ATTIAS

Arin had given me my way into the world of *King Lear* when she used the word "fracture". Fracture of the mind, the nation-state, the heart; a space opening between words and sound, sound and music, the inside and outside, reason and madness. So every sound in the storm sequence was doubled up, one part a reproduction of the real and the other its version in the mind; the music formed a bridge between the tempest actually raging on the heath and its metaphorical equivalent.

> Blow winds, and crack your cheeks...

For a moment of fearful exhilaration, we shared Lear's belief that it was his words that were causing the winds to blow and the thunder to strike – and being authored by Shakespeare, indeed they were; without them, there would be nothing, no storm, no stage, no theatre at all. But as Michael Pennington said early on in rehearsals, the storm must feel real: it can't just be an expression of Lear's approaching madness or the tricks of a well-designed sound system. And Lear's belief that he is himself 'the cause of thunder' is also about to fracture. If we're not both on his outside and inside, the devastating emotion won't carry.

## MARCUS DOSHI

Lear's confrontation with Regan and Goneril and exit onto the heath was the first point in the production where the light changed during the course of a scene. As Lear became more and more frustrated, the warm incandescence was slowly broken by a shaft of icy white light cascading over the corner of the upstage wall – a harbinger of the storm. The icy-white colour in fact came from arc-source fixtures, which are lamps that harness the light from arcing electricity like a mini-lighting bolt. After Lear's exit, as Regan, Goneril and Cornwall faced downstage, the light dropped to its most unnatural angle thus far, a direct ice-white light from the front that would be repeated in the storm.

So how do you put a real storm on stage?

Well, you don't.

In a pre-production workshop we actually rigged up a space with water and wind and strobe lights and leaves and such, to test what vocabulary could be useful in the theatre: the result was that it was all pretty lame. The rain was just a little water, the strobes looked like a bad disco, and the wind didn't work. It was nothing even close to the cataclysmic tempest that Lear was experiencing internally. Which was great, because it freed us to move beyond anything representational towards an abstraction that might actually meet the intensity of Lear's experience.

Still, I felt that some elements of a 'real' storm were critical to the telling of the story because the characters are experiencing and talking about it. It needed to be scary and dangerous and feel real even in its abstraction. This meant taking the natural phenomena of a storm and arranging them unnaturally.

So, the second movement of my design – from Lear on the heath through to the blinding of Gloucester – began with imperceptible light in the storm, barely illuminating Michael and the others, interspersed with moments of blinding intensity, shifts of perspective and focus, constantly in motion, their unpredictable rhythms all done with the merciless white of the arc source lamps.

Of course all this would be meaningless if it wasn't specifically curated with the text, so in working the sequence we were very careful about that. Elements were integrated into Michael's performance over the course of many technical rehearsals and previews: each day Arin and I added no more than one or two events to ensure that it didn't become overwhelming. For example, when Lear says

> Singe my white head! And thou, all-shaking thunder,
> Strike flat the thick rotundity o' the world

he was in a dim single spot cutting through a thick blanket of haze in the air. On the word 'singe', an extremely bright flash illuminated the entire space from an unnaturally low angle in front for one second, then faded over two seconds, leaving Lear in silhouette from a dim single spot behind him. On 'thou', the spot sharply crossfaded to another spot aimed diagonally from the front which then grew slowly larger in size. On 'world', lighting strobes cracked around high up in the flies, running through the next phrase – 'Crack nature's moulds…' before resolving back to a single spot. It was pretty much like this for the whole scene.

## MICHAEL ATTIAS

Throughout the show, the band used an expansive array of instruments. Each of the four strings on Pascal Niggenkemper's bass was separately miked, and also prepared with various materials, so that the storm textures he created – the cataracts and hurricanoes, the singe of sulphurous fires, and so on – could be dispatched to different sets of speakers surrounding the audience, to blend with Marcus Doshi's fog and lights.

To hold all this extreme sonic diversity together, all the bass textural effects as well as the melodies written to be sung by Edgar and doubled by Pascal in Renaissance style shared the same intervallic content. Satoshi Takeishi played a large archaic frame bass drum, glockenspiel, darbouka, hydrophone and gongs, both live and as samples processed through his iPad. We scored each of the hits of thunder precisely into the text. Hearing the subtle, powerful interaction between his percussion and Michael's invocations was for me one of the highlights of every show. I also triggered samples through my laptop, played alto saxophone, kalimba, ocarina (for the foul fiend that haunts Poor Tom 'in the voice of a nightingale'), whistles, and, for the blood impulse that propels the war towards the final duel between the two brothers, I introduced another archaic instrument, the shrieking double-reed zurna. Interwoven throughout were the sound effects created with my genius co-sound designer Nick Pope: thanks to their musically textural layers and although equally artificial, they were, by their very *difference,* able to take on the burden of reality.

Never once did we get to the intermission emotionally unscathed. Part of the brilliance of Michael's interpretation lay in the magnificent, always unexpected ways he negotiated these bifurcations. Seven times a week, he took the band through fire and rain. Like Gloucester, we learned to 'look with our ears.' With his voice as the soloist, and the other actors as members of the orchestra, we made a kind of concerto. And in fact, the whole of Act III, with its weave of voice, body, text, clothes, light and sound, from the tears of the old man becoming rain through to the explosion of blood at Gloucester's blinding – became as integrated a theatrical gesture as I've ever been part of.

## MICHAEL PENNINGTON

This week we begin to feel the set growing around us. When I'm now asked in an over-respectful way how I feel about having played King Lear, I curtail all the pieties by saying the main effect has been to leave me with sore feet. Sore knees too – just as they were getting better. Riccardo's set is made of metal with a slightly uneven finish, so unlike most wooden stages or sprung ballet floors, there's no give in it; each time you kneel or scamper around it's a little punishing. But it does look great.

While the floor is going down a wall is going up, with much attention to Health and Safety for actors and crew. The apparent upstage limit of the stage is in fact a large panel which can be opened to reveal a still deeper perspective of suffering – in front of it, Riccardo has designed a huge rusty wall made of the same immoveable metal as the floor, wide and high. This will, at two well-judged moments quite late in the evening, winch down by degrees until it forms a new slightly elevated floor, higher by its own thickness than the true one – revealing a sort of inner chamber beyond it, right against the outer wall of the building. This is actually designed as a tiny studio space for TFANA, but Riccardo's cunning gave it a different and somehow sinister meaning. It suggested a secluded torture room or an extermination chamber, the place where, in the barbarous extremities of Act Five, elders like myself were punished for being old by being beaten by Edmund's soldiers and Cordelia was humiliatingly stripped after the battle. It's as if we were about to be herded somewhere unthinkable.

How predictable is the motor that does the winching of the wall?

A stage is by definition quite a dangerous place. Trap doors can collapse on themselves and drop you several metres; if you look into the flies above you it really doesn't do to evaluate how many tons of equipment are held above your head – pieces of scenery, heavy lamps on electric bars – that just could fall on you from their restraining wires. And a wall like this that winches down, however slowly, is a thing that under no circumstances you want to stand under, even for a second; even locked off in its halfway position it looks positively precarious, for all its hydraulic good practice. You don't want to go near it, nor will you be allowed to.

The play's third Act begins with a shortish scene sitting between Lear's expulsion by Regan and Goneril – he would call it his decision to leave – and his confrontation with the elements. This is when the Earl of Kent hears from some Gentleman exactly what the audience is about to see. This newcomer reports that the King

> Bids the wind blow the earth into the sea,
> Or swell the curled waters 'bove the main
> That things may change or cease; tears his white hair…

He is accompanied only by

> the Fool, who labours to out-jest
> His heart-struck injuries.

Do you really want to hear about this before you see it? And who is this Gentleman and how does he know? Shouldn't he really be called a Soothsayer, as the King hasn't yet done it? In one sense he's a sadistic official setting the high-jump bar as high as possible for the actor of Lear. It's an extreme example of how Shakespeare's descriptive powers so far outstrip the technical resources of his theatre that such a thing may have excited its audience; but for us, it just seems daft. On the other hand it gave Richard Burbage and now me a few minutes' respite to draw breath while listening to what we are going to have to live up to. It's a miniature version of the Shakespearian Comfort Break, the famous rest for the hero in Act Four before he heroically returns to effect the play's climax.

In reply to the Gentleman, Kent has his turn. He has something to tell us too, a thing as unlikely as the moment in Act Two Scene Two when he said he had received intelligence from Cordelia in France. In both cases, how? He's disguised as a servant – or has he managed to retain from his days as the Earl of Kent a little secret workspace at the court, to which he can discreetly return? By what network of international informers has he opened what we might now call a thread to Lear's daughter, whom we have not seen acknowledge him when they were briefly together in the play's first scene?

By the time you've finished asking yourself these questions you've probably stopped listening; but the next bit is important. Kent reveals that there is "division" between Albany and Cornwall, and that the King of France has spies in their two households. He is preparing, presumably with Cordelia's help, for an invasion – in fact his army already have their 'secret feet' in the channel ports. Kent wants this Gentleman to get a message to Cordelia explaining how she may be reunited with her father, and assures him that he is himself a 'gentleman of blood and breeding' (presumably meaning himself rather than Caius). Still, as news flashes go, this is terse, and the Gentleman asks him, as if he'd forgotten his lines:

> Have you no more to say?

The director's blue pencil, which has hovered over the Gentleman's premature description of Lear, hesitates, as there is something here we're going to need to understand. Without this Cordelia Thread, we're going to be in trouble about the French invasion; and even with it we're likely to forget, as the army's continuing progress is so poorly tracked. When Cordelia returns, we may wonder how she's done it, and by the time we remember we'll have missed something else.


## ARIN ARBUS

So, though aware of the risk, we'll cut the scene.

## ACT THREE SCENE TWO: THE STORM

KING LEAR: I make the storm! I call it out of its corners and ask for more:

> Blow, winds, and crack your cheeks, rage! Blow!

Yes, a wind like the north wind of Boreas in Ptolemy's map with his fat old cheeks bursting, splitting the whole world like a village, scattering its homesteads and church steeples, silencing the cockcrow and the roosters. And here it comes, spitting at me like an animal. Those are my first commands, and then again:

> You cataracts and hurricanoes, spout...

And it comes again. Freedom! Freedom! Me and the thunder now, only, no mean little negotiations, no hinting and handholding, just the arching sky, a great blustering bowl above me.

I am the thunder and lightning; my syllables roll over each other, tumbling like a storm:

> You sulphurous and thought-executing fires,
> Vaunt-couriers to oak-cleaving thunderbolts
> Singe my white head

Singe is a word to sing out... And what does this fire burn? The tiny hairs on my old man's head, a hurricane to destroy a wisp. It's not an equal battle, but I have my power back.

> Rumble thy bellyful! Spit, fire; spout, rain...

No rights and wrongs out here. My bestial daughters owe me, but the weather not: it whips me only because I am here, out in it. This is its horrible pleasure, to harry a defenceless man. Or maybe in truth it's another of my daughters' ministers, like that Oswald, that Cornwall, those women's men. Wind and thunder, allied like Goneril and Regan.

> And yet I call you servile ministers
> That will with two pernicious daughters join
> Your high engendered battles 'gainst a head
> So old and white as this...

I wallow in this, and the rain pours off me.

On the ground, flat on my back on the ground. I must be still. I must be patient. I must start thinking again. The Fool must make up a song, to soothe me.

FOOL:
Clothe your bollocks
Instead of your head
Or you'll find a disease
In your wedding bed.

Put your foot in your head
And you'll make your brain sore
Your diseases will spread
And you'll never sleep more.

And by the way, what woman doesn't pout when she looks in her mirror?

KING LEAR:

> No, I will be the pattern of all patience.
> I will say nothing.

That word again, NOTHING.

Now Caius speaks. He widens my mind. I see a huge width, every point of the compass, as if my brain had come loose.

KENT: That Gentleman was right. Even when the bear, the lion and the hungry wolf keep their fur dry, he plunges on with his Fool.

Found him! Out here, like a judge of the world... He must go into this hard-hearted house, where I was stocked. And get a shred of courtesy.

KING LEAR: I think this. I think this is a pause for
thought. I look across the horizon, and I can see
the flat earth hiding its head, cowering below the
storm above. You can see your enemy here, and
they can see you. Here's a man who has a crime on
his conscience, and he knows he can't hide, though
he can run. It's some unthinkable thing: he can feel
the lash on his back in his waking dreams. There's
another who broke his sworn oath and sleeps
with his sister; another plotting a mass death; a
churchman who abuses his children. All these guilts,
all these crimes, out you come like the damned from
the madhouse and make your peace in this storm of
justice. As for me, wrong has been done to me, far
more than I have done.

These men with me look at me in a different way,
as the world spins. My boy is trembling, there is
something in his eyes that I remember from a
baby, a baby's look of... premonition?

My brain lurches. Have I lost something? I speak
to my Fool, I ask a question. I don't ask many
questions as a rule, so it feels strange. But I am
noticing something for the first time, that my Fool
is shivering. Why do I notice this?

> Come on, my boy. How dost, my boy? Art cold?
> I am cold myself.

My wits must be turning, that I should ask such a
question as I never asked before. A question that
doesn't solicit for me, or defend me. Or frighten
me. Just a question of him, as to what he is at.
Well, I'm cold too. So we should lie together – in
the straw, there's nothing else available. I feel...
sorrow. Sorrow, but calm as well. I am supposed
to be angry, angry with the storm, angry with my
daughters, so what is this sorrow worth? I think
it's for him. My Fool who's never seen anything
like this. He sings a simpler song. I know this old
song, they sang it in the streets and it makes no
sense but there is the wind and rain in it. No, it

makes no sense, but I tell him it's good, that it's a piece of philosophy, it's the very truth. We'll go inside.

FOOL: A night to freeze your balls, this, ladies and gentlemen. One more song:

When the priests are all talk
And the beer watered down
When dandies design
And lovers burn brown
Then Britain's re-written
And Gretna's Thames Ditton.

When all wrong judgments are absurd
When knights of the realm are not half-busted
When there's no such thing as a slanderous word
When a crowd is a place a cutpurse is trusted

When money lenders work on the farms
And tarts build churches and sing all
       the psalms
Then is the time, if you live that long
Your feet will go walking in time with
        my song.

Did you know Merlin's going to write that, some day in the past?

## ACT THREE SCENE THREE: GLOUCESTER AND EDMUND

GLOUCESTER: It's a dream that keeps coming back, a horrible dream. I'm being kept from the King at his worst of times. Cornwall told me to lock up the doors and Regan to shut him out this dreadful night. And I know the country round, there's no shelter, none, for many miles. That was enough, I thought, but no sooner were we all inside and I asked to seek out the King and take care of him, than the air froze. No, no, I couldn't. Did I understand? I couldn't. Why? Nothing. They sat in my chairs, they drank my wine, they have taken over my house, far more than the King tried to take over theirs. I wasn't to speak to him, or make the kindest move. It's as if they wanted him to die in the storm – how in the world can that be? To die? But it was only Regan and Cornwall, Goneril said nothing, perhaps because Albany wasn't there. He stayed at home I think, doing some home improvements probably. The Cornwalls are running this, whatever it is, this thing. But thanks be, I'd had a letter before they arrived, and I locked it in my desk: there's to be an invasion from France, on behalf of the King, for revenge. Edmund and I must defend him and be strong together.

So I tell Edmund all this.

I ask him to distract the Duke so that he takes that eye of his off me; to tell him I'm in bed, sick, while I go and help my liege lord. Strange, strange, strange, as Edmund says (thank God for him), savage and unnatural. Thank God for Edmund. This is a world gone wrong. All I know, I must slip away and look for my master. I hope I find him in time.

EDMUND: All I ever have to do is be there, and he entrusts everything to me, even his head to my noose. He wants me to collaborate with him; but in fact I can depose him better than I could before, better than with that Edgar trick. The Duke of Cornwall must know my father's guilt, and then the money is mine. This is the law of my goddess, Nature; the young spring up exactly at the same rate as the old fall. Well of course, it keeps an equilibrium.

## ACT THREE SCENE FOUR: POOR TOM

KING LEAR: Let me alone.

They showed me shelter from the storm, but I didn't want to go there, I thought I would never

*(Above left)* Michael Pennington and Robin Ellis [MW]; *(Above right)* John Shrapnel, Brooklyn Bridge [PS]; *(Below)* Prue Skene, The Polonsky, Robin Ellis [MW];

*(Above)* Michael Pennington, Prospect Park, Mark Pennington [PS];
*(Below)* Louis Pennington, Eve Pennington, Prospect Park [MP]

*(Above)* Act One Scene One: King Lear [CR];
*(Below)* Act One Scene Four: The Fool, Lear's Knights, King Lear [CR]

(*Above*) Act Three Scene Seven (The Blinding of Gloucester):
Regan, Gloucester, and Cornwall (Saxon Palmer) [CR];
(*Below*) Act Three Scene Two (The Storm): King Lear and the Fool [CR]

(*Above*) Act Two Scene Four: Kent in the Stocks [CR];
(*Below*) Act Four Scene Six (Dover): Gloucester and Edgar [CR]

*(Above)* Act Four Scene Six (Dover): King Lear and Gloucester [CR];
*(Below left)* The Duke of Cornwall [CR]; *(Below right)* Regan, Duchess of Cornwall [GG]

(*Above*) Goneril Duchess of Albany, the Duke of Albany (Graham Winton) [GG];
(*Below*) Act Four Scene Seven (Cordelia, King Lear and the Doctor) [CR]

(*Above*) Act Five Scene Three (Edmund and Edgar) [CR];
(*Below*) Act Five Scene Three: The End of the Play [CR]

come out if I did. It broke my heart, for I know it was meant kindly and I could never explain why I could not. They think, my Fool and my Caius, that this is just a matter of keeping dry, of a roof over my head: that's all this is to them, this insult to skin and bone. But I am crouched inside a greater storm, like the Fool under my great coat, though my mind is clearer now. The body cares only for itself, but the mind can zig-zag everywhere, this way and that, over the past and into the present, looking for a way to survive. All that hammers on in mine is my girls' cruelty, it's as if they'd dashed my meat on its way to my mouth, they are my mouth itself, tearing off the hand that feeds me. Like a bear in fact, you flee from a bear but if you run from it to the stormy sea, you'd have done better not to run at all but to feel the bear's breath in your last moments.

My daughters are that bear's mouth.

This is all perfectly clear to me.

But then I tip again, into the pit:

In such a night as this! O Regan, Goneril!
Your old kind father, whose frank heart gave all!

I saw clearly there, just for a moment, but now I see I'm creating positions for myself again, I'm sorry for myself again. My plan is never to weep but to avenge myself, after all I gave them, and then I feel myself tumbling through myself into some fire that's been scorching me since Cordelia left, it's as if I've not drawn breath since then; the view I had of things was driving me mad as the sea and wind, but now in moments I can see another picture: a picture of my Fool, who mustn't stay in the storm, he's no roof for his head, he has nothing to fight with. Myself, I might even sleep.

But then I see them out there, naked, poor and wretched, they have no roofs, their clothes are in rags, how can they think about ingratitude, about children? I see them. What have they? What can they hope for, stretched out in front of me, the homeless ones in their camps, in empty fields, their world shrunk to a few square yards?

I've not considered this before. I've not considered this enough. I should have gone out in the storm before, out of choice, to see what it was like for them, then I would have given away my gloves, my spear, my velvets, and paid my retinue of a hundred knights to stay at home; then my people would have known I loved them, they would have known there was justice on the earth as in the heavens. I could have done it with a flick of my sleeve, or like shaking the rain off my hat.

And here, just on his cue, comes a poor naked man, in all his looped and windowed raggedness. What he says makes no sense, as what I say perhaps makes no sense, but I see he has nothing, and that makes sense for him. He is naked and bleeding, he is sorrowful and proud, he is what I could become, a wise philosopher, he must have done the same as me, given everything to his daughters, and this is how you end up. He speaks a special language, a language of the court, but as if in a dream:

> Poor Tom, whom the foul fiend hath led through fire and whirlpool, o'er bog and quagmire, that has laid knives under his pillow and halters in his pew, set ratsbane by his porridge, made him proud of heart.

Proud of heart! How beautiful he is! He walks tall and naked, sees the world and gives me his benediction:

> Bless thee from whirlwinds, star-blasting and taking...

He has found his own state of grace, because of his pelican daughters.

The Fool makes jokes, but he doesn't interest me so much now. And the jokes are plain ones – that a beggar has a blanket so he's not naked, that everyone's mad but him. I ignore him. He'll need to do better than that. What does Tom say?

> Obey thy parents, keep thy words justly, swear not, commit not with man's sworn spouse, set not thy sweet heart on proud array,

Yes yes yes, and it seems he was a serving-man at court, so he's learned his lessons well: he

> curled his hair, wore gloves in my cap, served the lust of my mistress's heart

He knows what he speaks of: he did the act of darkness with her, broke his sworn oath in the sweet face of heaven, with wine, with dicing, women, he was an animal of many kinds, a hog, a fox, a wolf, a dog, a lion. How beautifully he speaks:

> let not the creaking of shoes nor the rustling of silks betray thy poor heart to woman...Still through the hawthorn blows the cold wind...

This is a man, a man of the world and not of the world. Is this what a man is? In a night worse than the grave, he owes no silk to the silkworm, no hide to the animals, no wool to the sheep. He's the thing itself, and I loosen my clothes to be like him.

But as I do, my philosopher tells me a walking fire ahead of us is the fiend. He would be the one to know. Flibberdigibbet, who blinds the eye and touches the face with sickness, who makes you no longer tell the difference between a moving fire and a man, who mildews the wheat and bestows the hare-lip. But I thought it was Gloucester coming, and perhaps it is. He asks our names. But I have lost my name. This is not Lear, remember.

KENT: Nor I Kent. Which only leaves Poor Tom, and he is raging now that he is frog toad tadpole newt and water... that he eats cowdung salads, and rats, drinks moss from the stagnant pool, whipped and imprisoned, though once he was a courtier with a shirt for every day of the week, his horse caparisoned and his sword at his side. Who is he? I almost know him from the past somewhere, and why is he so angry?

GLOUCESTER: I have to tell the King what his daughters did after he left, taking me from his side on pain of death. The cruelty of the women to you, and the cruelty of Edgar to me. Filial ingratitude will be the end of me and perhaps of you. But we must hurry – I have an outhouse on my land, exposed as it is, I'll bring you in and feed you. But you're talking to a filthy beggar.

KING LEAR: My philosopher, you mean, who knows how to set a trap for a rat, and clean himself of the fiend. And where the thunder comes from. He must have been trained, but in what? We make a chain together, hand in hand and all travelling in step, then all may be well.

EDGAR: What did my father say?

## ACT THREE SCENE FIVE: CORNWALL AND EDMUND

CORNWALL: I will have my revenge ere I depart the house.

EDMUND: This man is even stupider than my father, but more violent, like a rat. If I tell him it's terrible for me to put loyalty (to what? The principle of justice?) before my natural love for my father, he'll probably buy that.

CORNWALL:

> I now perceive it was not altogether your brother's evil disposition made him seek his father's death, but a provoking merit, set a-work by a reproveable badness in himself.

EDMUND: Does he mean my father's reproveable badness? I think he must. This man is a blind man lashing around in the dark, trying to keep his sentences clear and balanced, like some pedant running for office. He's a fool but he holds the sword that'll dub me one day. With a grand effort, as if I was pulling it from my gut, I give him the letter from Cordelia's spies that my fool father gave to me. I can afford some grandstanding too I think. Oh God, that it should be so! Oh God, my father! How terrible to be an honest man when it costs you your family!

That was a little much perhaps: all he can say to it is that he and I should go and see his wife. I don't know her, and she looks like a piece of work, so I'd best not rush. I'm approaching the heart of things. I sympathise with all the work that lies ahead of him. And now do I suddenly hear music?

CORNWALL: True or false, it has made you Earl of Gloucester.

EDMUND: Easy does it, don't get excited. Remember Cornwall has no brain at all, just imagination. I apologise for my too-much-goodness and I'm sent to find my father. Please God he's out there in the rain, looking after the King. That will bring the whole house down on him. I wouldn't like to meet these Cornwalls on a dark night – well, except possibly Regan.

Now what's he saying?

CORNWALL: Thou shalt find a dearer father in my love.


## ACT THREE SCENE SIX: THE HOVEL

KING LEAR: Eventually they brought me under cover.

It is like a dream when I have taken harsh wine. I sit and stare at some detail – my toes for instance. If a thought strikes me I let it take me away. But if I reject it and continue to examine my toenails, something important may still transpire. I've one more thing to say to my people, my subjects who have been through this night with me. After all, they have nothing, not compared with me, the rain comes down on them always, through the holes in their clothes, through their paltry roofs, onto their hungry bones. I owe them due process, that much I can do. So we must bring my daughters to trial. My companions will be these justicers I've found. We must have order, I cannot rest until I've seen the outcome: it must be proved beyond doubt that Goneril kicked her father. But why did not Caius trip her up as she ran away, as he did her servant that time? And why doesn't he chase Regan away now? Why has he let the dogs in to snap at me like hunting dogs, female hunting dogs?

EDGAR: This is my home, my father's farm house, I played in here at one time among these tools and implements, with that old man who looked after it and showed me how they bound up the hay. And here I am, like that boy who dressed as a beggar to frighten him. The same heady smell of hay but now mostly dank rain, the end of a storm.

My father's made a fire, good. He's gone for food, for whatever use that will do. But the warmth has hit the King like a hammer, and seems not to have helped him – he was better in the storm. He makes less sense now, he broods, he seems – untethered, somehow. And his Fool just keeps asking riddles, like a clock you can't stop, and none of them funny, they hurt. Whenever he speaks to the King the word 'madman' is in it. Is a madman a yeoman or a King, he says? A yeoman is mad if he lets his son overtake him, a gentleman is mad if he trusts a wolf to be kind, a horse to stay healthy, a whore to keep her promise, a boy (like him?) to love him.

FOOL: I have to make him see, but I only speak to him in riddles, I always have. If I showed him who I really am, as I am alone, in my stupid life, under the hedgerows, my tone of voice, my turn of phrase, he would be shocked, he might even denounce me, hang me perhaps. I have invented the character of a Fool and now it's my burden. But I must make him see, even now the truth is not funny at all.

My problem is this madman, whom I think I know for no madman. There's something about his familiars, his devils and even his songs, that I don't believe. He knows the start of one song, 'Come o'er the burn, Bessy, to me' but seems not to know how it goes on – luckily: it's a filthy song since Bessy's 'boat' is leaking, she has the pox. I fire the rest of the song back at him, but he looks lost. Because he doesn't really know these songs, they're my repertoire, although he's heard them a lot. Who is he? Could it be that he's...? Could it....?

EDGAR: It's as if we're all singing together. Sometimes the instrument just takes over. No one is playing in tune, but jazzing around, and I didn't know I knew of so many demons, so many sprites: Frateretto, Nero, Hoppedance, the black angel. I don't know what's coming next, the instrument is playing me, the player. I make up a song about dogs, perfectly rhymed but I don't know where I found it. Then, suddenly, I'm done. This is my godfather and my King – and look at him, gathering his imaginary skirts about him against the snapping dogs, imagining his daughters scampering like mongrels. My drinking horn is dry, and so's my brain. My father's found a way to get him off to Dover. I must be there too.

KING LEAR: I'll draw the curtains. Make no noise, thunder god, I'll go to supper in the morning. I've had none tonight. Ah yes. Yes. Yes.

FOOL : And I'll go to bed at noon.

❖

## JAKE HOROWITZ

The question everyone struggles with is, why does the Fool disappear? Where does he go, or how does he die? Or does he die? Productions deal with this differently. I have read of Lear accidentally killing him in the storm, being forgotten and dying in the cold, or being captured and hanged by Regan and Cornwall's soldiers, hot on the heels of Gloucester. These are all sad endings to the Fool's life, but each of them avoids one aspect of his disappearance that tragically buttons up his story, I think: that the Fool makes a *decision* to abandon Lear. I know Arin is thinking about him hanging himself. I too think his death is no accident; no outside hand plays a part. The Fool, for me at least, leaves to end his own life.

In Act Two Scene Four he sang a song to Kent, declaring "I will tarry, the Fool will stay." This loyalty and commitment to Lear is what gets washed away in the storm. He can go no further with this man who is running himself into the ground. It is too painful to witness. And so he breaks faith, and leaves.

The Fool's entire story questions what it means to be loyal, to be wise, to be full of sorrow and hope all at once; wanting, trying, needing to laugh, trying to be there for someone you love, trying to face a world which is crumbling in front of your eyes. And a few dirty jokes too. It never ceases to amaze me.

## JACOB FISHEL

There are three shifts for Edgar once he comes out of his hiding. First he tries to scare Kent and the Fool away. But when he recognises Lear at the mercy of the elements, he abandons his own safety and protecting him becomes the priority. Lear's sudden fascination with Poor Tom allows Edgar to calm and guide him. His third shift comes with the entrance of Gloucester. Instead of hiding from the man who wants him dead,

Edgar leaps forward and delivers a harangue on his suffering. His father has condemned him to death without even a word; that wound is deep. The knife twists when Gloucester fails to recognise him and refuses him charity. In our production, Christopher McCann as Gloucester whipped the begging Tom away, making Edgar feel the other side of the privilege he once enjoyed.

Gloucester reveals two things: that he still believes that Edgar sought his death, and that Lear's daughters also want him dead. It is not clear whether Edgar overhears either of these, but I found it helpful to.

Then, in Act Three Scene Six, Edgar and the Fool battle for Lear's affection. The Fool relentlessly supplies him with bitter truths, but they seem to plunge Lear further into madness. For Edgar, this is not the time for such things: co-operativeness is better, a view he articulates later ('Bad is the trade that must play fool to sorrow, Angering itself and others'). He is compassionate enough to see Lear's madness as a catharsis: the fracture in his heart may be paid for by the fracturing in his mind. Edgar used his explosive imagination to survive exile, and now he tests its ability to heal: he communicates with Lear through madness while the Fool talks sense.

### ACT THREE SCENE SEVEN: THE BLINDING OF GLOUCESTER

CORNWALL: Now this is private. Goneril must go post haste back to Albany to tell him of the French invasion, and that Gloucester has opened the door to them. But she has a thrilling idea before she goes:

GONERIL:
Pluck out his eyes.

CORNWALL: I like this. I like my sister-in-law for it. Better than hanging him, perhaps. But I'll take charge of it – I have the training; I don't want two women competing for the rapture. But Edmund, my new Gloucester, must leave too; this is his father after all, and there are limits for a son – aren't there? He always talked about his sense of justice playing against his family feeling. But Oswald's news is bad, bad, bad, that Lear is in Dover with – thirty-five? Thirty-six? – of that rabble of knights, to join

Cordelia's side there, I suppose they'll put him up the front, the figurehead of justice. Edmund must go to Albany and warn him to be ready to move fast.

And all this is Gloucester's doing.

I watch Edmund leave with Goneril before we start, we lock the doors fast and no-one can see us taking our pleasure, in the depth of the night. My wife understands me. Bring the old man in. Pinion him. There are times when due process must be put aside and a man's anger is his own glorious justice. Regan too knows we have no just cause in law for this, at least not to kill him – but we have enough to strip him, flay him, tear him and crucify him, or I shall never have peace. It's an act of war which all good men will understand. I cannot sleep while this man walks, sees, speaks.

GLOUCESTER: This is my house, my house. This terrible woman.

She straps me to the chair like a dog, worse than Caius in the stocks, she pulls one small hair from my beard as if that were all she was about. What a mockery, in my own house. All I did was to save the King, and who would do him harm? I am sure of it now, she would.

They know I've had letters though, they're right not to believe they are neutral. They know I would join with the King if I could, if I could only see him; they know that I was saving him from them. They know I have sprung him, out of their reach, out of their claws. What's to lose? I did it because I could not watch this dreadful woman tear his eyes out or her sister ravage him like a wild boar.

REGAN: He gives me an idea, and I feel fire creep through me, through my loins into my very heartbeat. He keeps talking about seeing. That's it, that's the clue, that's the climax.

GLOUCESTER: It comes fast, and I see it coming, I see its edge approaching like the sharpest light, I cannot move my head. This will be like nothing I've known. I stagger without moving. There's a buzzing, seething blackness and stars, a halo of thorns, while I sense, not see, with one eye now, his own servant take a knife to him, or perhaps it's my servant.

And now the flash again, the same terrible fire. Edmund! Edmund! What does the woman say? That he betrayed me to them? That he authorised this? Sharper than this knife, deeper than this darkness, I see that I was wrong. I knew Edmund all along. This strikes me down worse than blindness.

It is dark, quiet and still as if the room were empty. There is screeching in my head, a continuous whine as of an animal, but I know it's not from outside. There's nothing out there except my folly. And the bloodied Cornwall begging his wife to help him now he's wounded. But she says nothing. I think she has left, walked from him.

I feel kindness, some lotion for my eyes. And I will, I will, crawl to Dover. I will hear my King though I cannot see him.

I crawl on my belly. The clock stands still.

# THE THREE SISTERS

## MICHAEL PENNINGTON

Why is it that Act Two Scene Four is so often a major turning point in a Shakespeare play – consider *Twelfth Night* or *Henry IV Part One*? Here it was the point when Lear rushed into the storm, but it was also the climax of a partnership bordering on the telepathic between Goneril and Regan.

This was their finest, or foulest hour, and everything from now on will be a decline for them.

When it comes to getting us to this point, the pair of them together have shown they have real heft. Why is that? As a combination Goneril-and-Regan-and-Cordelia certainly don't. How has this affinity between the elder sisters come about? Is a point being made about the consequences of the mother's absence (and when was that?), one being faintly replicated in the Gloucester family, which has no female presence at all?

Cordelia is the youngest but we don't know by how much. She is kept until last in the love contest partly because she's the top of the bill in Lear's eyes, and partly because she is indeed the most junior. Now that productions no longer see her as a secular saint or the ideal pretty ingénue, she takes a more meaningful place in the tree: her own woman, resolved to stand her ground. The playing of the first scene is more complicated – and more satisfying – for Cordelia than it might seem. Not a wronged innocent (though she is both wronged and innocent), she is stubbornly unaccommodating: her remark about not loving a father as much as a husband is like a public gibe as well as a reasonable definition of terms. She is the most obvious chip off Lear's block, and her journey has begun even though she won't be visible again for a long time. She takes leave of her sisters rudely – 'I know you what you are'. What badness does she see – and implicitly always has seen – in them? Eventually she is not above blaming Lear for her captivity: even in her tenderest moment once they are reconciled, she takes an oddly critical tone:

> For thee, oppressed King, I am cast down;
> Myself could else out-frown false Fortune's frown.

When she returns from France she is stirred by Lear's miseries and may feel a dim regret that she was so difficult at the outset: perhaps it would have been better to compromise for the sake of peace. Now her obduracy is overtaken by her rekindled love for Lear and a new adaptability, quite different from the beginning, when she struggled with the very hardest thing for her temperament to handle. When Cornwall superbly condemned Kent as Caius:

> He cannot flatter, he!
> An honest mind and plain – he must speak truth!
> An they will take it, so; if not, he's plain

– you realised it could just as well apply to Cordelia. And the trick at the end is to find traces of what she used to be within her new rising devotion to her wayward parent. Recalcitrance and kindness mingle together.

But why is she so different from her sisters, so much closer to Lear than to them? Neither Goneril nor Regan have her sturdy independence of mind, which perhaps he used to like; they have a suspicious scorn for Lear, not necessarily without love until he jolts the play into being by cursing each of them in turn.

So what happened to the two of them and how lurid was it? It will never be visible to the audience, but may be of some use to the actor. There have been suggestions of abuse, which is really both too dramatic and too vague a charge. Judi Dench played Regan in the 1976 *Lear* with Donald Sinden in which I played Edgar. She had a stammer – a brilliant suggestion of fear of her father that might have had any number of causes.

Rachel Pickup is in her early forties, Bianca Amato a little younger and Lilly Englert graduated from the Stella Adler School a couple of years ago, so, allowing for gallantry, it's safe to say there's an age gap. Rachel I've known for many years (I remember her Cordelia ten years ago with Timothy West); she is the daughter of Ronald Pickup but since her mother Lans is American, she travels and works at will in both countries. In herself she has a loyalty so staunch that you would think I was the only actor, except perhaps her father, ever to have deserved to play Lear or to have succeeded in the part. Imagine the force and resolve of Goneril turned not against Lear but to his defence and you will sense what Rachel was like as a colleague and friend: I hope that for the sake of natural justice, she transfers her affections to her next leading man.

Bianca was born and grew up in Cape Town and has done a great deal of European drama, including the high style of Jane Austen and Noël Coward. Lilly – so infuriating as Cordelia in the opening scene and so stricken in the last – was born in London, but raised in Italy. So the casting of the Lear family suggests a mild variant on American speech, being inflected a little with the actors' backgrounds, which was perhaps helpful to an American audience. (Arin and Jeff have admitted to me that apart from good casting, this was a small insurance policy against any criticism that Lear was the only actor who didn't sound altogether American. In fact, in Shakespeare, I'm not sure those sorts of differences are important.)

Bianca's emerging Regan is restless, not naturally self-confident, suggesting a vortex of unrealised desires. She is dissatisfied, imaginative, inordinate, so profoundly insulting to me that on occasion I would fly at her and nearly end up in a punch-up with Saxon Palmer's Cornwall. By this time she is becoming the perfect candidate to blind a man.

Meanwhile Rachel's Goneril is lean, wounded, and has a ruthless edge in her sexual manipulation of Oswald to sustain his loyalty. Her cruelty to me is angular, cold, and absolutely unchangeable, and never less than stylishly administered. She has a natural elegance, and her characteristic – and to Lear infuriating – habit of swishing a scarf around her lends great point to

> If only to go warm were gorgeous
> Why Nature needs not what thou gorgeous wearest
> Which scarcely keeps thee warm.

What has gone wrong in the Lear family? There's only a line and a half that refers to the absent mother/wife; at one moment Lear makes his anxious joke that if Regan were not pleased to see him he would divorce her mother for adultery even though she's in her grave. As an only child I've always marvelled at the operation of siblings – usually for the good, sometimes for the painful, but never quite for the utter destructiveness that Regan and Goneril achieve, though not before they've played a magnificent doubles partnership to strip Lear of his defences.

## BIANCA

When my agent told me I was being offered Regan my first thought was "Why not Goneril? Who's playing Goneril?" At that time I felt that Goneril was bolder, more articulate, more dynamic than Regan, and I tend to play dominant and clear, as opposed to wily, slippery, or emotionally fragile. Then I re-read the play, and of course got excited about the younger sister, in her complexity and her murky psychology. Meanwhile Rachel Pickup – reed-thin, husky-voiced, thoroughbred – was wonderfully tremulous, like a violin string about to snap. I ended up darker and stealthier, calmer in my viciousness. A very good dynamic.

## RACHEL

Having played Cordelia I thought I knew the play, but I only knew Cordelia's play; now I was to see it as Goneril's. I recalled thinking how glad I'd been to be Cordelia; those other sisters, I'd never want to play them, they just don't make sense – no motivation, no reason, no justification; yet now, the moment I looked at Goneril, I just felt, How could I have been so blind? How misunderstood she is – Regan too, but Goneril still more so. This is the actor's instinct to understand, not judge.

Arin (who always gave the impression that we had all the time in the world), Bianca and I were very clear from the start that these sisters had to be real, human, deeply messed up but not evil. Survival rather than greed was driving us in this new world.

## BIANCA

I was interested in Regan's need to be validated and at the same time to stay in control: and underneath, her determination to punish her father for his inadequacies. She's up to her ears in middle-child syndrome, ignored by a distracted, irrational, self-obsessed, capricious and insecure father who is losing his marbles. Her contrived performance in the opening scene is the first of a series of last straws for her, inflamed by a seductive taste of power with her husband, and she loves it.

She revels in her volatile marriage. Cornwall and Regan need each other to feel they are being taken seriously – he sexually manipulative, co-dependent, ambitious, runty, she disturbed by desire and righteous in her violent perversion, a huge chip on her shoulder. When they blind Gloucester there's definitely a sexual thrill, and when Cornwall dies in the process, my Regan walks away from him like an animal leaving the wounded behind.

## RACHEL

And we wanted the relationship between the two of them to start out in tune with each other. But that breaks down as each clambers over the other to reach what they think they need. Regan starts and stops but Goneril is direct. The plot they pursue when Father arrives isn't premeditated, but when we shut the doors, we know the first threshold has been crossed.

## MICHAEL

Meanwhile Lilly 's position on Cordelia is direct:

## LILLY

All she wants in the first scene is for Lear to hear the truth: she's challenging him with a new idea, an idea of simple candour. She knows you can't measure love and when she asks her father how her sisters could love only him when they have husbands, she is questioning their honesty. Cordelia believes that marriage requires you to support and care for your partner, and she believes in bonds (she keeps using the word), both of the heart and the law. When she's banished and leaves her family they're broken. I think this leaving is extremely painful: relationships are complicated and between siblings especially so. I don't think she hates her sisters or that she is good and they evil. It's not emotion Cordelia is driven by: she loves her father deeply but she has an inner strength and her own way of seeing the world.

Not long ago I went to a fundraising event for an organisation that I certainly approved of, but I knew that as I was sitting at a table with nine potential donors, I would really have to express special excitement about it to be of any help, as if it was the very best organisation of its kind in the entire English-speaking world. What would Cordelia have done? She'd have said simply what she felt, without dramatic exaggeration. I grasped how brave and isolated she is and how much belief she has in her ability to reach her father.

## MICHAEL

And it all happens because Lear's inordinate vanity requires, and presumably always has, that love is rewarded with favours, according to his own judicious assessment. The love test is preposterous of course, and it also doesn't bring the best out in Cordelia: sanctimonious moral superiority with a side-swipe at the father. In a way he makes each of them into only children, for the worse not the better. The test that apparently gave them the liberty to express themselves (on the subject of him) in fact would have imprisoned them in gratitude, had it worked.

By this week the alliance between Goneril and Regan seems to be playing out in real life: I meet Bianca and Rachel one day coming down together from the gallery. I'd seen them up there gossiping for half an hour. I asked what about. Men!, they said. I couldn't get another word out of them, just exclusion and the confidence of two heads working as one in the battle of the sexes. I felt as excluded as Lear (well, not quite) and for a split second vaguely resentful, in that male way. After all, I'm a theatre colleague and so an honorary woman in a way Lear could never be. So I nagged my way into their talk. This was all good sport, but being sensitive to exclusion is also the root of much male jealousy, extending from *Lear* to *Winter's Tale* to *Othello*. It's the sense of a hidden life, of mockery, of a secret being held against you. And it comes to a head when you're a man who indulges a lifelong habit of setting his children in competition with each other for Daddy's love according to who does the best handstands.

# WEEK SIX

## SUSAN HILFERTY (COSTUMES)

Within the space of six months in 2014 I was to design two productions of *King Lear*, radically different in every way, one for TFANA and then Daniel Sullivan's at the Delacorte Theatre in Central Park with John Lithgow. It made it clear to me that there is no single way to design *Lear*, perform *Lear* or even hear the text of *Lear*.

Arin Arbus's version for TFANA shows a place out of balance, the masculine overwhelmingly dominant and the female repressed. It's a hierarchical culture and power goes to the male heir, never the female. It is wintry, brutal and cold; nothing grows and in a storm you feel sleet, not rain. The land represents power, not life. We made a world where you could feel these tensions before a word was spoken. Everyone was suspicious of each other, and there was constant eavesdropping and spying in the tussle for dominance; even sex became a power struggle.

In this totalitarian society the military is at the heart of the design: everything is stripped down as if ready for battle. Michael Pennington's Lear is a hard man of the army, always ready to fight, and his first appearance feels like that of a general as much as a king. His chest is thrust out, he has a short military haircut, he is jack-booted and wears a military fur-collared overcoat of a purple that indicates his rank, but doesn't soften his form. His whip is the extension of his gloved hand; his crown is made of rusting steel that seems both of the Iron and Industrial Ages. Set against a brutal metal slab, the Court surrounding him is also of this battle-hardened world. Uniforms and riding gear are my inspiration: at the opening, the whole court wears overcoats, boots and gloves like protective shells.

I use a palette of colours that come from rusted steel or that might appear in a bruise. There is no black. The overcoats do not match in colour, and other than the fur and crown on Lear, there are no outward signs of rank.

Lear's and his followers' return from the hunt to Goneril's and Albany's home has the grim look of a battalion after a skirmish, and Lear's men carry in the dead bodies of the animals they've killed with no sense of sport.

Until Act Four Scene Six everything feels filthy from extended combat and travel. Lear, for instance, after losing his purple coat, puts on a trench coat that gets increasingly dirty. It feels like night, until finally, in the field near Dover, it is as if a new day has arrived and there is just the touch of something living in the green around Lear's neck. The colours, texture and metals in the clothing are of a low glow so that they resonate in the darkness, like the chiaroscuro of a Caravaggio painting.

The English soldiers are always in battle gear, never in dress uniform. Edgar will take a uniform from a dead soldier and it becomes his outfit for the final battle with his brother, Edmund. Edmund is in a more prestigious uniform with a leather trench coat, but he has the same armour as the rest of his soldiers. In the last Acts, Gloucester, Lear and Cordelia all appear in natural linen, stained with mud and blood as their outer layers are stripped away.

The atmosphere of this kingdom is shadowy and thick with tension, as if the smell of gunpowder permeates the space. The clothing of the three sisters – Goneril, Regan and Cordelia – is tailored like riding costumes, with military overtones. Our young Fool is like a child who has been damaged and whose head is shaved like a cancer patient. He carries a red accordion matching his shoes and child-like Fool's cap. The red of the Fool's "coxcomb" is reflected in the blood that we later see on Edmund and in the blinding of Gloucester.

The production created a pressure cooker of tension building up inside until a spark of lightning caused the explosion of the storm that made a battlefield of the world. Edward Bond purportedly said that *King Lear* is a play "where people are getting on and off trains with a lot of luggage." This image sets the tone of movement and displacement. We emphasised Shakespeare's dramatic structure in which the whole family moves like an army on the run, setting up camp after camp and then moving on to the next battle.

## MICHAEL PENNINGTON

I walk down Fulton Street again, past the Greene Grape and the Greenlight Bookstore into my last days of work before the lengthy phase of technical and dress rehearsals begins. But something is different today, and not only because Prue has gone back to London for ten days. I've moved us into an airier flat, with equally noisy radiators (though with a different timbre) at the top of the house, approached by a staircase so rickety and askance that I'm reminded again of some provincial boarding house Harold Pinter might set a play in, perhaps remembering his own days in rep. Our shy

Lothario on the ground floor is long gone, perhaps wasted by his own excesses.

*The Wall Street Journal* is to do an interview with me today, but they don't want to proceed unless they can see some rehearsing afterwards. They don't want to come back to Brooklyn a second time just for that, so it does have to be today. (I see that Brooklyn and Manhattan – even the part as close as the Financial District – are still separated by more than the East River.) So we must accommodate them by rearranging the schedule to do a rehearsal involving Lear after the interview, even if it's not what we really want to do. In any case, it'll be a self-conscious affair: I don't know an actor or director alive who doesn't show off a bit under the beady eye of a camera or reporter, and we shall all give performances of ourselves rather than just getting on with it, as we really should be doing three days before technical rehearsals start.

As it turns out Joanne Kaufman, the *Journal's* feature writer, reckons that with my red sneakers, loose-fitting blue trousers and scruffy beard, I look like a vagrant in this "gentrifying" neighborhood (a Manhattanite speaks), but that perhaps that's just my way of getting into character. After all I'm playing a homeless man, an elderly imperious fellow down on my luck and down on my daughters. She's already got some warm tributes to me from Patrick Stewart ("brilliant, emotionally, technically and intellectually") and from Ian McKellen, who declares Brooklyn audiences are lucky to be witnessing the long-awaited Lear of "one of theatre's matchless treasures, whose acting style is modest and detailed, supported by intelligence and unrivaled experience." I'm not sure about the modest style, but I clearly owe a couple of drinks there.

However, in case I get too comfortable, she will end up telling a flat lie about my *Hamlet: A User's Guide,* reporting that I made Simon Russell Beale and Jude Law "swear on their swords that they'd read it" (actually they both voluntarily endorsed it). Still, what's striking is how long the piece turns out to be: twelve hundred words accompanied by a red-faced cartoon that might be a warning against high blood pressure, headed 'He's a Guide to Fellow Shakespearians". (We needn't have worried about the rehearsal, which I don't think she stayed for.) I was dealt with with the same amplitude later in the editing of video interviews I did with Jeffrey Horowitz and then with Ian McKellen; the same too when I did a piece in *The New Yorker* and experienced the priceless privilege it still extends of calling you back before publication to check that it was exactly what you meant to say.

As with the reviews later, the thoroughness and space arts journalists have in New York currently puts London to shame. We've reached a point here when *The Times* does virtually no book reviews at all and recently got rid of its respected Literary Editor. Its newly appointed theatre critic comes from a long career as a caustic political sketch-writer; the survival rate of its last four theatre critics (starting with the acknowledged doyen Irving Wardle, with whom I grew up) has gone from thirty years to eighteen to three to two. An august critical colleague (not an actor) recently observed that you don't have to know anything about the theatre in order to write well about it if you're a good writer to start with.

Jeffrey meanwhile has made a spirited attempt to get Michael Billington (*The Guardian*) and Benedict Nightingale (till fairly recently *The Times*) over to New York to cover the show and write a feature rather than a review. His instincts are right: they are the two critics, together with the retired John Peter, who might have the leverage to talk their editors into a trip to New York for the intrinsic interest of what we're doing. He reminds Michael how often he's said that he was eager to see my Lear and suggests he might even be able to place such a freelance article in *The New York Times*.

Regretfully, says Billington, these days, not a chance.

Another thing is different today. It's the first time I've come in late morning on this day of the week, and I'm weaving past the audience beginning to assemble for Frank Langella's matinee across the road at BAM. I can't help but be curious, not only because he has declined to meet for publicity purposes but because I've not caught sight of any of his company (most of them English colleagues) – though I've had an invitation to coffee from Jonathan Church his producer, with whom I've worked a good deal (and discussed *King Lear*) at Chichester. I'm not quite sure why (there being no such thing as a free coffee), but it's going to be hard to schedule anyway: soon they're closing. What I do know is that when BAM first heard that TFANA had scheduled a *Lear* at the same time as theirs they accused Jeffrey of having withheld the fact from them. But as the PA to BAM's Artistic Director reminded him, BAM hadn't notified TFANA of theirs either. Meanwhile the two versions, one nearing the end of its run and the other just climbing to its feet, are so literally up against each other that I wonder that I can't hear Langella's Storm Scene (he has a big voice) from my rehearsal across the road. This last week, though, it's rumoured he's been off sometimes, exhausted. And that he's gone on the record as saying he failed entirely to pull off King Lear. No, not entirely failed, but failed-to-pull-it-entirely-off. It's a standard phrase of becoming modesty to admit a little relative failure while suggesting the audience still got its money's worth; me, I've decided against any such self-denigration. I don't think I have to pull anything off; Lear is a part of my life and it will be complete whatever it is. For better or worse, I feel very confident today.

### ACT FOUR SCENE ONE: GLOUCESTER AND TOM

EDGAR : What did he say, my father, when we were out in the storm last night?

> Our flesh and blood, my lord, is grown so vile
> That it doth hate what gets it.

That's not me, surely, but maybe Edmund? No, he meant me:

> I'll tell thee, friend,
> I am almost mad myself. I had a son,
> Now outlawed from my blood; he sought my life,
> But lately, very late. I loved him, friend,
> No father his son dearer. True to tell thee,
> The grief hath crazed my wits.

And here he is, destroyed, caked blood and bandage on his face, stumbling and blundering, his arms waving in the wind.

OLD MAN: I've been in this household for eighty years: from a boy, in fact. I inherited a small holding here from my father. It's never been profitable, mismanaged more like. I knew the old Earl back then, and then this present one, and our dreadfully misused Lady and their boys, Edgar and the black sheep Edmund, whose birth brought on my Lady's death.

These Gloucesters! The father not only a ladies' man but always speculating on the stars and the eclipses, careful to oblige everyone at Court, making himself pleasant to the King, so we were always secure. Until the dark days came.

None so dark as the Earl's will be now, though, and for ever. Shall I ever forget these days? I have no time left to forget them, only time enough to die. That the Duke of Cornwall should come, and the Duchess Regan, and do such things. We staff always stayed together, so one of them killed the Duke, another made the lotions for these poor blind eyes, flax and egg-white, an old country woman's remedy; and here I am walking him. I even have to reintroduce myself as he seems not to know my voice at first, I have to show him again where all things are, re-acquaint him with his own estate, do his will, so that he'll think he sees the barn again, the outhouses, the harrows and the grain. But above all this, he's looking for poor Mad Tom.

EDGAR: I seem unable to speak for myself now, as myself, I'm like a player who has no lines of his own, a commentator, a stupid reporter of the facts. Not like this old man or my father, they can speak still:

> Old Man: You cannot see your way.
> Gloucester: I have no way and therefore want
>                                   no eyes;
>               I stumbled when I saw.

I am better as Tom o' Bedlam, he's taken me over entirely. Luckily, for the old man might recognise me, I've known him all my life. Here I go:

> Poor Tom hath been scared out of his good wits. Bless thee, good man's son, from the foul fiend...

My father knows me better like this than he ever did before. But suddenly he names me:

>                         O dear son Edgar,
>     The food of thy abused father's wrath,
>     Might I but live to see thee in my touch
>     I'd say I had eyes again

– yes, he names me, and I feel worse. But I see a way to give him back his eyes.

GLOUCESTER: Of course my memory is good now, and my hearing – I can hear that poor Mad Tom. Almost the last thing I saw with my eyes was him, and I thought of my son Edgar, something about him reminded me I suppose. Why is that my last memory? Hold fast to it, I say, because we are like the butterflies mammocked by children, the squealing pig chased for pleasure, the fly swatted from your brow. The beggar reminded me of my son for he too has nothing, he is a worm only.

I am better with this beggar, but my old man will have his eyes plucked out too by that she-devil if he's seen shepherding me about like this. The first thing is to get away, so he is never seen with us. My wits are sharp: now that I cannot see, I notice. He must find clothes for the beggar and follow us, he will travel faster than us on the Dover Road, but we must be separate from him, he will overtake us and then he will escape. After that, I don't know. I suppose the Duchess will lay claim to our house. I know Dover, in fact I know a particular cliff, where I once would stand and look towards France. I want to join the King if I can, to be with him and Cordelia again, but if not, I want to make my end on that cliff. The old man tells me my beggar is mad, he doesn't want to let us go, but he's just an old man. I've had enough of him:

> Above the rest, be gone.

A madman should lead a man with no eyes, for both our lives are inward, not seeing what the world sees. He will bring me comfort. I hope he knows the way, and I hear that he does:

> Both stile and gate, horse-way and footpath.

It was gibberish before, when he used to say the foul fiend vexed him, but now I see what he sees, Obidicut and Hobbedance, he is my man, he will go with me, we are the poor and the rejected, on the road, the mad and the blind. And I must stand on that cliff-edge with him.

EDGAR: Why Dover? Why that particular cliff?

## JACOB FISHEL

I wanted to run to Gloucester and deal with the practical issues – medical as well as political. Is the bleeding stopped, are the wounds clean, who did this and are they following him? But Edgar stays away and speaks of his own suffering:

> O gods! Who is't can say 'I am at the worst'?
> I am worse than e'er I was…
> And worse I may be yet: the worst is not
> So long as we can say 'This is the worst.'

My difficulty was Edgar's decision to stay in the character of Poor Tom. Why persist in his disguise when he hears that his father knows he's innocent, when he sees him tortured by his guilt, when he is in need of urgent care? These failures to act or to reveal himself seem excessively cruel. It's clear that Gloucester has fallen victim to the same plot that banished Edgar and he has paid a steeper price. So what is Edgar doing?

In fact I think Shakespeare is using this scene to acclimatise the audience to Gloucester's grotesque appearance. He was aware of the dangers of advancing the plot too quickly; and today, you have to allow for the audience flinching with horror or leaning forward to see how the makeup was done or cracking nervous jokes to their neighbours – all of which happened night after night. He used a similar device in *Titus Andronicus* when Lavinia's mutilation is revealed during Marcus's speech. There's very little plot development other than the information that she's survived. Both these two scenes feel like necessary expressionistic interludes before the plot speeds ahead again. So having Edgar reveal his identity or getting answers to all his pressing questions would be a risk. Surrendering to shock and grief allowed me to play the scene without obsessing on Edgar's lack of humanity.

## ACT FOUR SCENE TWO: MARRY, YOUR MANHOOD

GONERIL: My milk-hearted husband seems to be in a trance. He sits, says nothing of his own, if he's forced to answer he just smiles. France has landed and he says Oh Dear. Coward, coward. With him disgracing himself but Edmund by my side, I'm ready to count him out and go to Cornwall and my sister; now it will be Regan, Cornwall, Edmund and myself, with Oswald our intelligence. I believe Oswald despises my husband too. Yes, I see an opportunity here.

OSWALD: I'm very clear with her. That her husband took the news of her approach as a bad thing, but the fact that the French are invading as a good one. How is that? Albany keeps only scorn for me, and calls black white and white black. He loves our enemies, despises our friends. I am a faithful servant, and better still I know Goneril, and I think I know what will happen next. She is turning towards Edmund.

GONERIL: Edmund must go ahead, while I close up the house, with my sot of a husband in it. And I will claim Edmund. I'll call on him when I'm ready: in the meantime he has my promise, the way a woman can make it. He can have no doubt. A miracle, that both my husband and he both go in the catalogue for men – the one a fool fumbling about in my sheets, the other the object of my surrender.

EDMUND: With women like this I need do nothing. So I say I am hers until death (for the time being).

ALBANY: There are times in a life when you'd start the page again. My scum of a wife has driven her father wild, so has Cornwall the man he owes everything to. If she wasn't a woman, I'd take her apart with my bare hands. Fortunately my anger has loosened my tongue at last: I'll evade her no longer.

GONERIL: So at last you come when I call. I'm worth that much to you.

ALBANY: Far less. You're not worth the dust the wind blows into your face to blind you. You are outside nature, you who feel nothing for the source of your very life on earth. You pretend you don't understand. Your filthiness has driven a good man mad, a gracious reverend parent, he whom nature itself would respect but you are too depraved to, you and my brother Cornwall – how could he do it either? If you ruled the world, humanity would eat itself like a giant, like a war of the worlds, like the ocean drowning itself.

GONERIL: Child, child, child. You're missing part of your brain, the part that distinguishes our advantage from blind chance, that sees ahead of time whom we should punish before they commit any crime.

ALBANY: And you, your greatest deceit of all is that you're any kind of woman worthy of the name.

GONERIL: And now comes the news. Cornwall is dead.

He took my advice to pluck out Gloucester's eyes, and his servant killed him for it. It would have been me had I been there. The news is a mix: there will be no King Cornwall for sure, but Edmund is on his way to Regan, a widow now, and not so different from me in her appetites, more so as she's in practice, for Cornwall and she had a heat I haven't known.

There's only Regan and me now. Two Queens.

ALBANY: And now Cornwall is dead. There is justice. But Gloucester is blind. But didn't Edmund intervene, surely he did? No, he led the old man in, he cleared the space, he absented himself, to be sure

of it. He is what I feared, and so I have purpose in my
life – revenge.

## MICHAEL PENNINGTON

Astonishingly, in Act Four Scene Three the Gentleman who was so in on
Kent's secret in Act Three Scene One returns, though hardly by public
demand. It was he who helpfully told us that Lear was out raging in the
storm just before we saw it for ourselves; now (if it's the same Gent, and not
yet another secret ally of Kent's) he's back to tell Kent that Cordelia is in
the country, but that the King of France has inexplicably gone home soon
after he arrived with her, presumably because the playwright felt he would
get in the way otherwise. He then paints a picture of Cordelia so mawkish
that it almost makes the part unplayable. Listen to this: her reaction to
Kent's letters was

> Not to a rage; patience and sorrow strove
> Who should express her goodliest. You have seen
> Sunshine and rain at once; her smiles and tears
> Were like a better way…
>                                   Then she shook
> The holy water from her heavenly eyes.

The "better way" bit is lovely, with that swing and surprising modernity
that Shakespeare sometimes catches at the same moment; however, not
only is the rest hardly the Cordelia we last saw, but the imagery and the
ideas are Shakespeare on an off day. Likewise it's good to hear Kent describe
Goneril and Regan as Lear's 'dog-hearted daughters'; less convincing is his
claim that Lear is holed up in Dover and refusing to see Cordelia because of
his 'burning shame'. And in a moment we shall meet, directly contradicting
Kent, the reality: Lear not so much ashamed as asleep, and a new music and
a new character, a gentle doctor, as full of herbal remedies as Friar Laurence
in *Romeo and Juliet*.

## ARIN ARBUS

Still, in spite of the loveliness, we'll cut this Gentleman too.

## ACT FOUR SCENE FOUR: CORDELIA'S RETURN

CORDELIA:

> Alas, 'tis he: why, he was met even now
> As mad as the vexed sea, singing aloud,
> Crowned with rank fumitory and furrow weeds
> With burdock, hemlock, nettles, cuckoo-flowers,
> Darnel and all the idle weeds that grow
> In our sustaining corn.

I didn't know what I'd find, and now I see Kent didn't tell me enough. I expected some kind of readiness for battle from my sisters, but where could my father be and how would he be, how safe? And now I hear the worst – he's been wandering through the fields by the sea shore, bedecked in vegetation, what we would call quite mad, singing, crowned in a mockery of a King. We must find him, but what then?

DOCTOR: It's sleep, a matter of sleep, as the body slowly aligns with the mind again. And there is help. I've seen this before:

> Our foster nurse of nature is repose,
> The which he lacks; that to provoke in him
> Are many simple operatives, whose power
> Will close the eye of anguish.

## MICHAEL PENNINGTON

This short scene, unlike its predecessor, is Shakespeare at the top of his game. A sense of beauty, even of idyll, is bestowed on deep suffering in a way that neither minimises the one nor makes the other absurd. Cordelia's list of Warwickshire flowers is not there for prettiness but as a measure of Lear's madness; the 'high-grown field' is as visually explicit as it is possible to be in one phrase; there is danger, in that Lear's 'ungoverned rage' (as she imagines) could turn on itself and destroy the life 'that wants the means to lead it'. Cordelia is here on business, but in almost the same sentence is the simple desire to see her father:

> No blown ambition doth our arms incite
> But love, dear love, and our aged father's right.

And then – great Shakespearian cunning – there is no resounding final couplet about going to war, but the unmetrical simplicity of

Soon may I hear and see him.

In our production the arrival of this kindly doctor is the third manifestation of a truly remarkable actor that I've known for fifty years, ever since I was at Stratford in 1965. He played the Second Gravedigger in David Warner's *Hamlet* with me as Fortinbras, playing my first part of any size with the RSC and consequently taking an infinity of time to 'bid the soldiers shoot'. Even then Robert Lloyd (now Robert Langdon Lloyd) had a whiff of the special about him: it was the mystique of Peter Brook, for whom he'd played Puck at one stage in the legendary *Dream*, and indeed Edgar in the *Lear* film with Scofield. That he should tell me after the end of our run that I had supplanted Paul as his ideal Lear will of course be written on one of my tombstones.

When I went back to Stratford in 1975 I had bigger parts but I didn't know how to behave. I was suddenly Angelo in *Measure for Measure*, together with Ferdinand in *The Tempest*, in which Robert was Ariel. I knew this was the beginning of something, but I was all over the place. One day I had nothing to do for a couple of days and was preparing to go back immediately to London. But somehow I kept hanging about at the theatre. Robert was sitting in the corner of the Green Room. He asked me how I was, what I was up to, what I hoped for, both today and, he implied, in life. Three hours later I was still there with him, staring out over Bancroft Gardens and delighting in the talk – mostly about things I had on my mind rather than his, I fear, but I've never forgotten it. He gave me the feeling he had infinite time for me. I forget whether I went back to London or not that day. Bob is still a wonderful companion, as Benjamin Cole has testified on behalf of the ensemble of *Lear*.

He is also a man with such a deep sense of Shakespeare that even as the Doctor saying "louder the music there" in our production he is moving, apt and exactly right. His delivery of it will never vary through the run – it will turn out to be that rarity, something that should always be exactly the same. He has recently come from the very demanding part of Leonato in *Much Ado*, so we're very lucky to have him: he takes the view that he'll play pretty much anything for Arin Arbus, and thus is a little like the invaluable member of a state theatre company on the German or Russian model. During the run he will warm up before each show at 6pm, as most actors do, but in his case with strange little dances of his own that I somehow associate with Peter Brook in the Sahara Desert or the ruins of Persepolis. But then we all do strange things at this time of day, one way or another. One day Arin was taking the opportunity briefly to re-rehearse Lilly as Cordelia at this pre-show time on the stage, and Robert was uncharacteristically – and therefore impressively – incensed, not on his own behalf but on mine. It offended him that I didn't have the whole stage to roam about on at will at 6pm: I was doing such a great thing in their midst (I think he said "for" them) that I should have no restraints on space for my (actually rather cursory) warm-up. Apart from being hugely flattering, this outburst was clearly understood by everyone, including Arin and myself, to come out of love for her, her production and a sense of good theatre practice. It was like a momentary tantrum from your favourite uncle.

## ROBERT LANGDON LLOYD

I'm finding all my three parts worth playing. "There are no small roles" said Stanislavsky, but that's bollocks, obviously. However I do believe there are no parts of any size that don't welcome everything an actor can bring to them.

My biggest part in *Lear* is the soldier in the scene in Goneril's house (Act One Scene Four) when Lear comes back from the hunt. He has the least to say but he lives the most – furious at the offhand way Oswald (so brilliantly played by Mark Dold) treats Lear; fearful at what's happening to his master; joy when the Fool comes on and seems to cheer him (so I hope) but dismayed at his awful dangerous jokes which seem so absolutely not what's needed; anger at Goneril, powerfully released when I'm sent dashing off to saddle the horses, relief to be out of there. I live a lot in that scene. Total devotion to service, the serving of King Lear: I have been with him the longest.

I enjoy the Old Man in Act Four Scene One too, for his devotion to the now blind Gloucester. I don't know how many actors who play the Old Man choose to recognise Edgar, but I felt it was implicit in the line

I'll bring him the best apparel that I have.

Again, service to the family. And the Doctor – a healer, serving Cordelia and doing my absolute best for her father. Joy, wonder, and a tearful eye when he knew who she was. Michael was so great in that scene, it was a privilege to be part of it.

And all the time, Arin's production. I bless the day I walked into my first rehearsal with her. I've been in five shows she's directed. Do you know the Kinks' song, "Thank You For The Days?" That just about says it for me.

And, of course, thank you to that true man of the theatre, Jeffrey Horowitz, without whom no TFANA.

## ACT FOUR SCENE FIVE: STRANGE OEILLADES

REGAN: I smell the business. Albany's not coming with us – or is, but with such ado, as if he didn't want to. Meanwhile I find my sister has written to Edmund. I'm lucky to intercept this: it was almost on its way to Dover with Oswald. I could delay him, this Oswald. He'll do anything if he's worked on.

But I don't know. What is it? Why am I so uneasy? Why a letter? I saw her looking at Edmund, winking and hinting in her disgusting way with a man. And this Oswald knows it. I must tell him a lie. That Edmund and I have talked, made terms, I tell him, but quietly, with no grandstanding, just so he understands clearly what's really happening here. And I'll send Edmund this ring, it has dignity. Goneril must understand, he's mine now.

We should never have let Gloucester live. Oswald is promising to kill him if he can, but I know he can't, he's not a man, just someone for my sister to play with, as weak as Albany in the end. Meanwhile my husband hadn't enough foresight and let himself be killed, the fool. But he had other virtues: he's become a gap that I can only fill with Edmund.

## ACT FOUR SCENE SIX : DOVER

EDGAR: Now I must tread with care – and not just metaphorically. The two of us haven't found the rhythm of walking uphill, I haven't got the breathing right for it. Because it's no effort I'm talking too smoothly to my father, and he hears this polish in my speech. Suddenly he doubts who I am, now that he hears this 'better phrase and matter'. Above all he barely believes he's climbing:

> Methinks the ground is even.

I have to do it all with words, the best I've ever found. And make him uneasy: surely he can hear the sea, as I can? No? (Of course not, there's no sea.) I tell him that, unusually, his blindness hasn't led to a sharper sense of hearing. And so I fault him, as he faulted me for my accent.

I see what I have to do above all: help him fall further and further in love with the idea of his death, so he feels the height of the cliff, imagines a gatherer of samphire working half way down it, the distant fishermen, the sound of the sea on the pebbles, his own soft landing on the beach, so that then at the end he thanks the gods for his survival. All before the eyes of a friendly passer-by – played by another me.

And over he goes, but first he gives me money. Not only money but solace of a kind:

> If Edgar live, O bless him!

After a short pause, I'm that passer-by: I do this better. Poor Tom has fallen away from me, just turned into that man who climbed the hill, and now I'm number three, a local man, who does a hatchet job on the me at the top of the cliff:

> His eyes
> Were two full moons; he had a thousand noses,
> Horns welked and waved like the enridged sea.
> It was some fiend.

I could come to enjoy this. And as I have his blessing, he has mine:

> Bear free and patient thoughts.

But then:

> O thou side-piercing sight...

KING LEAR: The long grass on the dunes waves in the wind: I hid there for a time, that's where I saw field mice scurrying. Most people can't spot them, just as a small root or a flower can be seen by certain wild people half a mile away, too far away for anybody else. But I saw them. I am the King.

This also is as clear as it can be. You will say that this garland I'm wearing, these wild flowers, are not normal for a King, but I must tell you that since I am the King these have become the right clothes for a King. I can turn this leaf into a piece of cheese for the mouse for the same reason, and this feather is now my gauntlet. Somewhere I can hear that you're amused by this rearrangement. But at least I can't be accused of fantasy: I am exercising my imagination on behalf of my people.

I choose to be like the beggar I met, I've a crown of thorns, I've matted my hair. The man looking at me now is a beggar, maybe the same beggar. I remember him, he needs press money from me, but I need a password from him in return. In life there is always a password. He must be checked. He says "Marjoram". It is the right one. I think it is.

    Gloucester: The trick of that voice I do
                             well remember.
        Is't not the King?

I see a figure like a blotch of red and white, speaking to me or of me. Goneril. She's grown a beard. Or rather it's someone who looks as she would if she had a beard. The Earl of Gonster, daughter to the King. Another flatterer.

The wind wheels through the grasses. Where Gonster's eyes should be there's something that's like hellfire, the devil's red. Didn't my daughter say she loved me better than eyesight: it was a beautiful speech and then she betrayed me. Did she think I was a dog standing up on its hind legs for attention? From a child I've always been told I was wise, a wise child with white hair now. But when I was wet through – where was it? – when the wind howled through me – what night was it? – I called up the thunder but couldn't subdue it. That's when I learned that I was weaker than the thunder, that's what gave these flatterers away, I smelled their foulness then. I'm not what they say. I'm sick to the death like any other poor man's son.

But I am the King, every inch of me. It's in the marrow of my bones, in the tips of my fingers. You witnesses in the dark defer to me, you are in dread, I have your life and death in my hands. I make you laugh, you watchers in the fields. Everyone here seems to find me funny. That's all right. I have restored you to yourselves. Once upon a time before, you needed me: you crouched together, unclothed, shaking against the cold rain. I comforted you then. Now you're crouched again, in judgment, there in the half light, as if you were a jury of my peers.

What's this smell from within this Gonster's beard, this musky sex smell? Is it of adultery? The sex is all muddled. But I make the laws. If he or she, whichever it is, is an adulterer, they go free. What is adultery, other than what an insect and a tiny bird, a horse or a polecat do, and no-one indicts them? This reminds me of Gloucester and his bastard son, kinder to him I dare say than the true one was, truer than my daughters are to me. Anyway I need to swell our population somehow; the women are ready and in season with their matted hair and sweat, their acrid thing, their fire that burns and stinks.

So I advise this Gonster. He should buy some special glasses, some kind that have a complete new system of sight within them, rather than just improving his weakening eyes. Or use his ears.

Then he could see the evidence and lie in the face
of it – like a politician, like my daughters.

Thou hast seen a farmer's dog bark at a beggar?

GLOUCESTER:

Ay, sir.

KING LEAR:

And the creature run from the cur? There thou
mightst behold the great image of authority: a
dog's obeyed in office.
Thou rascal beadle, hold thy bloody hand!
Why dost thou lash that whore? Strip thine
                                          own back;
Thou hotly lust'st to use her in that kind
For which thou whipp'st her. The usurer hangs
                                          the cozener.
Through tatter'd clothes small vices do appear;
Robes and furr'd gowns hide all. Plate sin with gold,
And the strong lance of justice hurtless breaks:
Arm it in rags, a pigmy's straw does pierce it.
None does offend, none, I say, none; I'll able 'em:
Take that of me, my friend, who have the power
To seal the accuser's lips. Get thee glass eyes;
And like a scurvy politician, seem
To see the things thou dost not.

Gonster seems uninterested by this; so he should
do something useful like pulling off my boots.

All in all, this has been interesting. And now all new
men have arrived, with their kindness and their
respect. They kneel to me. They are not against
me. And this fells me at a blow, I can hardly speak
with gratitude. Everything that has happened
would turn any man into a man of salt, watering
his garden with his tears. BUT SOMETHING IS
WRONG HERE AS WELL, a knife has cut into my
brain, I don't know where I am. I have to run
away. I always wanted to die in action like the
husband I once was, so pleased with himself on
his honeymoon, so brave and so deceived. I point
out that I am a King and they agree, a most royal

one, and they should obey me. And then they kneel. One thing turns into another, the past into the present. I run and they chase me. And soon I am asleep.

EDGAR: Thank the gods, these men are of our party – a doctor and a loyal man from the court – I didn't think there were any left. They take him gently in, and away from the battle that the loyal man tells me is coming any moment now. I think we're near the end with my father. He asks me directly, as if he knew at least that I was hiding, who, in the end, I am, very simply, deserving an answer, even the right answer, but I won't give him that yet:

> A most poor man made tame by fortune's blows,
> Who by the art of known and feeling sorrows,
> Am pregnant to good pity.

That's how I tell him. Then a man comes to threaten him, demanding the surrender of the blind man. I must be another person again:

> Nay come not near th' old man, keep out, che vor'
> ye, or I'ce try whether your costard or my ballow
> be the harder.

What do I sound like?! What does my father think I am now? But this is not a joke. He fights me and now I know how easy it is to kill a man, one blow. For I see this is Goneril's manservant, both her man perhaps and her servant. His dying wish – to take a letter to my brother. Best I read it first. And for sure, this is an invitation to Edmund to murder our father and then to release her from captivity, from Albany's bed:

> From the loathed warmth of which deliver me,
> and supply the place for your labour.

World, world, world. This to my brother Edmund. Does he know of this woman's offer? She speaks about "our reciprocal vows". I fear, I fear the worst in him. Can he be in this wickedness so deep? I see I may have one more part to play, the avenging angel. I take my father by the hand, he must be made safe, for I hear the drums. I must not think about Edmund and what he may have done.

## JACOB FISHEL

Edgar deceives his father in an effort to purge his grief. It's seems bizarre, but it is his exploration of the power of imagination to heal the body. His intention is clearly to preserve his father's life and his deception makes that happen. When Gloucester eventually dies, it is not by his own hand. Then Lear's entrance into this scene, fully mad it seems, tears Edgar's heart open even further. He can only watch his father and his godfather, the ruined pillars of his family and his country, openly lament together. I found the passage on the 'image of authority' to be extremely pertinent for a young man deeply wronged by the law and soon to become the ultimate authority. Edgar is now ready to act. He has no qualms about killing Oswald, and we see again that he is competent with a sword. Then he discovers through the letter that Edmund may be behind the kingdom's demise. His actions are decisive. The philosopher/chorus has transformed into the play's able revenger.

### ACT FOUR SCENE SEVEN: BETWEEN SLEEP AND WAKE

KING LEAR: I seem to be wearing a rough red coat, and being carried around in a chair. There are voices, a woman and two men, and some music in the room. My head is still banging: I feel as if I was on a mill wheel, grinding. I don't recognise the coat or even my own hands. I don't know what's expected of me.

One man's voice is familiar and there's some kind of light around the woman that keeps drawing me to her. What set-up is this, what cruel trick? I'm old, older even than I am and I think my brain has come loose. Could this possibly be Cordelia, come for revenge or reproach or mockery? In any case am I even in England, or France, her country since she married the King? It's a trick, it must be, some wicked dream.

No, this is hell. Or a deception. Nothing good can come of this. While I am burning on a wheel some puppet-master is dangling the idea of my lost daughter in front of me, but not so clearly that I can see her features. Or perhaps it's a ghost I've summoned up. I wouldn't do this to a dog. But I am weak, they know I am weak, and I have no defence. Even at best, I must blink and blink for I can't believe how this could be, I'd rather drink poison and die than find this isn't true. For this woman hates me as much as my other daughters, and so she should. She has reasons and they have none.

Everything is dark outside of the light I see before me, moving towards me in her shape, her outline.

The light I saw her bathed in is burning my eyes now, stinging them into helpless tears. She reminds me a little of Goneril, and of Regan, but she is weeping, and they don't weep. There is a difference in her too, a difference of size, the set of the eyes, and the sound of the voice, which is gentle and agrees with me each time I speak. She wants me to hold my hand above her head, in a blessing, but I think I am the one to kneel. She calls me Your Highness, they never do. She is her mother's daughter too.

I think...

I think this is hell.

But I think it might be...

Her.

# WEEKS SEVEN AND EIGHT

## ACT FIVE SCENE ONE: THE INVASION

EDMUND: Two women, one husband and me. And this is supposed to be a battlefield. The widow is at me to have nothing to do with her married sister, on and on about it – talking of my maybe being 'conjunct and bosomed' with her – what was it – 'forfended place'. I nearly laughed in her forfended face. She says she intends 'goodness' on me. The husband changing his mind all the time, blaming himself for everything, I would think for not controlling his wife for one thing. Or maybe he knows something about the French that I don't know. Or maybe he secretly favours Lear and doesn't mean to fight on our side at all. But he's very polite so I am to him. He says he can still somehow defend England from a French invasion on principle, without necessarily being against the King. This man would cavil on the ninth part of a hair.

Now that Goneril is here, I see he has been preparing a great speech, wriggling this way and that. The King and others who mistrust us have fled to Cordelia; we must resist them because this after all is an invasion of our country, but we should be glad because the King is safe with them. I tell him he's spoken nobly, though actually he was like a corkscrew. They must consult their strategists, they say, but Regan won't leave here until Goneril does, they both want a word with me first. It's like a school dance, one woman confident and the other begging me. What's to be made of this? I may have some of my father in me, this ability to use a woman, but only if there is some benefit, and this is wearisome. And dangerous: if

I have one the other will turn against me, if I have both they'll kill each other, and we'll lose the battle with all that going on. It's not the having of them, it's whether my way still lies clear ahead of me and they're not across my path. Because they're really using me, not I them; there's nothing here for me until after the battle at least.

Well, what do you expect of me? I never had a mother.

## ACT FIVE SCENE TWO: THE END OF GLOUCESTER

EDGAR: I gave it to him, the letter to the cuckold Albany, the one I took from Oswald's body, Goneril's love letter to the bastard brother. Albany had to know, and he'll decide what revenge to take; if he wins the battle and lives, I can present myself as the champion to challenge my brother and bring him down in all his pride at last.

In the meantime my father must be out of the way, under this tree, enjoying the peace, or hearing the sound of war, more like.

Which Lear loses, in moments it seems. But my father seems to have grown roots into the ground, tangled up with the tree he's beneath. He won't move, might as well die here, a small tree under a great. After all that, after all we've been through. I draw a breath and try to sum it up. Him, me, all of us, what our condition is, all I seem to know, and it doesn't add up to much:

> Men must endure
> Their going hence, even as their coming hither,
> Ripeness is all.

It gets him up and moving, thank God. But we're near the end.

## ACT FIVE SCENE THREE: THE RECKONING

EDMUND: I know this is the night that either makes me or undoes me. So far it makes me: we won the battle, both women have set their caps at me, there's only Albany to deal with, and whatever part of the army supports him. I must be quick; before the women arrive – it is their family I'm removing, after all – and before anyone else can see, I hire a man to kill Lear and Cordelia, on the bribe of some future, unspecified happiness. I like this captain – he thinks this will be better than pulling a cart like a horse or eating the horse's oats.

KING LEAR: These men are not like the other men. They have hard hands. My daughter is frightened and I hold her in my arms to protect her. I haven't done this since she was a child. Quiet, I've said, we'll go to prison quietly. I could see we were defeated. We will sing, I tell her, we will be songbirds, and go over it again and again, I bless you and you forgive me, over and over. I'll tell you stories and we'll listen out for news, we'll watch while the others eat themselves up, we shall be like two halves of an egg – what was it my Fool said, that I should give him an egg and he'd give me two crowns, the bald one and the golden? No more of that.

EDMUND: And now it begins. It's like some mad, violent party when all scores are to be settled; no-one will leave it in the same state, if they leave it at all.

And what do I bring to the party? The extinction of Lear and his daughter, our defeat of the French, isn't that enough?

ALBANY: What do I bring? The news in the letter brought by the hooded fellow that my wife is propositioning Edmund, perhaps already has him, so the sickest feeling for a fighting man. Here we are, shoulder to shoulder, his body where it should never have been.

What else do I bring? Justice for them all, and a small hope for the future. The King re-seated if he is able. I must control these three, Edmund and the women: for a start they must give me their prisoners, as I am Commander-in-Chief, even if it's perhaps the world's weakest army. 'I' must become 'we', as if I was the General with Goneril not my faithless wife but my partner in arms, Regan in a nominal position and himself, the half-blooded fellow, as junior partner. Then I can obliterate him, if I can bring myself to, if that hooded fellow wasn't an illusion and responds to the call for a duel, produces the champion he spoke of, and does all his work as he promised in this letter. Though if there's a hand-to-hand fight and the anonymous man defeats Edmund I may entreat him to spare him after all – what use is another death?

GONERIL: What do I bring to the party? My control over Edmund, to whom I've now given nearly everything. He wears my favour, I told him it would stretch his spirits up into the air, and not only his spirits. I told him to conceive but perhaps that will be me. I am his in the lists of death, and it has to be done now, done publicly, done. And if nothing else, I have the means to dispose of Regan. If not, I'll never trust medicine.

REGAN: What do I bring? Very little, except my faltering hopes. Hope of Edmund. I said it: he is more convenient for my hand than for my sister's.

EDGAR: And what do I bring? The strange story of my life. My banishment, my father's eyes, my safety in his stables, my health out in the storm, my wits in keeping up with the King's rambling. Piece by piece, little by little, I have turned this into a strength – the physical strength of the warrior I never was, a right arm that can't be blocked. My name is lost. But I am courteous, admiring even, of the brother whom I now see clearly and whom I mean to kill; he has

> Strength, place, youth and eminence...valour and heart

– but he is a piece of utter wickedness. And he speaks back like a hero too: he calls me fair and warlike.

We both play parts here. So much so that he forgets in his repentance that he has ordered the execution of the King.

EDMUND: And what do I leave with? Darkness. But also one last joke, the one a bastard should leave the stage with:

> All three
> Now marry in an instant.

REGAN: What do I leave with? Excruciating pain, and darkness. Nothing.

GONERIL: Darkness.

ALBANY: With a little strength. I stand alone with Edgar. And we take hands over a vast span.

EDGAR: What will I leave with? The last word.

KING LEAR: Someone has broken her and the others have conspired in it. I had her for a moment in our new home in prison, I took care of her. I only had a moment. She's gone for ever. I must lay her out. I must cover that red weal round her neck, or it will hurt her, and link her hands together. I must straighten her, as I used to when she was sleeping at a bad angle. I must attend to her hair. I must say one last thing to her that nobody else can hear. I must tell her how I killed the man who killed her, yes, I did. I did.

And suddenly I can see her breathing. Did I dream this? No, there's no breeze, and a feather is moving on her breath. Do you see that? Can you see her? Can you see her? And darkness falls.

Enough.

Rest.

## MICHAEL PENNINGTON

The laborious but decisive process of getting the play into costume, shepherding it into place, kitting it out with lights and sound and setting it going for an audience, is one that in Britain you might do in three sessions a day for three days, followed by a dress rehearsal or two, then a preview on a Thursday, depending on the size of the show and the nature of the management. Maybe about thirty hours in all until the first preview.

In Brooklyn we had, including the final dress rehearsal, six days, some of nine hours' work, then, more intensely, of twelve hours. In all, over sixty hours. This was on a stage we had been working on for five weeks with the set going leisurely up around us. The moving wall had been there for weeks, the natural safety procedures and warnings in place. Its hoisting would otherwise have taken several valuable hours out of the technical rehearsal, or even postponed its start for the actors.

The obvious benefit was that the normal lurch from an outside rehearsal room into the technical – shock as well as pleasure – was smoothed down to a easy segue. So I take it that the relative slowness and thoroughness of the week's work, from first technical to first preview, is due to a tendency in US theatre practice to take a longer time and not just to the fact that Marcus Doshi's schedule had not allowed for very much pre-planning, when what was being aimed at with the lighting would have been agreed. It all happened now. Actors are used to staring at a blank and uninspiring stage in technicals, with plenty of time to despair about their costumes and their prospects; they're also used to being lit on the hoof during dress rehearsals. Added to that this time were quite fundamental musings as to how to begin to light a given scene; as part of this we would often be asked to run the lines, though not to performance pitch. This would be the cue for a lengthy *a priori* discussion among the creative team. Then we'd run the lines again, to see if what had been decided had worked – a process which naturally could repeat itself several times. Hours immersed in the venue are generally good for the actor; but it must be said that this, requiring a lower heartbeat of us rather than a gently quickening one, was tiring. For once the fierce injunction from Stage Management (a more powerful body than in England) to stay in the auditorium at all times was candidly ignored by a cast who needed a degree of comfort in the long pauses between being used.

Ah well, when in Rome.


## MARCUS DOSHI

Within the second movement of my design there were still moments of incandescence; the scenes with Edmund inside Gloucester's castle and then the hovel were lit very intimately and warmly. But the dominant figure overall was the white. It peaked in intensity and starkness at the moment of Gloucester's eyes being plucked out: a single diagonal back light over the wall, throwing long shadows, revealing the blood and the bodies, and making a cavernous darkness into which Gloucester could stumble.

The final movement began with Tom discovering his blinded father in Act Four. The scene was lit crisply and broadly, using the same white as the storm, but with much less shadow and no haze in the air. With the exception of Act Four Scene Two, which was lit with lingering warmth, the remaining scenes up to the battle in Act Five Scene Two were the same white light, a sort of overexposed Ansel Adams landscape. This culminated in an intense focus on Gloucester listening to the battle rage around him. The structure of this scene echoed that of the storm: multiple perspective shifts, tight focus, and flashes illuminating the space – the only difference was that the light was very intense throughout. At the crescendo of the aural event of the battle, the wall fell and revealed the space behind, wide open and empty, lit in a dirty manifestation of the light at the beginning. And so the final scene played out.

I went into this *King Lear* planning to precisely follow the arc from incandescent warmth to icy-white, with the storm as the turning point. But why then in the second and even third movement were there still moments of warmth, when the intellectual idea called for white? Because the infrastructure of my designs are methodical – in the studio I develop a design proposition for the show which is logical and organised and dictates everything, from the colour and location of the lamps to how I will plot out the cues. But then when I'm in the theatre I am freed to work very intuitively, to propose ideas through light that I might not if I were thinking too much. So, when I let the primitive warmth linger over

Edmund's antagonism because it *felt* right, it actually provided a visual counterpoint that allowed us really to *see* the white light that lays Lear bare. It made the arc-light work!

Not only that, but it turned out to be dramaturgically correct too, as Edmund's trajectory still occupied the story-space defined by the first movement's light. How this counterpoint worked compositionally and dramaturgically was the great lesson of the show; it was something I could not have figured out in the studio!

This production has been extremely satisfying to work on for a number of reasons. First off, Arin and Jeffrey are champions of my aesthetic – simplicity, essential choices, functional interaction, dramaturgical integrity and innovative beauty – probably because it has been honed at TFANA over these last many years. Second, the company of collaborators, performers, and support staff who went out on a limb in pretty much all directions throughout the process. He'll probably cut this [*Are you kidding? – Ed.*], but I really appreciate the spirit of collaboration Michael showed when we started tech'ing the storm in pitch blackness. And, finally, the show itself was so hard and rigorous and good. When I design a Shakespeare play I say, "I'm working on my third *Hamlet*." Or, "This is my second *Much Ado…*" Well, this was my first *King Lear* and I'm not really sure I'd ever want to do another.

## JAKE HOROWITZ

New ideas are being tried. I've started walking as if with a club foot, a birth defect. Already this limping walk, giving the Fool an interesting history in the world, completely frees me in the character. A whole new slew of impulses become available. I can scamper across the stage, hop, lean on Lear, and use the deformed foot to accentuate my jokes, anything really. This free and weird physical existence allows me to see everything in a new light. Part of what the Fool is trying to communicate is that Lear didn't realise how good he had it before he screwed himself! Well, here was a boy who knew what it really meant to be down and out. I looked sickly, startling, strange. And then I hanged myself.

❖

# THE DEATH OF CORDELIA

There's nothing you can do that can't be done…
— The Beatles, *All You Need is Love*

I f you meet an actor playing Lady Macbeth, you might mime washing your hands. And if you meet one rehearsing King Lear, you might ask How Heavy is your Cordelia? Professionals ask each other and compare methods. I asked the Lears I knew and they asked me too – all except Frank Langella, playing the part across the road at BAM, who kept up his silence. This conversation about a common problem marvellously dissolves any lurking sense of rivalry. The consensus is that in addition to being young enough to give the part the energy and retentive memory it needs, and old enough to know what the old man is going through, you need a third casting qualification – a secure spinal column and powerful upper arms.

Now Lilly Englert is not a big girl. Nor is she particularly small. As we addressed the question of how to stage this agonising final image, it soon turned out that she is right on the edge of what I, at my time of life, can carry in my cradling arms, at least in the classic semi-biblical manner, her head and feet bobbing pitifully. She offered to lose weight, but it would have been ungallant to accept and in any case there wasn't time.

So: how about a fireman's lift? Too expert for Lear to know about. How about the way you can carry someone on your back like a doppelganger, bending forward to form a double decker? Risky, if you get the forward bend wrong. How about the soldiers wheeling her on on a trolley? Lear, while he still had a breath in him, would never let this happen. Nor would he allow even the noble Earl of Kent to carry his precious daughter. So it remains Lear's problem.

What entrance should we come from? Upstage right or left? Upstage seemed good as we could start at the furthest possible point from the audience. We would then pass through a high wide empty space before reaching the eye of the storm – the audience's side blocks being a long way further downstage. A seemingly limitless pilgrimage for Lear, but a long way, and a nasty step to execute off that horizontal wall onto the main stage with your arms full of Cordelia.

So. In the other direction, from the front of house, along one of the diagonal runways? Still a long travel and very risky due to the runway's narrowness: there'd be a steep drop into the audience's lap if we were to fall off, and it could happen, and then someone would get sued as well as hurt. Which left the central auditorium route. But (given what you may remember about this) how? We'd have to come through one of the corner entrances, with little space to manoeuvre. The doors are heavy and someone would have to open them for us. Our unit of two bodies, one burdened with the other and rather wide overall, would still have a large visible distance to cover along the narrow channel behind the orchestra stalls to get to the start of the central runway. Especially as there is no masking there: we would travel visibly along behind the back row (as I did to make Lear's first entrance) and many in the audience would see the whole approach.

Here, solving at one stroke both the how and the where from, is what we did. We arranged that during the interval a long piece of black masking would be hung behind the back row of the central block, with a gap in the middle to allow for a clear route down the runway. On an agreed cue, Lilly took her place inside the corner door at audience right and I in the audience left airlock. I knelt on all fours, opening my door myself as I did so. I then crept into the exposed corner area of the auditorium and turned right towards the camouflage of the masking along the back row. Had you been looking, you might have assumed that Lear was, in some symbolic way, crawling on his belly like the serpent from the Garden of Eden. It was more difficult for Lilly: she needed to get across the exposed area at her corner as best she could (dressed in white): she must have seemed to be walking in her death-sleep.

Quiet as a mouse I went. Sometimes en route I would encounter a discarded programme or even a bottle of water, halt before it as an animal would, and brush it aside as if with my snout. Lilly and I would meet, she upright (her choice) and me crawling, just short of the central split in the masking. (I was still crawling out of habit, even though we'd taken the trouble to hang it.) At the *moment juste* – before we reached the peripheral vision of someone sitting in the back row – I purposefully, still sort of in character, got to my feet (Lear rising like a phoenix from his suffering), and slid into a position facing the back wall, with Lilly up against it in front of me, gripped her beneath her ribs with both arms and without a pause came shuffling down the central runway, dragging her after me, backing towards the stage, core muscles locked to protect back and abdomen, eyes ruthlessly trained on the road behind me (except that I was also facing it). It was like backing a vehicle without a rear mirror, but with a fanatical attention to angle and distance so that we wouldn't go over the edge, this, like the other runways, being barely three feet wide.

And all the time hoping there was no obstacle on the runway. Once in a while my feet, attuned to every bump and tear in the stage cloth beneath them, would encounter a slippery-surfaced programme; but as the run continued, we found, as Bottom says, a device to make all well. The noble Earl of Kent, entering a few seconds ahead of us, would rudely foot any such vulgar thing aside, as if he were preparing for the Palm Sunday procession into Jerusalem. He would have done the same if the obstacle had been – God help us – an umbrella or a coat. By some miracle this never happened, not in this second half of the show – though it did in the first, where it was occasionally a nuisance to jump over someone's handbag while running out into the storm with "O Fool, I shall go mad". At least the audience couldn't stretch its legs across your path, as they can at the Donmar in London.

We reached a given point on the main stage that I recognised by the co-ordinates of light and latitude – that particular bump in the floor, that seam in the stage cloth, that pillar in the side seats – and I put her down, which was much more difficult that bringing her on. It was uncomfortable for Lilly, but it looked very suitably messy – Lear is not used to dragging heavy weights around, and yet no-one would have presumed to help him – and we continued.

The whole thing was probably worse for Lilly, unable to help and enduring all as an inert dead body, but I did feel the audience were willing us on in our shuffling. I was also seeking to do justice to one of Lear's defining moments, one of the handful you're judged on:

> Howl, howl, howl! O, you are men of stones!
> Had I your tongues and eyes, I'd use them so
> That heav'n's vault should crack…

and to get her onto the floor smack on 'crack'.

Perhaps, if it could ever have been welcome for Prue to go back to London for a few days, this was the time for it: for the first two weeks of March she would have felt she was on a solo holiday in Brooklyn, and my appearance at any time of night would have seemed an unexpected surprise. And now she's back, sailing through Border Control with another ninety days' allowance on her visa. Glad to be installed on the top floor, she immediately comes to meet me for dinner at Caffe e Vino, our (and Jeffrey's) favourite joint near the theatre, and immediately feels she lives here again.

### *Friday, March 14th: The First Preview*

The deal is this: after our week of technical and dress rehearsals we play twelve previews from now until March 26th, rehearsing in the day the while, from 12 noon or 1pm.

However, beware the interpretation of the word Preview. In the UK this is definitely a critic-free phase; if ever a reviewer asks to come to a preview because they have another premiere that clashes with yours but to which their Editor insists they go, they can come. However it's thought good practice if it's acknowledged in the review, especially if it is at all negative, that this was only a preview (most but not all previews are at a reduced price in acknowledgment of their status).

New York is different, in some ways more relaxed and in some more anxious. It's open season from the moment of the first preview. A critic can come to any performance thereafter and base their judgment on that, and to hell with English chivalry; however the notice itself won't be published until after the official opening night, which is for donors, sponsors, whatever A List the theatre runs with. This certainly spreads the load – *The New York Times* might be in at a certain performance, but equally likely not, and the management of the Polonsky won't tell the cast which. A standard press night, especially in a theatre of 265 seats, would be quite an unnatural audience, with an atmosphere you could either cut with a knife (unnerving) or over-enthusiastic (friends there to counteract the critical chill).

The fact that some of the technicals ran from noon until close to midnight (once or twice a little longer) was also a standing reminder of the fact that the subways in New York run all night, as they have for over a hundred years, while they still don't in London. So it was felt reasonable to keep people longer than their British equivalents. This was the period that I worried about Graham Winton, Tim Stickney and Chris McCann, the intensified complexities of whose travelling must have resulted in an almost complete divorce from anything resembling normal life. I also noticed that occasional actor lateness was surprisingly tolerated at our rehearsals, no doubt out of compassion.

At least the far-flung Earls of Kent and Gloucester and the Duke of Albany must have found the preview period a slight improvement on the technical, since the play came in at just over three hours and by 11pm.

### TIMOTHY STICKNEY

After performances I had to dash to the Port Authority at 42nd Street to make my bus connection to New Jersey or be stuck in Manhattan all night. Which explains why I was only rarely available for meeting out front with folks or drinks after the show.

### GRAHAM WINTON

Often, on the ride home late at night, I'd crack a couple of beers, put something nice on my headphones and decompress. By the time I got home I was ready to wind down. Coming from Brooklyn I usually got there around 1:15am. Well, I like trains.

### LILLY ENGLERT

I just got one subway to the Upper East Side and it took me around 40 minutes, though sometimes, if the express line wasn't running, it could take a lot longer. I always got home pretty late because it took me a while after the performance to wash off all the blood and mud.

### CHRIS MCCANN

Well now, I had several choices. Depending on which I made, I could find myself home in roughly forty minutes. If I chose poorly (because of false intuition, or some deceitful subway app announcing non-existent trains) it could be an hour and a half. Let me explain: I could travel on the G Train that runs through Brooklyn into Queens, and then transfer to the Number 7 or the E – but though that transfer happened at the same G station, the distance between both trains was not tiny, and it did happen on at least one occasion, one very sad occasion, that I chose to transfer to one, missed it, and then made fast tracks to the other and missed that as well. Or: I could take a No 2 or No 3 from the theatre into Manhattan, to Times Square, and transfer there instead for the No 7. The advantage would be that I would be hopping on the No 7 at its starting station and would always get a seat. Or I could hop on a D to Manhattan and transfer to an F which, the very first time I tried it, worked splendidly – I was home in about half an hour. Needless to say it never worked the same after that....

## MICHAEL PENNINGTON (INTERRUPTING)

All that hopping, Chris... I specially like the touch of the dithering Earl of Gloucester in this, looking for his best route, ears alert and presumably stoical about his ghastly injury.

## PRUE SKENE

On the afternoon of the first preview I go to Brooklyn Fare to buy some salads and eat them with Michael in the Polonsky foyer, meeting members of the cast for the first time. They are tremendously welcoming and friendly, in that great way of actors, though I'm well aware of everyone's nerves. It's clear that this is a very successful and buoyant team that has been created in only six weeks.

And it was thrilling to see Michael accomplish his dream.

## MICHAEL PENNINGTON

We have a celebratory drink together at the Berlyn afterwards. This German-inflected bar (beer garden in the summer), immediately opposite the theatre, presents itself as the Polonsky's local, though it's as difficult to get a table there as it is everywhere else, and rather a fast turnover of staff means there's not much recognition factor, which would maybe help. This part of the evening is only momentarily spoiled by a *Star Wars* fan clutching a heavy folder of photos and posters for signing. His slightly aggressive approach, essentially a vociferous chasing of me from the theatre to the bar a hundred metres away, might be due to the fact that as it turned out he was an ex-cop, collecting for his Federation Pension Group. I expected shots to ring out.

*Saturday, March 15th: The Second Preview*

## PRUE SKENE

At lunchtime (timed for European evening showings) I went to a live screening of the Metropolitan Opera's *Werther* at BAM – a much-criticised work that's been described as Massenet dousing Goethe's original in French scent. The Met is acknowledging disappointing attendance figures at the moment, but the *The Met: Live in HD* series of worldwide cinecasts may be boosting interest and generating revenue. For this new production they have called in today's most in-demand tenor: the wonderful Jonas Kaufmann, directed by Richard Eyre. No trouble getting the London critics out to New York for this one. Having Kaufmann on stage ensured it had been standing-room only in the 3,800-seat house on the opening night.

I loved what I saw of the production and the singing but have to confess to dozing through some scenes, thanks to delayed jetlag hitting me at afternoon siesta time.

Then I have an early dinner after *Werther* at Caffe e Vino with Moss Cooper and Maggie Whitlum (long-standing friends from Arts Council and other days) who are going on to see *Lear* while I go back to the apartment to catch up on my sleep. Or perhaps to view a good documentary on TV or the Charlie Rose show: he has excellent guests and I like to see a more polite – and therefore more revealing – interviewing technique after the confrontations of Jeremy Paxman.

## MICHAEL PENNINGTON

Meanwhile Lydia Stryk is in for the second preview – the first friend to see the show. She's the dramatist daughter of my friend Lucien Stryk, the poet, who died last year, in town because she's gone to the Memorial Service of an old friend and mentor Stanley Kauffmann – no relation to Jonas the singer or to Joanne from *The Wall Street Journal* (who is in a spot of hot water now about her chronic habit of leaving first nights at the interval). Stanley was a passionate advocate of new theatre writing (including Lydia's) and foreign film, and as a critic he helped introduce the work of Truffaut, Bergman, Chabrol and Ozu to Stateside audiences. Think of a cross between Pauline Kael and Kenneth Tynan, but living to 97. Lydia has had too many losses, and her response is subdued for that reason I think and I keep my vanity out of it.

## Sunday, March 16th: The Third Preview

This morning I get a text from Orange, my mobile phone provider. Unlike, say, the average twelve-year-old, I understand it only a little:

> "You're currently protected by a £42 (ex vat) data roaming price cap, you've reached that cap based on our standard rates of £8 per MB... If you have a bundle, don't worry you'll be charged at your discounted bundle rate."

It goes on to say that if I want my cap removed I should text the word YES to 387.

Such is my state of mind that all I can think of is the Fool offering his Fool's cap to Lear in place of the crown he's given away, an act both of self-abasement and of folly. This turns out to be right on both counts. Do I want my Orange cap removed? It seems to me, that unlike for the Fool, it must be a good thing, this going capless, in case I am ever called from England (my son or my agent or anyone else who might have difficulty getting through to the Tracfone.) So I enthusiastically tap YES. You'll be sensing where this is going, I dare say.

But not exactly. Two days later, on the morning of the fourth preview, I wake up to two messages from the Fraud Department at Santander, one of the two banks where I hold accounts and who now need to speak to me urgently. They have also called my London agent, and the RSC, who were my most recent employers. One message, from the Senior Portfolio Manager, Fraud Strategy, originates in Bootle; the other, from the Senior Fraud Investigator, Fraud Operations, in Milton Keynes. The accents may vary but like most everybody I encounter in the somnambulist drama about to unfold, they have a training that has left most of them with an absolute unanimity of vocal styling, content, and strictly controlled attitude, as close to automated as they can get.

I don't have access to a landline in New York, and calling the UK on the Tracfone is touch and go. When I do get through to one of the Santander numbers, I get a third person who is now on duty. This is Sue and I will become quite fond of her, so surprised and relieved am I by her reasonable, uniquely untrained tone, that of a kindly surrogate aunt perhaps. She tells me there has been a big and multiple hack on my account the previous Friday, 14th March (the day of the first preview). It's taken the form of a large cash withdrawal, seemingly over the counter in the Edgware Road branch; its transfer to a new account in my own name but unknown to me; a card payment to a Jewellers in North London and another to a supplier of body building equipment nearby. Sue promises an immediate refund, which the next day, 19th March, indeed goes through. She also advises me to check other accounts, as a precaution.

Waiting to get through and brooding, I've started to do that by checking my account at Lloyds. I find that online access to it is blocked; however there's a number I can call. Now I seize up my Tracfone again and reach Charlotte who confirms that Yes, there has been a hack here too. She gives me a reference number as a victim of Fraud, a security code and another code (a code for the code?) and says it'll probably all be sorted out within two weeks. She is polite enough, but says firmly that there's no question of any refund before that, indeed I will have to go into the branch first with my ID and show them all my codes. I explain that being in New York I can't do that for the next two months. She acknowledges that seems a problem, but there's nothing she can do: them's the rules. I realise in my general perturbation that I've forgotten to ask her why Lloyds didn't notify me of the unusual activity on the account, as Santander did – and as, I should have thought, any halfway decent bank would have done. Presumably it's a rhetorical question.

Charlotte has also confirmed that the account is now frozen, which means I have no way of accessing it to see what's actually happened. Later, back in London, I will learn that eight days before this conversation, withdrawals had been made close to the size of the Santander ones, and in some cases through the same techniques – cash withdrawals at two branches, cards at the same Jewellers and body builders. All this happened on the Monday before the Friday of the Santander hack. Why in the world had Lloyds not called? The similarity of the two methods is a little sickening: I go to work imagining the rising jubilation of a chancer travelling from the Strand to Victoria to Edgware Road making the hits, the rush of blood at having achieved them. Not to mention the marvelling, which I now shared, that a bank could allow someone to walk into a series of branches and out again with sums of money of that size – a thing I'm sure I couldn't have done myself, and I'm legit. And then that they could go and do the same at another bank.

Orange and the two banks soon become the incommunicative triple pillars of my current world. I can see that two of them – Santander and Lloyds – are connected in their failure; but what have they got to do with Orange and my raised cap – or should it be coxcomb? Because I now see I've been charged a total of £1,075. 38 by Orange in two weeks.

I move into a period – seven more weeks in New York and then a further four months in London until the business was pretty much laid to rest – in which my default posture was, I think, a sort of incredulous brooding, perhaps not unlike that of Lear when he finds himself denied or contradicted in his progress through life. Certainly when Arin Arbus greets me at the theatre, it's as if she had indeed met a specially boding King Lear on the stairs and goes white at the news, as if I'd been struck down by a particularly nasty disease – *hysterica passio* or *tremor cordis* perhaps. She asks me if there is anything she can do. I think I saw her reaching for her purse.

## Thursday, March 20$^{th}$: The Sixth Preview

Prue joins me in contemplating the workings of the criminal mind by going to a matinee of *A Gentleman's Guide to Love and Murder*, in which Jefferson Mays plays eight roles – the source is that of *Kind Hearts and Coronets*; it closes as I'm writing in 2016. I wonder what the perpetrators of my bank fraud look like. Not like stage villains, I'm sure.

## Friday, March 21$^{st}$: The Seventh Preview

Robin Ellis is my very oldest (in the sense of longest-standing) friend – we met within the same five minutes on the day I left school in 1961 as I did John Shrapnel, in a rehearsal for the Youth Theatre; they both took me under their wing. A few weeks later we went off to Berlin and dauntlessly crossed to the East via the newly installed Checkpoint Charlie to see a dress rehearsal at the Berliner Ensemble; then we went through Cambridge acting together. Robin's here with his wife Meredith, and they almost smell of their idyllic house and garden in the Tarn: its bouquet arouses more European nostalgia in me than any thoughts of London. Robin sits with a quiet beam on his face: no need to make any speeches, he's just specially delighted to see his old friend making sense of the work done since I made the Russian guards at Checkpoint Charlie laugh at my passport photograph at a moment of supreme East-West tension. So we go to Berlyn again (I've only just noticed the coincidence), this time without a Brooklyn cop behind me. The bank business has sat between my two visits there. So did the cop know something? My mind is beginning to do meaningless calculations, like a hapless fiction-writer trying to corral random events into a convincing plot: we went to Berlyn after the first preview, which was two days before Orange removed my cap, which was two days before the banks called about crimes that had been committed in the days before the first visit to Berlyn. O Fool, I shall go mad.

### Saturday, March 22nd: The Eighth And Ninth Previews.

I take up my trusty Tracfone and call Lloyds again, determined to get some proper action. I reach an extremely terse girl called Brooke who repeats the message – no ID, no refund. I point out that Charlotte had understood the difficulty about that. She says there's no record of my talk with Charlotte, and there's no one called Charlotte in the department anyway. I go off like a bomb. She informs me I have no business talking to her like that. She then tells me she is in a different department, not 'Fraud' like Charlotte, but 'Credit Card Fraud', very much as if I should have known the difference. In any case I didn't yet know that a credit card had been involved. I refer to my fifty years as a customer, and that I dislike being treated like the criminal, not the victim. But she is ready for that: Mr Pennington, Did I say that? When did I say that? Always the surname to start with – that's how it's done in this comedy of manners. Feeling like King Lear deprived of the name and all the addition of a King I slam the phone down as if she was Goneril – have you ever tried to slam down a mobile? – and gape into an alternative universe. I'm busted, more or less cleaned out, and thus unable to pay further bills, mobile phone ones for example.

When Bianca Amato's Regan explains to me tonight that there will inevitably be a clash of authority in her house if her staff and mine are vying to look after me, I want to kill her. She has a way of saying:

'Tis hard, almost impossible….

as if she was speaking to a child, with a sort of infuriated pity. It's an outrage. She also has a little habit of putting her finger to her temple and sort of twisting it as if tightening a screw that's going into her head. It's a sort of "doh". Brooke probably knows it and does it invisibly on the phone about the customers.

I flew at Bianca as if to do some terrible thing: Cornwall (for her) and Kent and Gloucester (for me) started forward to intervene. Bianca jumped out of her skin and recoiled. Well, of course I never would actually hit her: in acting you live on the very edge of the unthinkable. If it comes to you to do such a thing, you must immediately start racing to the edge of the precipice and as immediately stop. It can be thrilling: a form of electrical shock, and I love it. Saxon Palmer (Cornwall) says there were nights in *Lear* he was physically scared – and he's quite scary himself.

As it happens Rachel Pickup has, quite independently, discovered the exact same screwy gesture that Bianca has. So here I am with two daughters both doing the same "doh" thing at me. So on some of the nights to come, all in all, I'd rather kill Goneril: she has a sort of soignée way of flicking her shawl across her shoulder as if mildly incommoded by the weather or the atmosphere. Well, here's what I say about that:

> Thou art a boil,
> A plaguesore, an embossed carbuncle
> In my corrupted blood…

– whereas Bianca gets only 'Regan, said you so' from me, because I'm a little afraid of her.

On the last free Monday before we open, we have dinner with Nicholas Wapshott and Louise Nicholson. Jim Dale is a guest – delightful – and Chandler Williams was invited but couldn't come "for personal reasons", thereby ensuring all sorts of speculation, some of it quite lewd. But he's a Bastard, after all. The show seems a long way away, but it's definitely developing its own traction. And spring is beginning to show itself. To be warm is gorgeous.

## *Wednesday, March 26th: The Twelfth Preview*

My old friend, the great horn player Timothy Brown, having yesterday played the *Eroica* under Joshua Bell in Florida and about to do it tomorrow at Lincoln Centre, comes to the last preview with a party of musicians, one or two of whom I know. At the outset of his career fifty years ago, Tim was in the RSC's band and played the crucially delicate music cue for Lear's awakening to find Cordelia, hand-stopping his horn to achieve the necessary muted sound.

I am hugely soothed by this wave of friends. And of course they completely understand about tone and modulation and notice everything.

## PRUE SKENE

This afternoon I'd been to see a rehearsal at the Mark Morris Dance Center, almost next door to the Polonsky. I'd had an invitation to the company via Ballet Rambert and was intrigued to see the master at work. I also wanted to see the building, having been instrumental in getting Rambert's new headquarters on London's South Bank off the ground: these had opened a few weeks ago and I was inordinately proud of them. I was shown round by a very nice and friendly girl, Jenna Nugent, but my enthusiasm waned when Mark Morris himself entered the rehearsal room. At first he seemed to ignore my presence but then preened up and immediately started making some dismissive remarks about the new Rambert building, calling out to his Production Manager "What did I tell you was wrong with those Rambert floors?". But then he started rehearsing and although ghastly rude to his dancers – they didn't seem to mind and indeed many of them have been with him for a long time – one could see by the tiny changes and insights he made why he is such a great choreographer. A fascinating experience, made the more so by my dislike of him alongside my admiration for his work.

## Thursday, March 27<sup>th</sup>: Opening Night

A premiere is the most important night of your life/year/month, you tell yourself. You will judge your work (with a little help from others), and make your case again to whomever you may need to. To your worried parents perhaps, some thirty years after their deaths, so that they can rest in the knowledge that it wasn't a mistake to go to the Noguchi *Lear* and all the rest of it. Or just to the boy or girl you love up in the gallery, Waving their handkerchief, Merry as a robin that sings on a tree.

Or you could consider it just another night, just another opening, another show: three hours in the evening of an ordinary day while the world goes about its own indifferent business and you complete a small piece of carpentry, or plumbing, or fixing the TV, whatever you're good at. A task which it would be better on the whole to succeed in than to fail, but in the end only a task, one which you started some time ago and still have several opportunities to improve.

The main thing is how you brief yourself, preparing for nerves that generally last for a few early moments and then drop off you like a coat as you get going. In my case this took the form of not eating all day for fear of being sick – a bad decision. But I did do some thinking about this famous slide show called The Eleven Scenes of King Lear. How, I ask myself, am I doing with them?

# THE ELEVEN SCENES OF LEAR

## Lear's First Scene (Act One Scene One)

There's a trade wisdom about first scenes: you don't have to account for your whole character all at once. All of Cleopatra's mercurial variety, the entire emotional mechanism of Hamlet, a signal of what your Lady Macbeth is going to be like compared to another.

Audiences generally don't remember the first scene when they get home, although *King Lear* is a bit of an exception in this respect as its towering overture casts a long shadow over the play, so clearly does it contain the seeds of the tragedy to come. Critics invariably find a convenient keynote, so that they can write "From his very first entrance, tottering but watchful..." or some such, and audiences remember it too, understanding its full meaning in retrospect.

With *Lear* there is a further thing, and like most dilemmas in the theatre it's pragmatic: this is probably the most difficult scene to stage, both for *Lear* and for Lear. Even more than the matter of carrying Cordelia on at the end, practical questions swing down like automatic barriers. If Lear wears a crown, what kind of society – ancient or modern or something in between – does that suggest? Is the audience part of the public, being addressed about his resignation, or are they as usual eavesdropping in the dark? Do the people on the stage have cocktails in their hands or are they hieratically on their knees? Is Lear more like the CEO of a corporation with a business plan in his hands or is he a pagan tyrant?

Then, where will he come on from – upstage? Not necessarily. Will he sit on a throne? Not necessarily: if he does, he will look a bit – well, Shakespearian. Try each alternative. What is his apparent mood and is it the same as his real state of mind? The time will come when Barack Obama will weep on television at his lack of progress on gun controls while declaring his fury at the deaths of the most recent victims. How does Lear, despite any number of tearful self-doubts or regrets he may be hiding, manage to dominate the scene with the fullest authority of his office – while allowing each of the daughters, as they are summoned, a good position in which to feel uncomfortable as characters but comfortable as actors? And above all, has he decided on the love-test before he arrives, or does he make it up in the heat of the moment, an extra unscripted joke up his sleeve to ratify what he's already carved into the map? And is the map visible, and should it be a huge carpet on the floor, or a little gazetteer under his arm?

If there's one more powerful entrance in the theatre than upstage centre it is downstage, especially if it's straight through the audience: they're immediately implicated. If you come on up centre as Lear you're likely to be invisible behind a throne or some such, unless you do a little loop, known as a "banana". Not very dignified. Alan Howard used to peek mischievously out from behind the throne as if he'd been hiding there while the court assembled. But in some productions he might have found the Fool there as well, ready to leap out at the end after hearing the terrible things being done to his friend Cordelia and making himself scarce. A downstage centre entrance, if it's available, subconsciously brings you in from the real world that the audience has just left. And the chutzpah of not straight away showing your face is not to be underestimated. The Minerva in Chichester has a particularly good entrance like this, because it's sudden – there's no long approach through the stalls and immediately you arrive there's audience above and ahead of you. It has such surprise value that everyone wants to use it: though downstage, it's known paradoxically as the Star Entrance because it puts you very much in charge, if that's appropriate.

The stakes are immediately very high: Lear is talking not of retirement from office in order to spend more time with his family (though he hopes he will), but explicitly because he wants to crawl unburdened towards death. This so calls a spade a spade that it's very unlike modern politics. And so is the love contest, a caprice that puts everybody on their extreme mettle: in reality it's a competition in improvised public speaking, a thing at which Lear himself, being a professional, has probably always been good. It's clear what follows: satisfaction with Goneril, partial pleasure with Regan, affront and rage at Cordelia. Yes of course, but the assault on Cordelia particularly needs vocal variety, flexibility and range – it's spiteful, sullen, furious and bitterly disappointed all in one. You might threaten her physically, or not. What can then be tough is dealing with the protests of Kent: Lear is enraged with his suddenly disloyal servant, but it's an entirely different kind of rage than at Cordelia, being professionally required rather than paternal: it's difficult to feel as strongly about banishing Kent as being affronted by your favourite daughter. The residue of it all then spills over into Lear's attitude, peremptory and then ingratiating, towards her suitors the Duke of Burgundy and the King of France.

As for the hinterland: what, in truth, does Lear feel about turning his back on her forever? She is by far his favourite, and how alike he and Cordelia are! He even flings her 'Nothing' back at her when Burgundy begs for a little bit of dowry to go with her hand:

> Nothing. I am sworn. I am firm.

Well, father and daughter are nothing if not firm. Cordelia is as unyielding over what might seem an unimportant gesture to her father, cheap in the giving, as Lear was in demanding it.

In this demented competition to attach the country to the most attractive price tag, Lear is in another sense at his best. When he then goes on the road, never to come home, his utterance, though often very powerful, will be plagued by faltering conviction, wavering self-confidence, sudden outbursts and retrenchments. But his command of this first scene is expressed in absolutely regular, fluent and highly accomplished verse. Extreme as his feelings now are, they resolve into balanced antitheses and confident rhythms. You can see how impressive he would once have been, when his judgment was better and less dangerous. In fact, he is still strangely elegant:

> The barbarous Scythian
> Or he who makes his generation messes
> To gorge his appetite, shall to my bosom
> Be as well neighboured, pitied and relieved
> As thou our sometime daughter.

This is part of your difficulty as you negotiate the opening. The emotions claim you and haul you around the stage and up and down your voice while requiring you to deal with quite highly-wrought verse. This is certainly when I think I shout too much, or too little, or the wrong kind of shout. Or that I've forgotten one of the main things about the job (tricky as it is in this play), which is spotting the contradictions: even at the height of his fury with Kent, Lear has the statesmanship to allow him a judicious five days' grace to pack and prepare, in order

> To shield thee from disasters of the world.

Later on he will even 'entreat' rather than simply advise the King of France not to marry Cordelia.

The only thing the first scene needs to be is complete to itself, an arresting overture and first view of the mountains. In a way, the more self-contained it is the more it quickens the spirits and summons up the blood. As Lear, you've staked out your claim and every night you sense what you need to do next. If you're not pleased, there's all evening to balance things out: if you kept hitting a D instead of an F, play in D Major for a bit. You've dumped your piece of clay on the board or mixed your initial colours, and they don't, some nights, look quite as you expected.

And much as I reproach myself, by the middle of Lear's next scene I've quite forgotten about it.

### Lear's Second Scene (Act One Scene Four)

Shakespeare is embarking on a remarkable musical fugue in the matter of Lear's diction. When he arrives at Goneril's with his controversial private army, he still commands all right, even in areas where he has no prerogative any more; but his metrical virtuosity is a little challenged by events – particularly by the adjustment to conversational prose forced on him by the newly-disguised Kent and his Fool. Unexpected repartee from the former – probably to deepen his disguise: I don't associate Kent with jokes – and the latter's need for a feed to trigger his various punch lines and provocations, means that for once in his life Lear is not in charge of the conversation. But he is dimly aware – an awareness he can suppress until someone else, such as the Third Knight, voices it for him – that he is missing the 'ceremonious affection' he is used to and that there is an 'abatement of kindness' not only in Goneril but in his 'general dependants'. He even admits, uncharacteristically, to a certain 'jealous curiosity' of his own that may be causing him to imagine it all. With the Fool – much missed and now turning up out of nowhere – he goes in and out of focus: feebly threatening him with the whip if he goes too far, half-listening, obligingly giving him his cues. There is a possessive affection here but a little uncertainty about the right note to hit. Until, in fact, the arrival of Goneril, whose message is very unwelcome but with whom he can least trade flowing sentences. Lear is clearly more comfortable cursing than conversing; and he's at his morbidly rhapsodic best when he calls on Nature to neutralise her as a woman.

Then, having cursed her so well, he returns to say it all again, his mastery more than a little stained with petulance. It was a good exit, but he's either had a change of heart or got some fast bad news – this is the much-debated moment when he's offstage and loses, or doesn't lose, or is told he's going to lose, half his retinue.

Goodness knows it's hard for the audience to follow what happens in the few moments he's been away. Has Oswald told him of the new rule, he who has so shockingly brushed him off during the scene as merely "My lady's father"? But does Oswald have that kind of authority? Or has Lear just got muddled (perhaps like his author) about what Goneril has actually said (which was nothing about 'a fortnight') and overcome by what he's just done to her? Is he alarmed at or proud of his intemperance, or momentarily penitent before losing control again? Perhaps he simply wants to rub in his already explicit message. This is a *pensée d'escalier* forced into the light – the compulsion to return to the scene of the trouble to add the perfect, devastating summary, or just to pick a bit further at the scab.

## Lear's Third Scene (Act One Scene Five)

In Peter Brook's 1971 film, the little scene between Lear and his Fool after the denunciation of Goneril took place not as they waited for the horses that would take them to meet Regan, but bumping along behind them in a carriage over the unforgiving terrain. The physical movement of the rickety carriage had an obvious effect on the actors' bodies and became a factor in how the scene was spoken. This was a good idea: the relative peacefulness of being out of the house, out of the heat of a debilitating quarrel and with a little time to reflect (to the extent that Lear has the capacity for it) began to syncopate with the rhythm of his transport. The elements were as they had been: some regret over Cordelia ('I did her wrong'); a weakening flow of curses ('To take it again perforce... monster ingratitude'), and something new – fear for himself, a thing he can only admit to his Fool. It is – at last – a quiet disclosure by a man who is rarely quiet, and he goes into verse for it. There could even be a little charm in the last phrase, that to stay sane would be his preference:

> O let me not be mad, not mad, sweet heaven!
> Keep me in temper; I would not be mad.

He is also listening a little better and joining in more astutely. Having paid out a lot of slack to his Fool ('No... tell me') something wakes up in him. He swiftly considers the Fool's enquiry as to why the seven stars are no more than seven, and comes up with the answer:

> Because they are not eight.

This lack of effort is like a reference to time gone by, when the two of them were a proper double act. The Fool recognises it as a good joke stolen:

> Yes indeed; thou would'st make a good Fool

– as if there had been a talented heckler in his audience. All the same, the two of them are going headlong into the unknown: the world has jolted out of true for them both.

## *Lear's Fourth Scene (Act Two Scene Four)*

It's easy to mock Shakespeare's geographical waywardness: he can be as far off-course as the famous non-existent coast of Bohemia in *The Winter's Tale*.

In Act Two Scene Four it doesn't do to look too closely at why and how everyone is turning up at poor Gloucester's house at the same moment – but with Lear bringing up the rear (slower horses?). Of course Shakespeare knew his business in a far more important way. He sensed that Lear's direct, head-butting style when he wishes sterility on Goneril needs to be followed as soon as possible by a variant in which he must take on Regan and Goneril together; then he must twist and turn, negotiate, feel the ground slipping beneath him, compromise, beg, wheedle, and feebly bully, all to reach exactly the same point of defeat. It really doesn't matter about travelling time: on a stage with no scenery, the tonal contrast was all that interested Shakespeare. His form of logic goes straight as an arrow.

The first thing Lear encounters is entirely surreal, even more surreal than not having his horses standing there waiting for him when he left Goneril's. Caius, the new servant dispatched to announce his approach, is sitting in a pair of wooden stocks in the courtyard of an apparently deserted house – no Gloucester to be seen, no Regan, no Cornwall, nobody.

A semi-comical No/Yes routine breaks out between them, a bit in the style of the first scene, when Kent was Kent. It might remind you of the Beatles – You say goodbye, I say hullo. (I'm not sure if, as I go indoors, I'll be able to resist the temptation to say "Follow me not" to the immobilised Kent – most Lears seize on this one unambiguous joke.)

For the first time Lear feels physically ill, sick with sorrow; 'hysterica passio' is probably what we would call an anxiety attack, an extreme apprehension like suddenly facing a man with a gun. It needs, I would say, to be played specifically; Shakespeare was imagining a disturbance rising from the pit of the stomach (the 'mother') to the chest and the head. Action is his release: he charges into the house and returns with Gloucester as his only prize – shifting from foot to foot, trying to see both sides of every quarrel. They are sick, says his host, they are tired, and the Duke of

Cornwall is a famously stubborn man, fiery in fact. But he has "informed" them that the King is waiting for them.

Wrong word to use (you never know which the dangerous words are going to be), and not good for a rising sorrow. Two wrong words, in fact: 'fiery' and 'informed'. Well, not as 'fiery' as I am, let me tell you. I am *Mister* Fiery. And 'informed' sounds as if Lear has put in an application for an audience. And then from nowhere – don't overlook it – a moment of appeasement, even understanding. If you're sick you can do nothing, he says, the mind shuts down with the body (Lear will contradict this in the storm). It's almost kindly: these moments are already like gold dust to me in rehearsal, one of the moments which endear Lear to Gloucester, Kent, the Fool and even us. It doesn't last: he catches sight of Kent again (having momentarily forgotten him), and goes off bang. Damn it, he'll stand here until they come out.

The long negotiation that follows with Regan and Cornwall and then Goneril as well will track about and about as I nag, insinuate, thunder and bargain, trying everything in turn – even an apparent sweet reasonableness, and a wry humour here and there. Complaining to Regan about his other daughter in her absence, Lear casts himself unwittingly as the wronged child, launching instantly into denunciation – 'Thy sister's naught' – only to find Regan as tough as nails. He is old, he must learn to listen, he must learn to obey. This is quite unlike Goneril's sinuous implications, and most unlike the Regan the audience has seen up until now. Instead of answering, he goes for Goneril again – 'my curses on her' – only to be told that he's too old to have an opinion. He can't afford to flare up again, even though worse is on its way: he's being told to ask for Goneril's forgiveness. He retaliates with an elaborate mime of humility, begging like a little frail old man for a crust of bread. This is good, but only a preparation for horrendous images of defacement and infection (at least he doesn't go for the womb again) that he thinks will allow him to turn flatteringly to Regan, who would never deserve such a thing. His transition is a little lumpen and certainly ineffective: he should have left it at that.

Something is sinking in like an accelerating stone as I wheel and pirouette clumsily through the final manouevres, the last before Lear's life – and mind – changes forever. It's like a steady drumbeat: Who put my man in the stocks? Goneril arrives, and immediately lines up with her sister, hand in hand. Who would have thought two women holding hands could be an act of aggression?

Lear can see that the final bargaining is a far from even fight. Facing such a partnership, all he can become is petty, trying to drive a limp wedge between the two of them. The number of his permitted followers goes down and down: he scrabbles to hold on to the cliff-face but the avalanche has started. Goneril is denounced again but it has no effect except to unite them further. He calls Goneril all the names under the sun but then assures her he won't reprove her: it should get some sort of a laugh. Rather than stay with Goneril with fifty I'll stay with Regan with my hundred. Regan says no. For her, too many knights means too many chiefs in the house and not enough Indians and she drops the offer to twenty-five. The auction has gone into reverse. I go back to Goneril for fifty, but her offer's closed. With virtually no followers I already feel no more than the naked unaccommodated man I will become: but in fact I'm only having my outer layers flayed off in preparation for the real thing.

Then from right at the bottom, King Lear soars.

What need one? Don't configure it. Nobody needs anything except a coat to keep them warm. Not even Goneril's fancy clothes, they keep nobody warm. What he needs is patience only, and divine retribution. He will punish them dreadfully himself, though he doesn't know quite how (note: dare the audience to laugh). Above all, he won't give way, or above all cry. He will go mad, but he won't cry.

This is Lear's greatest moment, a *tour de force* of defiance. He prays no longer for shelter but for anger. He finds the force to drive him through the next third of the play. It's the reason we take to him in spite of everything: his default mode is to keep on, to keep on keeping on, to keep going.


## Lear's Fifth Scene (Act Three Scene Two)

Who would have thought the famous Storm Scene would be only eighty lines long? Shakespeare sometimes wrote single speeches as long as that. But everyone has to remember it, and the Lear is unlikely to forget it. This is where the accumulated tensions, improprieties and pent-up grievances, all the intricate and unworthy bargaining, all the impotent energy, find a new and extraordinary form. The evening lifts off together with Lear, and rather than continuing to trace the exact circuitry between the characters, the audience experiences the play as a sort of secular mass, in the musical sense of the word as well as in the weightiness.

Have you ever been in a storm such as Lear describes? How near have you been to such a thing? You would have been very unlucky, and perhaps not be here to tell the tale. How wet have you ever been, have you ever been thrown off your feet by the wind, or opened a door to meet a wave pouring through to engulf you, have you ever lost your home to a flood? Have you ever imagined what would happen to an elderly man or woman, however tough, who then applied what energies they had left to changing the course of the weather?

The play becomes, in a good sense, remote as well as riveting. Actors and audience are less in the business of relating to their life experience than making a huge leap of the imagination. Lear brings to the leap a form of utterance of quite astonishing fluidity, as if he were a one-man orchestra. He constructs new compound words as if he was working in German. But they are held back from time to time by Shakespeare's old monosyllabic trick:

> Blow winds, and crack your cheeks, rage, blow
> …Till you have drenched our steeples, drowned the cocks.

These are soon submerged under an avalanche of syllables: cataracts and hurricanoes, sulphurous and thought-executing fires, vaunt-couriers of oak-cleaving thunderbolts. This, certainly at the time, was a revolution in what can be done with language in the theatre; it still is, whether you accompany the Storm with a lot of sound or none, with music or not, with flashing lights or "real" rain. And who would have thought Lear would now begin a tentative social critique (partly aimed at himself) – warnings to the unpunished criminal, the justice who punishes the crimes he is guilty of himself (he'll return to this subject later), the conspirators who plan the terrorist attack, every kind of wrongdoer? Or that as the storm subsides and he's offered shelter, he declares that his wits are beginning to turn and in his next breath kindly enquires about the welfare of his Fool. Is he cold, as cold as he is?

> Poor fool and knave, I have one part in my heart
> That's sorry yet for thee.

It's the first time he's shown any interest at all in anybody else's feelings, and he calls it the beginning of madness.

And who would have thought the whole process could have taken only five minutes?

### Lear's Sixth Scene (Act Three Scene Four)

By the time Lear and his very small new entourage find Kent's shelter, the weather is much the same but he has calmed down a little. Now he wants to be alone. He has, in fact, begun to think, and it would break his heart to be interrupted. A storm is not as bad for the body as disillusion is for the mind, he says. If you ran away from danger and found yourself heading for the edge of a cliff, you'd turn round and offer yourself to what you were running from. If the mind's OK, the body may hurt, but if the mind hurts you forget about the body.

I now have to play this logical Lear (or recover him from before the play's start) as he pursues elementary truths – elementary because he's never done such a thing before. For his daughters to assault their father is like someone dashing the food from his mouth when he was a baby. His absolute goodness on the one side, their absolute wickedness on the other. This oddity sets Lear thinking, and he talks as simply as he can to us in the theatre:

> Poor naked wretches, wheresoe'er you are,
> That bide the pelting of this pitiless storm,
> How shall your houseless heads and unfed sides,
> Your loop'd and window'd raggedness, defend you
> From seasons such as these? O I have ta'en
> Too little care of this. Take physic, pomp…

His revolutionism is rather provisional: pomp will still exist and simply take its medicine in his new world, the poor will always be poor, just have a poor roof over their poor heads, and all will be well. It's a start.

With the arrival of Poor Tom, Lear can accompany his tutorial with an illustration. Here is a poor man who was once at the court, who had mistresses (including his patroness), who gambled at the casinos, drank with the best, and who has been brought low, lower still than Lear, by his daughters – what else could explain his present state? It's better so, better to be naked, to owe nothing to a soul. I will join him.

This tone of curious enquiry has bequeathed us its funny side. The moment of Lear's disrobing, which Shakespeare clearly meant to be interrupted by the arrival of Gloucester (the "walking fire") before it can become too revealing, has been seized on from time to time as a cue for nakedness, drawing intense critical scrutiny – inevitably – of the personal provision of some of our favourite leading actors. It's OK, but I would prefer that Gloucester simply didn't miss his cue.

## Lear's Seventh Scene (Act Three Scene Six)

– in which Shakespeare continues to reinvent theatre.

Inside the hovel the only people who talk workaday sense are Kent and, briefly, Gloucester. They're easily upstaged by the Fool, the madman and the pretend madman, playing fiends and staring at visions, in only one of which the King actually believes. For him, the presence of the Fool and Edgar is assurance that there are two judges for the lawsuit he has in hand. For him this jointstool is undoubtedly Goneril, and her crime is that she kicked him. Regan runs away, and her place is taken, in a great dissolve, by a pack of dogs all barking at him, and they in turn by a man in elaborate Persian clothes, arriving at the very moment that he wants to call in a surgeon to find out where the cruelty gene is lodged in Regan's brain.

Even now, the staging of this has been giving us some trouble at the Polonsky: for once Arin's general method of starting by allowing the actors loose to go where they will doesn't seem to be paying off. A three-sided stage requires certain things as a matter of course. To state the obvious, wherever you stand on it someone will not see, or only just see, your face. Therefore you have to change positions pretty regularly, just as you need to be careful to be audible to people sitting behind you. In this scene it would be best if Lear, Edgar and the Fool are mesmerised by their own visions. Lear sees Goneril in the dock, the Fool identifies her as a joint-stool, Edgar is attended by a demon telling him that Nero is an angler in the lake of darkness while Hoppedance cries in his belly for two white herring. In its relative warmth after the storm the scene parodies the comforts of an interior in Gloucester's house, just at the moment that house is about to become a chamber of torture.

We don't much want to diffuse it with expedient moves hither and thither: its one small drama is best done as an intent and deadly thing, surrealistic and comically serious. But in the end we've had to settle for a position far enough upstage for everybody to have a view of sorts, so it's rather distant from the front block while only slightly favouring the sides. Like Act One Scene One, I'd like to have another look at this one day.

## Lear's Eighth Scene (Act Four Scene Six)

In *Measure for Measure* Claudio, under sentence of death, paints an astonishing picture of where he's going:

> Ay, but to die, and go we know not where;
> To lie in cold obstruction and to rot;
> This sensible warm motion to become
> A kneaded clod; and the delighted spirit
> To bathe in fiery floods, and to reside
> In thrilling region of thick-ribbed ice.
> To be imprison'd in the viewless winds
> And blown with restless violence round about
> The pendent world; or to be worse than worst
> Of those that lawless and uncertain thought
> Imagine howling; 'tis too horrible...

You see and feel every moment of this, so much so that you forget it is one thing you're never going to see or feel. In Act Four of *King Lear* Edgar does much the same when he describes the sheer cliff on which he pretends he and his father are standing:

> The crows and choughs that wing the midway air
> Show scarce so gross as beetles. Half way down
> Hangs one that gathers samphire – dreadful trade!
> Methinks he seems no bigger than his head.
>                     ...The murmuring surge
> That on the un'numbered idle pebble chafes
> Cannot be heard so high. I'll look no more...

It's not real – neither of them can see any such thing – but realised as completely as if it was. Moments later Lear aspires to do the same thing as he describes the world as he sees it now – the crooked judges, the politicians with their glass eyes and opaque consciences, the man of God who lusts after his parishioners, the women in constant heat.

This is the Dover Scene, one of the great attractions of the part. For me it's been slow to yield. In fact it's been one of two or three – the Trial Scene in the hovel and the start – when I would have welcomed being told what to do for the best, but Arin has felt sure I'd find them without – perhaps in the previews even. My indecisiveness has extended from how to play the scene to how to look as I do. Lear enters 'fantastically dressed with wild flowers', and it occurs to me that this is one of the moments you get the production photographs from, together with images of the Storm and the death of Cordelia. It's as if they explain certain things to the potential customer. I've seen Lears carrying on like still barmier Ophelias, giving flowers to everyone; or crowned with them in a way that wittingly or unwittingly suggests a crown of thorns. But there's something about that I don't like – because, after all, who wove this crown? Lear himself, with great concentration – which in this scene he doesn't display? So far I have a little woollen hat and a sharp necklace of thorn branches like barbed wire, and old pairs of trousers and shoes. I've retained the Fool's red concertina from the Hovel scene, where he bequeathed it to me, though this might be a red herring. I'm pottering around like a barmy gardener in weekend trousers and I talk mostly in a mild and sensible way, though –

> Ha! Goneril with a white beard!

– is sharp enough to make Gloucester simultaneously laugh and fall to his knees in shock. And whether Lear could really say the name Goneril with any kind of calm I'm not sure.

But I think it's probably all too humble, too domestic at the moment, not jagged and untethered enough. However it's come some distance with the preview audiences, which is just as well: this is a Becher's Brook in the part, and I might as well not have started if I fall here.

How is Lear speaking now? His organisation of the verse and prose at first features stabs of apparently random things:

> There's your press money – This fellow handles his bow like a crow-
> keeper– draw me a clothier's yard… look, look, a mouse…Peace!
> Peace! This piece of toasted cheese will do it…

– then moves into a prose as beautiful as verse:

> When the rain came to wet me once, and the wind to make me chatter,
> when the thunder would not peace at my bidding, there I found 'em,
> there I smelt 'em out…

– then, naturally enough, it elides into the gracefulness of

> Ay, every inch a King;
> When I do stare, see how the subject quakes…

– an unusual form of verse which characteristically runs full-line/half-line/full-line/half-line:

> The wren goes to't and the small gilded fly
> Doth lecher in my sight…
> The fitchew nor the soiled horse goes to't
> With a more riotous appetite…
> But to the girdle do the gods inherit,
> Below is all the fiends'…

Sexual horror upends this into prose:

> There's hell, there's darkness, there's the sulphurous pit…

This is followed by a more beautiful form of prose, and finally a verse that musically supports the recognition of Gloucester, the quiet climax of the scene.

Of course none of this is as random as it seems, it follows Lear's emotional graph. It's just that the ideas are stripped of their normal content and have linkage only in his imagination. The ideas of archery, of challenging his enemies (the most persistent, as if this were now preferable to the Trial he conducted in the hovel), of official corruption, the interchangeability of the judge and the criminal which has taken hold of Lear since his wits first began to turn in the storm, of (particularly female) adultery, are developed impressionistically, without outside stimulus. The sexual disgust seems to be an overspill from his shock at his older daughters, since there is a distinct lack of sexuality in the character from any other point of view.

It's all right if people laugh at some of this: it defends them from anything worse. Lear distributes bits and pieces of this and that and then asks Edgar for a password, which Edgar offers off the top of his head – 'Sweet marjoram' – an answer Lear finds completely satisfactory. He sees a mouse in the long grass of the field and tempts him with a piece of toasted cheese, which in reality is – what? Well, a leaf, probably, cunningly laid in the imaginary mouse's imaginary path. Then he hurls down a challenge at someone (also a leaf?). Then he sees Gloucester, and mistakes, or pretends to mistake, him for Goneril with a beard on. Don't tell me this isn't funny; but you also know that at any moment laughter can be made to die on its own breath.

The central image is sensational – no Fool any more, but a blind man, a madman and a phoney madman (who also utters Shakespearian exclamations of shock to the audience). As Jan Kott suggested, this is as much like Beckett as the preceding scene of the fall from the cliff. Lear and Gloucester could be Vladimir and Estragon, entertaining their wretched selves with a little vaudeville:

> No eyes in your head, nor no money in your purse.
> Your eyes are in a heavy case, your purse in a light...

But Gloucester and Lear – one unable to see, the other unable to cope – nevertheless find each other, and at the discreet climax you should be ravished by one of Shakespeare's great moments:

> I know thee well enough; thy name is Gloucester.
> Thou must be patient: we came crying hither...

I have an idea that Beckettian bleakness is the easy bit; the emotional mass packed behind it carries the whole thing, and so far I may not have caught that: I'm still not sure what tones, what pitch, what pace, how agonised or otherwise. And in fact I think I've provided the answer in this section by anxiously quoting so much of it. If the part of Lear starts like a bucking horse that wants to throw you, by now it's a thoroughbred: just stay in the saddle, listen to the Shakespeare and it'll probably carry you home.

## Lear's Ninth Scene (Act Four Scene Seven)

Bob Lloyd, now playing the Doctor attending on Lear, does something so beautiful in this scene with the most insignificant line. When Lear is carried on, still asleep, Michael Attias's music is as spare as it could be, just light chimes, but the Doctor judges it a little too soft, soothing but not quite assertive enough for what he knows may happen. Lear will awaken to find Cordelia there at last – and who knows what effect, for good or ill, this will have on him, on his heart, for instance. So Bob says:

> Louder the music there.

In his tone is a request, an order, a sympathy with the musicians, a deeper sympathy for Lear, and an authority, all expressed almost in sotto voce. It is a perfect piece of Shakespearian acting bestowed on what could almost be a stage direction. This is what you learn – he has learned – in sixty years of work and instinct. From it I've already discovered what the texture of this whole scene is – so fragile that it could rupture at any moment, sensual in the most discreet way, so gentle without piety.

Lear feels his way to each word, let alone thought: he returns to the same idea, of being "abused", that all this is a dream or a trick. He is never at peace, though the surrounding cadences are like calm water. This is in any case not so much the Reconciliation it's said to be, but a preparation for a reconciliation which we don't see. I've seen Lears all dressed in miraculous white, all clean, the storm forgotten. In fact, all that's needed is that he should be asleep. The fact that he's quiet and his eyes are closed is all the audience need to be moved: they see immediately that there has been a modicum of rest from horrors which may now gradually be forgotten, though they certainly aren't yet. He finds he can't greet Cordelia without comparing his wrong to her with the wrong her sisters have done to him, and he begs again not to be misled, not abused. It is a scene that ends with his anxiety slightly relieved, but not much.

To start this process of recovery, which in fact will lead to his death, what I see is that if any pathos has been allowed into the previous scene at Dover, it must be very very sparing indeed; now is when we might be allowed some sorrow for him, a crumpled man in a chair who once sat proudly on his throne, in his seat at dinner, his family around him. But it's only the beginning, and a warning of devastation ahead.

### Lear's Tenth Scene (Act Five Scene Three)

happens almost by accident. No sooner does Lear find some peace than war breaks out. There is no sign that he understands why Cordelia is here at all – he is unlikely to be *au fait* with the political situation. All he knows is that he was in a field at Dover, fell asleep and had a vision of Cordelia, and now everyone is fighting. But he does become a parent at last. Everything pours into Cordelia, as if she's just been born – humour, protectiveness, pride. It's the last time they'll see each other's faces.

### Lear's Eleventh Scene (Act Five Scene Three)

I mentioned at the first day's rehearsal that playing Richard Strauss in Ronald Harwood's *Collaboration* was what, one day, made me think of playing King Lear. Strauss, appearing before a Denazification Tribunal, ends the play in mid-sentence, as the tearful composer tries to accuse his friend Stefan Zweig (preposterously – Zweig was Jewish) of being a collaborator with the Reich as well as a collaborator in Strauss's music. In other words, he tries to shift the blame. He gets as far as "You are the...." and collapses in tears at his own dishonesty. And the play ends.

It's an inspired line, an inspired way to end any play. But Shakespeare could never have done it, even though he once put in a stage direction for Coriolanus to hold his mother's hand and remain silent. This writer has to do everything with words, and even the most volcanic emotions behind them have to find a form. Nothing is inexpressible, nobody runs out of language until death takes them or they leave. They never fail to have something to say. No Beckett, no Pinter here, no Harwood, with their withheld thoughts. So what do you do with all these words? Make sure they make sense in themselves and don't sob all over them. (And, of course, notice when they're monosyllables.)

> Howl, howl, howl! O you are men of stones;
> Had I your tongues and eyes, I'd use them so
> That heav'n's vault should crack. She's gone for ever.
> I know when one is dead and when one lives.
> She's dead as earth. Lend me a looking-glass...

That's five lines, all (if you discount the third) of monosyllables until you stumble over the practicality of the "looking-glass". Then:

> If that her breath will mist or stain the stone,
> Why then she lives.

And so it goes on, only relaxing as far as the occasional disyllable until the final speech of all, which breaks the pattern for a special repetitive effect and that unexpected button, too tight for comfort:

> And my poor fool is hang'd. No, no, no life;
> Why should a dog, a horse, a rat, have life
> And thou no breath at all. Thou'lt come no more,
> Never, never, never, never, never.
> Pray you undo this button, thank you sir.
> Do you see this? Look on her! Look, her lips!
> Look there, look there!

Sorry to labour the point to myself, but that's two hundred and thirty-two monosyllables, only thirty disyllables, four trisyllables and two words of four syllables for Lear in the whole final scene, and that's the end of him. Even in Edgar's final speech there are only three non-monosyllabic words. Did Shakespeare plan this, or was it all instinct?

> The weight of this sad time we must obey
> Speak what we feel, not what we ought to say
> The oldest hath borne most; we that are young
> Shall never see so much, nor live so long.

# WEEKS NINE TO FIFTEEN

Prue writes to her sister Lucy:

'It was a terrific performance on the opening night, but as soon as Michael put his head round the door afterwards into the foyer (full of guests for the party), he surreptitiously beckoned me behind it as if to impart a terrible secret. He said he thought he'd have to see a doctor in the morning because he'd nearly thrown up in the storm scene and hadn't known how he was going to continue. So a quick dash through the party (only really stopping to greet Roger Rees who was wonderfully affectionate – these RSC colleagues from the 1970s!) and a cab home where a humble bowl of granola made things better. Of course after some sleep and some breakfast he's fine and now very happy about the whole thing. And he's cancelled the doctor.

Unusually for New York, where the sun so often, even when it's very cold, seems to be shining in a brilliant blue sky, it's a grey day, but at last the temperature seems to have risen above viciously freezing and yesterday it poured with rain. Probably by tomorrow spring will be in the air, which will seem fitting. I've seen a few crocuses and snowdrops – so very much later than in the UK but then only a week ago there was snow. The cold was exhilarating at first but enough's enough.

Though the critics were there last week, this is when they publish. So an email from Lesley Duff, Michael's agent, saying "Good review in the NY Times" made it possible to look up the notices rather than pretending they weren't there, just a glance away. And yes, *The New York Times*, which is the one you need, is very good; there are other good ones and one stinker, but apparently that paper (a Murdoch one) is always bad. And now I look at it, it's not that bad.

A recuperative day writing emails and not much else, and now very happy, not least because I hope Michael can start to enjoy a bit of life here too. And it's lovely that so many friends have been passing through or have found excuses to be in New York – or even come without excuses – to see him. This weekend we're having an early supper with two old friends of his: the writer and director Guy Slater and Carey Harrison the writer. They're coming to the Sunday afternoon show.

I'm so relieved.'

## MICHAEL

I'm afraid it's true about the opening. I felt sick as a dog, and you wouldn't want a belching dog at a gala reception.

Perhaps the arrival of Carey Harrison's email after we met up that weekend completed the cure: it made me feel like a dolphin gently turning in warm water, with that daft newborn look they have, even when, as they're able to, they've not slept for two weeks. Carey speaks of feeling serene today in the face of perfection, of the blessed state an audience gets into where anything the actor can do seems exactly right. He's extremely kind about certain matters of rhythm, pitch and variation and speaks of the Lear of our generation being his friend. That's all I'll quote, but what really makes me gasp is the extent to which this is not the grand old man of Woodstock, the lecturer at Brooklyn University, Professor of English at the City University of New York who once shared an office with Allen Ginsberg (and even came to look like him), but palpably the Carey of half a century ago who used to explode into my room at Cambridge like a rearing stag, hooting with the laughter of discovery and with only one thought in his mind, that we should immediately set up a production of Pinter's *Birthday Party* or Brecht's *Galileo*; or with some outlandishly funny story of female rejection he'd just experienced, or maybe a new Beatles album that needed instant playing (though usually I had that before he did).

But then this, to forestall the sin of pride, from *Time Out:*

"An unfussy *Lear* contains good performances, but is slow to boil. The Arbus-Pennington isn't the best I've seen, but it's very, very far from the worst. However, the pivotal scene where he rages against the elements is marred by odd choices. From that point on, his performance grows increasingly less compelling."

In this way I achieve a kind of balance.

Guy Slater is here to put on a remarkable piece of work he commissioned and directed in London, *Don't Wake Me: The Ballad of Nihal Armstrong* by Rahila Gupta. Superbly performed by Jaye Griffiths, it's the true story of the author's fight for her intelligent, disabled son Nihal to be valued by society. It opens next week at the 59 East 59 Theatre, and I'd be astonished if it wasn't a triumph for all three of them. To give himself over to a little tragedy of the imaginary kind for a change, Guy came to *Lear* with Carey, and was as ever shrewd, appreciative and loyal; he does me the courtesy of coming to see virtually everything I do and is always enlightening about it, usually over a bottle of retsina within a few days. Rita and Jonathan

Lynn (whom I've known since before his glory days – *Yes Minister* (three BAFTAs), *Nuns on the Run, Cousin Vinny* and *Sergeant Bilko* – in fact we played Vladimir and Estragon at the Edinburgh Festival of 1963) have with enormous generosity given us open house throughout our time here, and have come with Greg Mosher, a long-time associate of David Mamet's and former director of the Lincoln Centre. I can see Johnny isn't entirely happy, though he found me OK, and is anxious lest his response disappoints me. This is much harder work for him to hide than for me to hear: you feel terrible when you know you're being unconvincing after a friend's show. Johnny, it's fine.

Then John Shrapnel (Lucky in that early *Waiting for Godot*) arrives, with all kinds of pretexts for visiting New York (relatives to call on, etc) so that I don't have to feel entirely responsible for his remarkable effort in coming. In fact, he's also here on a reconnaissance for an apartment for himself when he comes back later in the year to do Ken Branagh's *Macbeth* at the Park Avenue Armory – another strong alibi for his visit had he detested our show. The plain truth is he will stay for seventy-two hours and when not at *King Lear* spends most of the time talking and eating with Prue and me. We take him to the launch of a new biography of Edwin Booth by Nora Titone called *My Thoughts Be Bloody* at Avi Sharon's favourite Century Club (you could be at the Athenaeum in London). On the way home John and I talk so vigorously about *Lear* – Booth's and mine – that we miss one of the public art miracles of the subway, Bill Brand's *Masstransiscope* on the Q line from Manhattan near DeKalb Station. It's a brilliant parody of the principle of the moving image: a series of panels that you watch from the train window as you speed past and so experience the effect of a movie, except that you're doing the moving and the frames are still. Brand says the idea was easy to sell simply because nobody took it seriously, but it caused him some discomfort – to renovate it, as he had to do himself, he had to descend into the tunnel via an abandoned station. Despite its familiarity, New York commuters don't look at the *Masstransiscope* with the normal stunned subway eye but take real pleasure in it. (I tried to concentrate on it another day, but the train slowed down at the crucial moment, turning it all back into still panels.)

Shakespeare's imminent birthday also brings out of my past Robert Cushman, formerly theatre critic of *The Observer*, whose reviews at university helped me to my first job. He is now domiciled in Canada as a freelance theatre writer, and he's preparing an article called the *Year of the Lear* (not to be confused with James Shapiro's book *The Year of Lear*, also approaching the presses). I meet him for coffee but we spend most of the time gossiping rather than advancing his piece, so we have to follow up with this brief correspondence:

Dear Michael

When you came back from the hunt in the Goneril scene, you made me think of a vigorous English country squire, physically not ready for retirement whatever he may have told himself and other people. In "Reason Not the Need" – or rather, before that speech actually happened – you seemed grimly aware of the absurdity of measuring the daughters' love by the number of retainers they permitted – even, in a masochistic way, relishing the absurdity of it. Isn't this a crazy mirror image of "which of us shall we say doth love us most", except that the scales are off his eyes this time?

It seemed to me that you played not exactly a kinder, gentler Lear but a more humorous – and, in that sense, a more intelligent if not a wiser one – than you described in your book, *Sweet William*. In the production, I loved, a little later, the lightning flash and the thunder stopping just before "my wits begin to turn". I did wish the staging of the mock-trial scene had been less huddled in a corner and I didn't quite understand the Fool's suicide later on – why would he do it?

Going back to Lear's humour, I liked the playfulness of the Dover scene leading up to "I know thee well enough, thy name is Gloucester." This sudden moment of lucidity has always seemed to me one of the play's great shocks – a really sublime moment, shattering the conventional stage idea of madness.

Oh, and by the way, this production was the first I've seen to make anything of the play's opening line: of course Lear would have preferred the Duke of Albany to Cornwall! I totally agree with you about the importance of Albany. Like you, I remember the excitement of the terrible behaviour of the knights in the Brook production – the overturning of the table is still a memory that thrills. I've come to wonder though whether the text really justifies it. After all, Lear's word is probably as trustworthy as Goneril's; at the very least, she's *looking* for grievances. When we do get to hear the occasional word from a Knight or Gentleman, they sound rather civilised. Isn't what impresses Lear about the disguised Kent that he's capable of behaving as obstreperously as Goneril has complained his fellows have done – that he is, in fact, the first one with the balls to do it?

Lear having no soliloquies points to him, as an absolute monarch, never having had to develop any talent for introspection – and when he does he goes mad instead. An even more extreme example is Timon of Athens, who in the first half of the play never talks to himself, and in the second does virtually nothing but. I should think this must be one of the major problems of acting and directing that play – the complete change of tone and register. But you tell me!

Once again, it was wonderful to see you in New York.

Best wishes

Robert


Dear Robert

I'm struck by what a big baby Lear is, utterly spoiled and unaware of it. If I've anything original to offer to the ongoing story of Lear it's that he's such a child, such a dangerous child. This seems to me a useful line to the audience as we all know what big babies are like. It also gives the opportunity for him to be momentarily enjoying himself at the beginning of the hunting scene before everything goes wrong – in terms of the overall performance, that's money in the bank. On the other hand, as things get worse and worse for him, apart from some rather dramatised self-pity, I find his stamina impressive. He invariably takes the tough line.

I also made the unsurprising discovery that nothing proceeds in a straight line. Lear is of course never quite one thing: the "madness" comes and goes. Throughout the play he seems to shuttle between piercing good sense, riffs of madness, and a sort of overt mental torment. Though he didn't know what we know about brain chemistry, WS obviously had a sense of the truth of this. So the wonderful 'Poor Naked Wretches' outside the hovel comes right after him believing 'that way madness lies'. I'm glad about the sense of humour you noted – it's more a wry perceptiveness that he sometimes hides behind his bluster; some sense of irony that suggests why he may once have been popular, intelligent and good company. I also found Lear much more mercurial than I expected. I don't think the famous reconciliation with Cordelia is really the emotional heart of Act Five – Lear finishes the scene still afraid and unsure – the real beauty of the reunion is in 'We two alone will sing like birds i' the cage' when he takes care of his daughter as he should for the first time, and even tries to entertain her.

I too wonder what we'd think now of Peter Brook's knights: what they're really like is an open question. You should perhaps feel that both Goneril and Lear misrepresent them: they're neither the louts that she describes nor the 'men of choice and rarest parts' that he does.

As for Timon, it depends what you call a soliloquy. Timon's solos in the second half are mostly invocations to Nature or against the city rather than confidences to the audience, just as Lear commands the winds to blow and crack their cheeks. I didn't find the contrast between the two halves of Timon much of a problem, though the interviews in Act Two are of an uneven quality. I think the change is all part of the play's (to me) charm and interest. You play each moment for what it's worth, and hope the assembled images add up to some kind of whole. Same with Lear – there are eleven Lear scenes and the best you can do is to show them distinctly, particularly in the second half.

All the best

Michael

After the ten previews, we played forty-two performances. Seven shows a week could be thought a small mercy compared to the English eight, but it did involve four performances in just under forty-eight hours between dusk on Friday and cocktail hour on Sunday, there being matinees on Saturday and Sunday. Hallelujah Sunday evening, of course: dinner, conversation, home, visiting, though that was sometimes better done on Monday with a good night's sleep behind.

In the working week I rested for England, going warily about in the mornings on one small mission or another, but leaving the afternoon well out of it. Thus photographs exist of King Lear watching *Thomas the Tank Engine* on PBS Kids at teatime without a kid in sight. In this and in other ways, I just gave in to a great and pleasurable slide, amazed that I found the part much less tiring than I'd expected or been told it would be.

Far more tiring than Lear was Orange. Having removed my cap a couple of weeks before, on April 2nd they block my UK phone as the bills are getting so high. A kindly gesture you might say, suggesting a dim awareness that to take over £1,000 off a customer when his phone may have been sitting in a drawer for two months is not the best public relations. Now that I've inadvertently exceeded caps both voluntary and compulsory, bundles and all (and still don't understand the diabolical Data Roaming – which, as you'll have realised, is what this turned out to be all about) the phone will do nothing at all.

But before they disappear, soon to be absorbed by EE (the future wasn't so bright with Orange after all) I thought I'd have a word with them. After all, they don't know the circumstances and will be sure to understand and make a gesture. So I go online, and am referred to a website memorably called

explore.ee.co.uk/forms/we-are-listening

Well, they are, in the sense that I'm advised to leave my contact details on the site and to describe the nature of my problem so that they can then get back to me within three days. After five, they do, with a response that offers an interesting approach to cause and effect, the kind of false antithesis that a Shakespearian actor knows well, since Will sometimes (being a master of genuine antithesis) uses it for comic effect. They say that as they are improving this service they are unable to deal with my request.

To distract them from their quest for perfection, I call Orange from the theatre's Production Office phone, my only practicable choice. After a lot of Herb Alpert, I get through to Stephanie in Accounts and explain that I only use my mobile over here for occasional emails and texts and have never browsed the internet with it. So given the proximity to my double bank heist, might this huge bill be a fraud of some kind? She enthusiastically agrees and will at once make out a report and pass it on to the Fraud Department. As it is not possible for a customer to contact Fraud directly (I will increasingly wonder if this Department actually exists) I'll hear from them shortly, she says.

I never did. A gesture to be sure, but not quite the one I'd hoped for. My rather one-sided correspondence with Orange, a phone company, would remain entirely written, not spoken, just as that with the banks, where the written word is so often thought binding, was generally done over the phone. The only impression I made that day was in the TFANA Production Office, who said they had found King Lear as scary on the phone as on the stage.

Later in the run, its rituals having become more or less a habit, I give up Thomas the Tank Engine and boldly lunch with friends. Meantime Prue chalks up twenty exhibitions, eight films, twenty–five shows (only two with me) of which five were our performances, two concerts, two evenings of opera, two dance evenings and two lectures. As often as not, *King Lear* being longer than most plays, she would then meet me after the show at the Polonsky to catch a cab home together – was ever a Mr Lear so well equipped with a Mrs Lear?

Life continued as if I had been transplanted: perfectly satisfactory, not unlike home, just on a different site. In that sense lunching was a way of imposing a normal routine, but remembering to look to the left before stepping off the kerb. When my son came over for a visit with his two children, I made a deal with TFANA and we moved for a long weekend into ridiculous splendour in Union Square, where my grandson Louis (not quite seventeen) told me he was reading Kierkegaard and that he was going to live for ever. They came to the show and ten minutes after curtain down were across the road at the Barclay Centre to see the Brooklyn Jets continue their habit of beating Orlando Magic, this time by 97-88.

The director Ron Daniels cuts rather an ascetic figure at breakfast in Dizzy's Diner on Brooklyn's 9th Street, especially as there is some quite noisome garbage on the front step. Thirty years ago he used to assure my son, who wanted to be an actor at that time, that it was perfectly OK in the theatre to acknowledge that he was the son of one who was reasonably known – he'd advised his own boy in the same way. There was always a little of the monk about him, though at the RSC in the 1970s he unkindly earned the soubriquet (in defiance of good spelling) of The Man Who Put The Ron Into Paranoia. He helped me enormously, allowing me to play certain parts he and his colleagues couldn't really see me in, on the proviso that if I failed, my game would be up in all their eyes. He also told me I knew too little about the necessary skill of uniting a company when you happen to be playing the leading part. Having directed, among many other things, Roger Rees's RSC Hamlet, Ron moved to the US and turned his hand both to the new and classic repertoire as easily as he had done at the RSC, both as a freelance and for some time as the Associate Artistic Director of the American Repertory Theatre based in Cambridge, Massachusetts. He directed a movie too, which premiered at the HBO Latino Film Festival in New York.

Time has done a certain amount to Ron, though not physically. He has always had an exceptionally wide range as a director, while in himself and in those days he struck me as more tentative and self-effacing than he is now. He became part of the diaspora of directors that followed Adrian Noble's succession from Terry Hands at the RSC, together with Barry Kyle and to an extent Bill Alexander – associates who found themselves out of a job and heading for the US. As well as dramas and a possible second movie, he has more opera work booked around the country now than he can count, in Boston, Houston, San Francisco, Colorado, Florida and Washington. So he flourishes here, but feels very cut off from his children in the UK. We part affectionately, but without embracing – there being people you just don't. By the same token, though I know he's come out, I rather untypically evade that conversation too. We part friends but still strangers. On the way home I'm startled to remember that he shares the exact same name with the friend who found Tim Hardin dead on the floor of his apartment in 1980.

Restaurants are where much provisional theatre business gets done: it surges and quite often dies, like Cressida's love, 'on the birth of its own labouring breath.' Having come back from Ron armed with his desire to do *The Tempest* with me in Washington DC, I go a few days later to Rucola's Italian in Boerum Hill to meet up with Arin Arbus. We discuss doing *Long Day's Journey Into Night* at TFANA next year, if she and Jeffrey can get the rights, which are clutched to the bosom of the producer Scott Rudin. From a commercial producer's point of view, this is a play in which you first capture your female star to play Mary: it could be called Waiting For Meryl. As for James Tyrone, the actor manager, I very much like the chutzpah of bringing an English actor to play O'Neill in New York, but taken aback – until she insists on the logic: the Tyrones (like Arin's own maternal grandparents) were Irish Americans, so I have as much right, just about, as any other to play one of them. I feel rather more enthused about this than about Prospero. Also, Arin is an extremely discreet and private person, so I'm delighted and complimented when she breaks confidence and discusses the strengths, vulnerabilities and personalities of each actor in our cast – especially as she has known and worked with many of them for a long time. We agree about every one. This is all very pleasant, this juggling with ideas that may never happen, seasoned with a high level of gossip, all as a slight release from the efforts of putting on a big new production. I get the sense that – a rarity – Arin is taking life a little easier, though as she's one of the year's judges of the Tony Awards, she still has to be in a theatre most nights.

We agree that after seven weeks' rehearsal and two months of playing, *King Lear*'s first scene is the one we would most like to review – will definitely fix if we do the play again, as we hope to. Trouble is, we don't know, even across a table, how to do the fixing. Perhaps I should have had a throne after all.

Sure enough, the Washington *Tempest* hasn't transpired and we couldn't get the rights for the O'Neill away from Rudin: now (spring 2016) it's opening with Jessica Lange and Gabriel Byrne on Broadway.

## Wednesday, 16<sup>th</sup> April

Three weeks from home and to keep me on my toes, the bank hackers strike again, implying another connection between Santander and Lloyds. A new Santander account has been opened, and the remaining balance of my Lloyds account switched to it, leaving it empty.

I get on to Lloyds, asking how this was possible when they'd assured me the account was frozen. No-one seems to know. All the bank feel able to do for me now is remove my own access to the account – which I didn't have anyway. It's as if they were thoughtfully protecting me from staring at the glaring £0.00. So both accounts are frozen, and there's nothing in the Lloyds one anyway. The weather continues fine.

Next day two hundred and seven emails arrive in my inbox, and in those of many other Virgin customers. Virgin are calling this royal cock-up a "distribution list error": anyone clicking Reply to their recent customer emails found themselves messaging everyone on Virgin's mailing list. The Information Commissioner's Office, an independent body that enforces the Data Protection Act, is cautious, saying that it is looking into an "alleged breach" of the rules before deciding if action is necessary; Virgin Media say it is "investigating exactly what has happened". They don't say Sorry, but like the horse racing away from the stable door, they gravely warn that anyone pressing "Reply" and entering the email chain was exposing their own details to thousands of others. Yes, we noticed.

To transcribe many more letters to and from Orange and the banks would drive a long nail into the coffin of this book. You may have similar stories, in which case you'll be familiar with the music: a consistency of tone bordering on the indifferent, though the gas beneath it goes up and down depending on your own mood. In the correspondence, I know that I relapsed into a style inherited from my lawyer father, which I made more lurid by adding showbusiness threats of exposure in the media – a course my father would have disapproved of, but which was endorsed by that other showman Jonathan Lynn, who said it always worked for him, which I suppose means he's more famous than me. I think Orange are trained to deal with that too, putting their hands over the receiver and grimacing at their colleagues about yet another vainglorious customer's threat of media exposure.

At one point I sketched out a one-act play in which a character called FFOM (Foolish Fond Old Man) strides about his bedroom while a succession of men called Parkinson or Morrison (not unlike Briggs and Foster in *No Man's Land*), come in and out, repeating mantras. Each begins by expressing gratitude that (as frustrated seekers after truth) I have given them the opportunity to deal with my complaint. As they leave they repeat their thanks and state as a simple fact that Orange is the biggest and best mobile phone provider in the UK. (This play is of the fashionable verbatim type, like *London Road* or *Stuff Happens*: these unvarying announcements came word for word from the beginning and end of each email to me, giving it a whiff of the *pro forma*.) Meanwhile the FFOM rants about Kafka and there are Pinteresque pauses of several days. The phenomenon of the Chief Executive's Swerve (the natty way a CEO passes all complaints at great speed down the chain of command) is also touched on, as is the probable nonexistence of Fraud Departments. I thought of calling the play *Ban Ki-Moonshine*; thus far is has not been performed. Too much like real life, I suppose.

One Sunday Patrick Stewart comes to *Lear*. We've been playing telephone tag for some time. I very much want to see him: he's approaching the end of his run, he plans to travel, and as ever he has work upon work beyond. As the show is a matinee I have the pleasure of looking forward not only to the end of the working week but also to the paradisal free evening beyond it – a bottle of wine, a meal, Patrick's company. I see him in the foyer and his face is very complicated: I can read approval, reservation, affection, criticism, a Where-Shall-I–Start preparedness for the evening ahead – all of it just as he would have done on mine. Prue and I go with him and his young wife Sunny Ozell to Marco's on Flatbush Avenue, a very original quality restaurant, run by a young family that at the time had three places on the same Avenue. This is where Patrick and Sunny met: Sunny, a brilliant jazz singer, was waiting at table. Now she's recording her second album and appearing at The Marquee Club. The obligatory exposed brick interior, lemon soap in the bathroom, crème fraîche gelato, wood-grilled oysters, 'slightly complex' tagliatelle, chicken liver bruschetta, charred duck hearts and gizzards skewered and drizzled with a mostarda made from Concord grapes. And so on. In the end Marco's aim can't have been quite true – it's now been converted into a burger joint, albeit an upmarket one.

Patrick and I were only ever in two plays together at the RSC: *Hippolytus* with Natasha Parry (directed by Ron Daniels) and then Bulgakov's *White Guard* at the Aldwych with a novice actress straight out of RADA called Juliet Stevenson. We also played in Trevor Nunn's first Shakespeare workshop which in turn led to John Barton's series *Playing Shakespeare* in which we all pretended to act badly so that John should show us how to do it better. However, like Roger Rees and Ian McKellen and Ron Daniels, we are marked by the badge of Nunn, 1970s vintage, seemingly held together for life not only by the acknowledged goldenness of the age – the Donmar, the Aldwych – but some bond that leads us to fall on each other's necks wherever in the world we are – like veterans, like reunited family. I know this is mockable talk, but it absolutely is the case. When I was asked later to do one of those How We Met kinds of piece for *The Observer* to publicise a book of mine, I turned straight to Patrick, but as we discussed it we realised that all our memories of Stratford – to do with observing illicit midnight migrations along the Waterside cottages – were completely unprintable in a family newspaper. I did the interview with Judi Dench in the end, who could never be accused of such things, at least after she met Michael Williams. Over the next two years this was to be a generation meeting the scythe; for the time being Patrick tells me incredulously of a piece in *The Guardian* outing him as gay because some happy snapper has caught him in a typically collegiate actor's embrace with Ian McKellen.

He seems delighted with *Lear*, declaring it's a long time since he has had to wipe his eyes in a theatre. I suggest there's something I've spotted about the part that might be useful to him when he comes to do it; he says not to worry, he's already noted it and pocketed it for future use. This kind of piracy is genuine. American citizen as he now is, he misses the Cotswolds, even in the grey-green winter, and longs to walk through his own front door there.

As it turned out Pat would crop up quite a bit in the next couple of years, though always *en passant*: he is not in the least Mephistophelian but I did feel sometimes like Faust receiving a visitation. He's extremely sprightly and I notice something in him that I don't quite in Ian McKellen – that in two brilliant careers, while Ian has done all the Shakespeare he could want (he spurns Falstaff), there's an endearing hankering in Patrick for Timon and Lear, which explains why he could cheerfully pinch an idea from me in preparation. (I hanker for Romeo, the only one I've missed now Lear has joined Timon, but comfort myself with the knowledge that I can do a bit of it in my solo show and no-one will mind.) Patrick even achieved a remarkable sleight of hand by playing Othello with an all-black cast – much work for them and a once prized part for a white man becoming his again. I am sure it would be an easy matter to achieve his ambitions, so it's hardly a neurosis; but I like that he still feels there is more to do. Meantime he's been nominated for a Golden Globe for *Blunt Talk*, playing a character whose name is quaintly borrowed from a small part in *Henry IV Part One*.

In the extremely convenient front of house bar at the Polonsky which is the only real exit from backstage I meet and re-meet people I admire, including Austin Pendleton, who wants me to play in *Ivanov* with him, and Zoe Caldwell, who was Charles Laughton's Cordelia: a series of surprises that made it impossible not to be happy as these precious weeks raced by. And though I hope to live for many a moon yet, I also admit to having a feeling of completion. The press continued excellent, and refrained from comparisons which came out in subtler ways: *The New York Times* said Langella was a loud Lear but I was a quiet one. I certainly wasn't, but the peculiar debating-chamber nature of half of the stage was allowing great intimacy where you might have expected pyrotechnics. I'm sure there were dissenting voices, but I didn't hear them.

## A CONVERSATION WITH IAN MCKELLEN

*(From A Video Moderated by Jeffrey Horowitz)*

IM: Do you have a throne in the first scene?

MP: No, I got rid of the throne, it bored me. And wonder now if I was wise.

IM: You don't sit down at all?

MP: No.

IM: Poor old fellow. Poor old legs.

MP: Now I have a little desk I stand behind…

IM: I had a throne AND a little table I stood behind…

MP: Yes and the stage is metal, so my main symptom of wear and tear so far playing King Lear is I have sore feet.

IM: Oh, poor old feet… I had a chair as well as the throne and the table.

MP: Had it every which way in fact. Good.

IM: Yes.

MP: What did you do with the daughters, when they have to speak, and they need a good position?

IM: They came up and joined me.

MP: Thus pleasing everybody.

IM: Yes that's right.

MP: Well, it is a public scene.

IM: Is it domestic or is it public? Well, I made it a bit of both.

MP: Yes, I talk to the customers too, as if they were the court... and the house lights stay up. And make a joke about how I can now "unburdened crawl towards death" as if waiting for them to say "no you're not old enough..." You know, Lear has done this sort of thing before, he knows how to use his audience. Or thinks he does.

Lear is sort of locked off inside the play, isn't he? No soliloquies.

IM: Well, I found a couple.

MP: Like that one-liner ... "I have ta'en too little care of this"?

IM: Yes.

MP: Does that count?

IM: Yes.

JH: *(Interrupting.)* OK. We're rolling.

To begin at the beginning: I know you worked together in 1976 as Mercutio and Romeo, then *Venice Preserv'd* at the National...

IM: Oh, my goodness me...

MP: Ian, you haven't FORGOTTEN!

IM: No no, not forgotten, just sort of put it aside...

JH: Then *The Syndicate*. So you enjoy working together.

*A pause.*

MP: Well, it's as if we sort of check in on each other every few years.

JH: How do you mean, check in?

MP: Well, checking up. Anyway, coinciding with each other...

IM: Yes.

MP: Yes. With pleasure.

IM: Yes, coinciding with pleasure.

*A pause.*

JH: And you've played the same parts: you've both done Hamlet, Macbeth, Leontes, Timon...

IM: Not Timon, me. You're welcome to him.

JH: And Coriolanus, Richard II, Richard III…

MP: Not Richard III, me. Thank God.

IM: Well. Our experience does overlap, after all… For instance, we learned certain ideas about how to speak Shakespeare at Cambridge…. Do you know that the Bloomsbury Group and Virginia Woolf got very exercised by the poor speaking of verse on the professional stage in the UK, and they contacted Dadie Rylands – he was a very un-donnish Cambridge don, Jeffrey, who was close to Edith Evans and John Gielgud and Michael Redgrave too, and with Rupert Brooke he formed the Marlowe Society in 1907, dedicated to the right treatment of Shakespeare's text. Many directors – John Barton, Peter Hall, Trevor Nunn, actors like us – were influenced by him.

JH: What was there, before Dadie's Revolution…

IM: Henry Irving, Edwin Booth, the plays as star vehicles… the *raison d'être* was to see Irving, or Edwin Booth in the US… lots of scenery, not much production in the interpretative sense… and always in very large theatres for economic reasons. The actors had to deliver in a style congenial to the back row, not the front. I think Shakespeare is still too often done in large spaces. But blank verse is often conversation.

MP: Then there's been our enthusiasm for running companies, as Ian did the Actors' Company in the 1970s, which was run democratically, they hired the directors and cast themsleves, they were all paid the same…

IM: And your English Shakespeare Company was unmatched, and said something about you, in the rigorous approach to making an ensemble: you set an example the National Theatre could well follow…

MP: Yes, but it gets tough doesn't it… touring … Arts Council meetings… managing it all… you know: an emergency budget meeting at 7pm then playing Henry V at 7.30.

IM: Well with Michael it's not just a matter of him at the centre, but the whole enterprise guarantees a level of performance, it's a long way from Henry Irving.

JH: What do you say when people say *Lear* is an unbearable experience to watch – I mean the play not the performances? Do you find audiences are depressed or tired at the end?

MP: No, they seem rather exhilarated. It's like the blues, the bigger the blues the better they'll keep, the deeper you go into Lear the better you feel.

IM: The play has the reputation of being an impossible thing. But it reflects the time it was written in. It's full of cruelties, but there's probably not much in the play a Jacobean audience wouldn't recognise from Tyburn or every street corner in London.

And in a way I think Lear's death is a relief in the play, not because we have a train to catch but because he's so clearly, painfully, had enough by then. But there are survivors. There's not much in the play about the condition of England, as there might be in a History play, but it's there, a hint of a possible new order…

And maybe it's a happy end for someone who's always depended on the gods for his authority; he ends up an atheist!

MP: Yes, and sane… his precious gods have let him down; he appealed to them in the storm: "You put me here, and now you pour buckets of water on me…"

IM: In the old days he wouldn't have noticed the rain.

And when is he craziest? At the outset.

MP: You bet! Lear likes to think of himself as the "barbarous Scythian" who cooks and eats his own children! Or as wrathful as some mythical dragon, a being that never existed.

IM: Yes, I think there is some hope at the end. Those young people have lived through the reign, now it might be the will of more than one man that decides things. Edgar and Albany are better equipped for the new world than Gloucester and Kent. I find it not so tragic. After all, he's sane now: believing he was God's man on earth was the insanity!

MP: What I do wonder about in the play is his generation's loyalty to Lear – why? Because he wasn't a bad King for them. But he's a certain kind of man who's never bothered to understand women, no sexuality, a wife who, however badly the rest of the family's malfunctioning, is hardly mentioned now she's dead. One thinks of a patriarch or even the old-fashioned CEO of some corporation. His sexual disgust is something to do with the daughters, but I don't think he's a misogynist in general, just indifferent to women.

IM: He doesn't like their power. And a world in which women need sex as much as men doesn't fit into Lear's view of things!

When I played Kent to Brian Cox's Lear we went to Prague and met Václav Havel. He said that just as he became President he'd been writing a play about Lear (not many future Presidents break off from doing that!). Now he saw that international relationships, fortunes of nations depend on the personal relationships of their leaders.

MP: Shakespeare was very interested in power vacuums. What happens when there's a vacancy? All sorts of extreme behaviour.

JH: Do you think Lear and Cordelia find love at the end?

*[They hesitate.]*

MP: Filial love, yes, but it's so brief, only the briefest moment of reconciliation, two or three lines of tenderness and relief, and then her neck is snapped. A little window has opened and then closed fast.

IM: Then he's howling for her, the second kind of howling in the play: the first scene and last. Lear no longer demands power or possession. By then he's the thing itself, he's been through the worst. Imagine a Pope in all his ridiculous clothes, kneeling and kissing a smelly foot. Lear's done that.

MP: Retirement wasn't a bad idea, even if his behaviour to his daughters was. He retired before he's forcibly retired: he's not so competent any more, there are other big dynasties in the kingdom. It shows a certain self-knowledge. Now he can hunt the boar or do his gardening, and think afresh about certain things. But his method is disastrous. Everybody knows what he's already decided, and now the girls have to sing for their supper. It's as if he puts his kids on a table top like some stupid entertainment, it's a beastly thing to do, when everyone else is in the know.

JH: And he has huge rage at Cordelia because he thought she would stay and look after him in his old age?

IM: Maybe in a Nurse's uniform bringing little potions...

ALL THREE: "I thought to set my rest On her kind nursery".

IM: Oh, but she wasn't consulted about that, and she's getting married. All fathers think it's the end then. When I see tears in the eyes of fathers at weddings it makes me think of Lear. He knows he's going to lose. He's jealous.

MP: He doesn't like France or Burgundy much, but he has to find a husband for her. It seems cruel that Cordelia says: why have my sisters husbands, if they say they love you all? But he's designed the future without consulting anyone. But why didn't he expect Cordelia to behave as she does – he knows her, after all.

IM: But you know, I don't think Shakespeare was interested in character in that way, though as modern actors we have to be. But this play has a certain whiff about it, it's a Once Upon a Time Play: Once Upon a Time There Was an Old King, who decided to retire...

MP: Yes, and lots of the play is a big dark bedtime story... but being Shakespeare it also reaches into us in terms of our own family, in fact I suspect that's its first hook into a modern audience, this exemplary tale about inheritance tax planning...

JH: Ian, when you played Lear, did you think about Samuel Beckett – you're in *Waiting for Godot* just now?

IM: It's the other way round really – when you do Beckett you might think, oh yes, I see, he got all this from Shakespeare.

MP: I never think of other writers while doing Shakespeare, because there's this one big difference – no pauses; not like Beckett, Pinter, Chekhov, in Shakespeare you're dead if you're not speaking. Everyone steps up to the mark and is ready, Shakespeare's audience wasn't interested in watching people ruminating, thinking, deciding what and what not to say. Yet it's overwhelmingly human.

IM: And specially in a theatre like this, where the smallest shift of thought is picked up. And any good play is about the lives of the audience, or otherwise what's the point? Shakespeare uniquely asks for a commitment from the actor of his own experience, standards, beliefs, morality, not many plays ask you for that – you find out about yourself, it's very rewarding but also very tiring. Great plays go on by being sustained by the commitment of the performers to believing in the story and wanting to tell it.

JH: And playing these other great parts, how have they affected your Lears?

*A long silence.*

MP: It's your practical experience that helps. Ralph Richardson once said playing Lear was like lying on your back with a machine gun aiming at eleven targets on the ceiling. And there's a real slew of them at the moment.

IM: A larynx of Lears…

MP: Anyway: Coriolanus is a brute, a rockface like Lear. There are certain parts—some nights you look at them and you can't think where you're supposed to grapple on at all. Of course, then you start and you find a way of doing it, but it's not an easy entry, ever.

IM: Except Richard II – you can't really fail; it's very, very simple. All laid out for you, if you're reasonably pretty, and you get a move on with it.

MP: I don't think I found it as easy as that. I think I seriously tried to make it a play about revolution…

IM: Ah well, there you go…

MP: Whereas in fact it's a big, showoff lyric tragedy. But to answer your question, Jeff, sort of [Looks at McKellen]: this guy has, in the most genial way, set the bar so high all my working life— that's my big speech, and I won't make another one—and it matters a great deal when he comes to see *Lear*.

IM [gently touches MP's arm] Aw…

MP: I went to *No Man's Land* and came home thinking, I must attend to that. Not that Spooner's like Lear, but there are certain aspects of being an actor…

IM: That always happens if you are enjoying a show, doesn't it? If you see someone really inhabiting a part, and you don't want to work out how it's done, you just think, Well, *I* can't do that. And then the actor who has been doing it comes and says the same thing about you. So lovely! Lovely.

MP: With Lear as much as anything it's a big physical and practical call you're preparing for, and also one of planning: you risk repetitive vocal patterns, and it's difficult to avoid a kind of continuously complaining, noisy, self-pitying mode. So you use all your wits, I mean the wits you've gained from experience, to find a different way through. I was once complimented in another play, it was very nice to hear, that I was completely different in every scene but always the same person. Maybe like Ian and me sitting here for the last hour, different bits show at different times.

IM: I also think the saving grace of Lear is his sense of humour. His closest professional associate is a Clown, that's who he chooses to spend most time with, and he accepts his gibes with very good grace. It's a redeeming feature. You wouldn't joke with Stalin.

MP: And madness makes him a vaudevillian, he criticises the naked Poor Tom about his "Persian attire", he wanders round Dover covered in flowers, then he sees Gloucester blind and streaming with blood and declares it's Goneril with a white beard. Then Gloucester and he do a double act, a sort of wisecracking Flanagan and Allen routine. The audience loves it.

IM: And needs it.

MP: And then a great joke about politicians' glass eyes, how they seem to see things they do not. That's great for the audience in any country. Lear is funny, autocratic, even wise sometimes, tender on occasion.

IM: I think there are three things for me. First of all, you're usually talking about the nature of kingship. So you must believe you're the most important person on the planet. Which is quite a hard idea!

And then, after Richard II or Romeo it's helpful to reach Shakespeare's mature plays and find him playing with language, jazzing it around, complicated and thrilling. But you have to see it coming, treat it in a new way.

Thirdly, *Lear's* the leading part but not the only one. And Hamlet doesn't have to be full-out all the time, there are lots of others, the play is about Denmark, after all, about everybody Hamlet knows or thinks about and meets. *Lear* must have thirteen terrific actors, then your responsibility is reduced, sometimes you can let the others get on with it and have a rest. Even when you're on the stage and you do speak you can rely on it as it's Shakespeare. You don't have to work flat out. Such a play is collective, even this one.

MP: Yes, and I hear, Ian, you fell asleep before playing the Dover Scene one night? All wrapped up on the sofa in your dressing room.

IM: The play just stopped. They said, 'There has been a technical hitch.' I was just by the stage by then, and the person who said that said, 'Oh, no, here he is.' Enter technical hitch.

MP: They thought you were just a bundle of rags in the dressing room...

IM: No more of that, my lord, no more of that...

*All laugh. End board.*

❖

Prue emails to her niece Tish:

"It's been a fantastic time. The first week I was the standard tourist. I walked across Brooklyn Bridge and visited the Ground Zero site: since my last visit in 2010 the waterfall pools on the site of each of the towers have been put in place with the names of the dead etched around them, together as near as possible to the place where they had been that awful morning. You couldn't but be moved in spite of the towering skyscrapers that were already encroaching onto the area like a jungle creeper that can't be restrained. And there had to be a trip to MOMA, its atrium filled by an Isaac Julien installation and a special exhibition of Gauguin prints which exhilarated me, as his work always does.

But after that I got a grip. I was going to use the time to explore parts of the city I didn't know and would start with Brooklyn. The exhibition space of the mighty Brooklyn Museum was given over to a Jean Paul Gaultier riot of fashion and its permanent collection included Judy Chicago's ultimate feminist artwork *The Dinner Party*, interesting to see as I'd studied it as part of an Open University course. The Museum was on the edge of Prospect Park which over the weeks offered good walking – including sight of the Quaker Cemetery, a 12 acre patch which you can only enter, alive or dead, if you are a Quaker. There are apparently more Quakers in Brooklyn than any other part of the State – approximately six get buried there each year, the graves marked by little oblong stones hardly bigger than a shoebox. Perhaps the most famous contemporary resident is the actor Montgomery Clift who was buried there at his Quaker mother's request.

It was during a snowy tramp on one of our first weekends that we discovered the Cemetery, alerted by the excellent *Secret New York*. Area by area the book uncovered unusual places – a tiny museum, a doorway, the entry to a subway evacuation tunnel disguised in a brownstone terrace – and was an irreplaceable guide.

For wider exploration, all I had to do was to set off from Brooklyn on the C train to Manhattan and get walking. For instance, an early trip to the Upper East Side started with some miniature dwellings nestling on a second-storey window ledge at 942 Madison Avenue, the work of artist Charles Simonds who says he creates them for the Little People who are migrating through the city. A few steps away you find in the Bemelmans Bar at the Carlyle Hotel an extraordinary mural depicting dressed-up animals such as a rabbit in a smart red tie smoking a cigar – these were the 1947 work of Ludwig Bemelmans, who used his animals to represent four seasons in Central Park and lived with his family rent-free in the hotel for eighteen months while he was painting them. A little further up, a huge sculptured head that once adorned the demolished Ziegfeld Theatre lies near the trash cans in a basement in East 80th Street. Straight on into Central Park and just behind the Met Museum stands the Equestrian Statue of King Jagiello, victor over the Germans at the Battle of Grunwald in 1410. This was a centrepiece of the Polish pavilion at New York's World Fair in 1939: stranded when war broke out in Europe, the statue was presented to the City of New York by the Polish Government in exile. Back on 5th Avenue and up to 104th Street you come to the Museum of the City of New York, where the final sight of this particular tour is situated: the dollhouse created by Carrie Stettheimer during the first half of the 20th century. Carrie and her sisters were very much part of the New York artistic scene – the tiny works within the dollhouse are all originals, the most noticeable being a miniature version of Marcel Duchamp's *Nude Descending a Staircase*.

There was another benefit in visiting that Museum at that time as it was showing an exhibition about Hurricane Sandy which had swept over the city in 2012: among the photographs showing the destruction and turmoil was a video of people standing – or swaying – outside as the storm broke. When Michael was later wondering about how he would deal with the effect of the storm on Lear I was able to suggest that he went and looked – which I'm pleased to say he did.

The Events listings of *The New York Times* were also good for theatre. I quickly discovered that the crowds queuing at the half-price ticket booth in Times Square could be avoided by going to the side window that dealt in Plays where only about three or four other people were to be found (Musicals took the money). There always seemed to be a good deal for any Broadway or off-Broadway show and during my time in New York I saw over twenty plays. Best remembered include *All The Way* about President Lyndon Johnson's machinations to get his Civil Rights bill passed: this starred Bryan Cranston (whose *Breaking Bad* series we didn't discover until our return to the UK and who was thus unknown to me). I was particularly struck by the audience being silenced during the end applause by one of the cast stepping forward and announcing that as this was the week when Broadway raised money for AIDS research, the prosthetic ears worn by Cranston to achieve his LBJ likeness would be auctioned. When the bidding reached $1,600 it was generously agreed that the spare pair Cranston had in his dressing room would go to one of the two remaining bidders so they both left happy – a form of fundraising that has yet to reach the West End of London. (Incidentally, if we think the West End is bad, Broadway's attitude to physical accessibility shocks: in one theatre the Stalls' Ladies was down a flight of stairs and then through a tiny anteroom. It was then surprising to see a sign on the middle of the three toilet doors stating "Wheelchairs Only".)

But it was discovering New York's smaller spaces that was the most fun and which offered the most interesting fare: in the Irondale Center, a converted church hall just off Fulton Street in Brooklyn, I saw *The Box* by Marcus Gardley, a devastating portrayal of black prisoners performed in rhyming couplets – it clearly made the point that to be black in the US considerably raised your chances of being imprisoned and rammed it home by being disturbingly funny.

I have to confess to not always being a fan of Caryl Churchill's work but her *Love and Information* at the tiny Minetta Lane Theater in the West Village was terrific. Consisting of fifty-seven short scenes it covered the problems of communicating in this speeded-up world – something the set and lighting complemented by setting each of the different scenes with amazing speed. As Ben Brantley said in his *New York Times* review "It's the multiplicity of these scenes and their fragmentary nature that make *Love and Information* so exhilarating and exhausting". I also loved *Buyer and Cellar*, a wonderful monologue performed by a camp Michael Urie in which he fantasises about setting up shop in Barbra Streisand's basement.

Just in case I was feeling homesick I was able to catch up with some hit shows from London: *A Doll's House* with Hattie Morahan, playing in the excellently "distressed" theatre of BAM, just across the road from the Polonsky where Michael was settling into his run; *Red Velvet* with Adrian Lester at St Ann's Warehouse also in Brooklyn; and

Punchdrunk's *Sleep No More*, still packing them into the McKittrick Hotel after three years. To enjoy this kind of immersive theatre, wandering through stupendously dressed rooms and coming upon groups of actors performing snatches of *Macbeth*, I think you need company: I usually rejoiced in the freedom of being alone but on this occasion wanted a friend by my side to compare the experience.

Often my theatrical evenings ended back at the Polonsky, waiting in the foyer and enjoying the praise I overheard from the exiting audience. The cast members would drift down the stairs to meet friends or quietly slip out to home, and then a bundled-up, becapped figure would appear and I could see those remaining members of the audience suddenly realise that King Lear himself was amongst them.

As I'd visited the Brooklyn Museum near the beginning of my stay, so it was the scene of one of my last outings: a big Ai Weiwei exhibition which featured some of the work that was to be shown to huge interest at the Royal Academy in London some 18 months later, including *S.A.C.R.E.D,* containers depicting the 81 days of his imprisonment by the Chinese authorities (familiar to me as the setting for Howard Brenton's play *The Arrest of Ai Weiwei* which we'd seen at Hampstead Theatre about a year before), the stacked bicycles and the coloured vases. I also remember a room filled by a poignant snake made up of the tattered schoolbags rescued from the Suchuan site where an earthquake had destroyed so many lives and buildings, the latter through faulty construction. I wasn't aware that the exhibition, the first major showing of Ai's work in New York, would create the storm it did when it opened at the Royal Academy in London later, but then I was altogether more remote from the artistic buzz.

Now it's the end of April: the snow has finally disappeared (much later than usual) and about two weeks ago spring arrived literally overnight: where there had been bare twigs there was heavy blossom and the scrappy front gardens in this street were suddenly full of bulbs and flowering shrubs. The wonderful Brooklyn Botanical Garden is bursting with spring, the magnolias and cherry trees releasing their reined-in blossoms in spectacular array. I went there last weekend: I thought very much of you because there's a huge cherry walk and I wondered whether the ones in Battersea Park had come and gone as we're weeks behind here. It's the suddenness of it all that surprises – plus the vagaries of the weather because there was a weekend of sun and high temperatures and two days later it was snowing again. Yesterday we went on the Staten Island ferry in T-shirts and today I need a winter coat.

And now it's come to an end, and I'm leaving a day before Michael because he's agreed to stay on for a gala dinner and I can't change my flight. So often in life you only appreciate happiness in retrospect but I

think I've known throughout these four months that they were special
and I'm fortunate to have lived them."

# MICHAEL

I stand having a natter with F. Murray Abraham after the TFANA Gala
on the steps of the Capitale, a *beaux-arts* national landmark that used
to be the premises of the Bowery Savings Bank and is now a night club,
"event space" and restaurant (venison with chocolate oil, bison at thirty
dollars). The Bank survived the Bowery's notorious century as the wretched
skidrow of Manhattan – abject poverty, brothels and flop houses – though
its marble walls and floors, its portico of Corinthian columns and general
air of a Roman temple must have seemed a calculated insult to the vagrant
population. Despite the spokesmanship of Joe DiMaggio among others,
the Bank couldn't compete with deregulation, which forced savings interest
rates up, and has been sold on quite a lot: it now belongs to Capital One.

It's to be hoped that many dollars have potentially changed hands
here tonight at TFANA's annual fundraising bash. As these things go, it's
been an extremely civilised event. The format of being the one performer
at a round dinner table of a dozen potential donors can sometimes
be hard to get going, but on this occasion, the women on either side
of me (and generally it is the women who set the tone) were inspired
conversationalists and genuinely curious and friendly. Leonard Polonsky
and his associate Georgette Bennett have been rightly lauded from the
platform for the Foundation's generosity in getting TFANA's new theatre
open – their donation looks to me to be the equivalent size of their
normal charitable gifting for a whole year. Murray meanwhile, who apart
from playing Salieri in the movie of *Amadeus* and a dizzying number of
Shakespearian principals, has been closely associated with TFANA ever
since he played Shylock and Barabas in *The Jew of Malta* in 2007 for
them, and has rightly been given an Award for Lifetime Achievement.

So he too has been thoroughly celebrated in song and story – a classic Jeff
Horowitz speech, video footage of his work, the passionate admiration of his
colleagues – but still he has a brooding air as he waits for his cab. He confides
that he hates ageing and can't help being a little uneasy with the brilliant
young actors he sees around him. This is a familiar trope, and I rib him that
he sounds like Solness, Ibsen's Master Builder, frantically anxious about the
next generation of architects coming up (for which, read playwrights younger
than Ibsen). I recall that when I did this play I complained to the director

Philip Franks that I didn't understand Solness's envy of younger brilliance in his field. Philip remained silent, until I looked up from my reverie to see him grinning broadly at me: "Did you say you don't know what it's like at your age to feel jealous of the young in the arts?". I laughed, Murray laughs now, and I laugh yet again on the way home at how, among actors, one touch of nature makes the whole world kin.

The next day I go home. Jeff Horowitz insists we have lunch before I leave but is delayed – as he was for the critical meeting with Arin after the workshop in 2012. I can't mind, then or now – he runs a theatre. He arrives fifteen minutes before my car will be here to collect me. Quite astonishingly he contrives to take me to a restaurant and, as with our debriefing after the workshop, we eat probably the fastest course yet served in the establishment – and this is the Old Sichuan, which is not a short-order place. Jeff has loved Murray's Master Builder story and reminisces swiftly about coming to Chichester to see me in the play; he also continues a theme of so much of the last four years by making me an offer: Falstaff in *Henry IV* sometime. I try to answer but am stuffing so much in my mouth with Falstaffian speed that I can only nod enthusiastically.

I'm still thinking of Jeff as I head to the airport – particularly for some reason of his early frustration at not being able to get Michael Billington and other English writers to New York to cover the show. He was recompensed a little later in the run by a piece in *The Times Literary Supplement* by Lucy Munro – not only our only coverage in the UK but much longer than the Arts page of any broadsheet review would have allowed. In it she compared and contrasted us with Sam Mendes's production at the National Theatre with Simon Russell Beale, which opened on the day I left for New York (a pure coincidence).

> "This is, it seems, a year of Lears. In the same week that I saw Sam Mendes's revival on the epic space of the revolving Olivier stage, I also attended Arin Arbus's more intimate production for Theatre for a New Audience. Both productions centre on bravura performances from their respective Lears. Each makes similar decisions in the matter of the text, drawing heavily on the earlier, quarto, version, with its greater hostility towards Goneril and Regan and its greater sentimentality towards Cordelia. Both include the astonishing sequence in which Lear imagines putting his elder daughters on trial. But they also turn to the later, folio, version for Lear's final words, in which he appears to believe that Cordelia has returned to life. Each attempts to account, in its own way, for the Fool's disappearance towards the end of Act III.
>
> Yet the atmosphere and impact of each production differ markedly. Where Mendes's production is large-scale and raw, using visual

spectacle to shape and underpin its human interactions, Arbus's is small-scale, stark and alert to the capacity of sound to shape our emotional response.

In a classic study of *King Lear*, now nearly twenty years old, Kathleen McLuskie argues that in order to experience the proper pleasures of pity and fear associated with tragedy since Aristotle, spectators must accept that fathers are owed particular duties by their daughters and be appalled by the chaos which ensues when those primal links are broken. For all its considerable nuance, Arbus's production embodies this approach. Pennington's Lear conveys a clear sense of his role as paterfamilias, touching the stomach of Goneril (Rachel Pickup) as he bequeaths part of his kingdom "to thine and Albany's issue" and seeming almost as shocked by the violence of his response to the resistance of Cordelia (Lilly Englert) as she is. Yet the complaint of Regan (Bianca Amato) that Lear "hath ever but slenderly known himself" could apply as much to his relationship with his daughters as to his self-knowledge. In contrast, the three daughters seem to know each other all too well. Cordelia's criticism of her sisters as she leaves for France is clear and pointed, while Regan and Goneril seem eager for the chance to brutalise their father and anyone who stands in their way. Indeed, the presentation of the elder daughters is epitomised by the involvement of Regan in the viscerally staged blinding of Gloucester (Christopher McCann): she holds him down, and his blood splashes across her face; at the end of the scene she leaves the dying Cornwall (Saxon Palmer) alone on the stage, her attention already shifting away from him and towards Chandler Williams's Edmund. The heart of Arbus's production lies with the older men: Lear, Gloucester and Kent (Timothy D. Stickney). In a superb *coup de théâtre*, the battle between the French and British is presented from the point of view of Gloucester, who stands alone on the stage. Instead of the usual bandage across his eyes, ingenious make-up imitates the empty, brutalised sockets, and instead of seeing soldiers, we hear the noise of combat. In the final scene, Pennington enters through the audience with Cordelia, his howls of protest resounding terribly in the small auditorium.

Where Arbus encourages us to pity Lear and Gloucester, Mendes refuses to let us identify with either man or to excuse their children's violence. If Arbus's staging shocks in its fine details, Mendes's seems more calculated to inspire outrage. It does so through a striking reinterpretation of the title role by Russell Beale. Lear begins the play as a military leader, and Anthony Ward's design points up the connection with authoritarian rule and dictatorship by presenting us in Act II with a monumental statue of Lear in heroic pose. Lear's knights – numbering at least thirty – are a brooding presence throughout the early scenes. Meanwhile, the programme presents pictures of a range of twentieth-century dictators: Tito, Gaddafi, Ceaușescu, Stalin and Mubarak. Yet the parallels are suggestive rather than overpowering.

In the first scene Regan moves out from the long table behind which the sisters are placed and sits on Lear's knee. Cordelia (Olivia Vinall), seems profoundly shocked at the effect of her refusal to play along with Lear's game. She is placed on a chair when Lear offers her to France and Burgundy. Throughout, Adrian Scarborough's Fool watches from his vantage point on the walkway into the audience.

Lear's movement into retirement is marked by his change of dress from uniform to cardigan, a choice that underscores the incongruous nature of his desire to keep the trappings of rule but not rule itself.

It is difficult to fall wholeheartedly behind either the older generation or the younger. Stephen Boxer's Gloucester is, like Lear, comparatively chilly and violent, taking Edmund (Sam Troughton) by the throat when he questions him about Edgar's supposed conspiracy. His sons are vividly differentiated: Edmund, neat, suited, initially bespectacled and as tense as a coiled spring; Edgar (Tom Brooke) relaxed and somewhat complacent in his early scenes. Disguised as Tom the beggar, he clearly signals his unease with the role he has given himself to perform…"

I remember that when this arrived, Jeffrey had it enlarged and put in the foyer at the Polonsky. He allowed himself one edit, a pictorial one: in place of the portrait of Simon in the part he managed to paste an exactly equivalent one of myself. This was, after all, the American version of the journal.

I shall miss these people, very much.

# WEEKS SIXTEEN
# TO A HUNDRED AND SEVEN

*Friday, May 9ᵗʰ, 2014*

Ishould probably have shares in Le Pain Quotidien. I even like the
cappuccino in bowls; and after all, if Shakespeare is my daily bread, I'm
now trying to prolong its freshness. Sitting down with Philip Franks
at the branch in Highgate I naturally have a reflex memory of Hudson
Street in 2010, when Arin Arbus leaned across the table and put me straight
about *The Taming of the Shrew*. The New York Pain Quotidiens seem to
me uneasy places, and too content, in my opinion, with high levels of air-
conditioning. I've also found that they pump themselves up a bit compared
with London's, like Revivalists at a Trappist meeting trying to whip up
some excitement. Oddly, at the moment you can get a Flourless Chocolate
Brownie, a Pecan Swirl or a Detox Salad in London but not in New York;
and Tuscan White Beans, Quiche Lorraine and Paris Ham in New York but
not in London.

I'm having a debriefing meeting with Philip – wearing his director's
rather than actor's hat – within a week of coming back from Brooklyn. In
this relationship he and I have worked together over the last seven years
with extreme pleasure, on Ronald Harwood's *Collaboration* and *Taking
Sides* and then on *The Master Builder* in London and Chichester, as well as
on a couple of his radio productions. This flurry of work came after a period
of several years when, with great dignity and courtesy, he had sometimes
suggested projects to me and been patient with my deferrals. Meantime he
has discreetly made me aware by example that, in case I was thinking of
myself as Shakespeare's representative on earth, he can out-quote me on a
number of plays and has a better memory of many productions. He joined
the RSC as an actor in 1982, just as I finished my main stint there, and by
the time he left six years later he'd played Hamlet on their small-scale tour
and Bertram in *All's Well* on Broadway. He's also been in Howard Barker's
*Seven Lears*, and we remark often on the fact that two of the cruellest
playwrights of the age (in the imaginative sense), Barker and Edward Bond
(*Lear*), have both done terrific variants on Shakespeare's tragedy. Which
is what, in pointed particular, we're discussing, as we have been off and
on since we first worked together and thought of doing the play one day.

When a director and actor find each other and have any kind of a classical bent, it's a common enough topic.

Initially we thought perhaps of suggesting Stalin's Soviet Union as the court of King Lear, or indeed Lear appearing as any one of the dictators Lucy Munro speaks of: anything resembling an unfamiliar "invented" world seemed to us too vague for the play. This is an opinion we changed about the time that we stopped meeting at the Café Rouge and started favouring Le Pain Quotidien.

A person's views on *Lear*, as on many classics, are better clarified by talking about the productions they've seen than by any theoretical credo. For better or worse Pip is very interested by the one I've just done; and he's anatomising the most recent productions he's seen himself, including Sam Mendes's at the National. He makes me especially pleased to be back home and remembering how much we share, about good theatre and bad and everything in between, almost to the point of predictability. He has a touchpaper reaction to any form of cant and to bad Shakespeare. I remember his thoroughness when he directs, his memory and range of reference, his taste, his huge A4 book in which he records his work meetings like Prospero. He's opening a new one of these now. When the New York production cut into my life our discussions of *Lear* paused; now they seem to be re-booting.

I'm circumspect though, because there's an unfinished story surrounding the TFANA show and Philip should know about it. For much of the New York run, I and Jeffrey Horowitz, a man of commendable directness now somewhat baffled by the British codes he found himself trying to decipher, had conversations with UK parties possibly interested in importing Arin Arbus's production lock, stock and barrel. It's not cheap to move a unit company like this, but on the other hand there might have been sources of sponsorship at the American end, had there not been enough in the UK. We even had a speculative budget in our hands to demonstrate how it could be done.

There was some show of interest from the RSC, who had a three-week slot in the Swan next spring. Meanwhile I was in touch with a commercial management whose New York Executive Director, after several invitations, cajolings and follow-up calls, did finally come and see the production in Brooklyn. His leaked report was that without the RSC's imprimatur he didn't see how his company could afford to take it on. It took a little while to figure why my being an Honorary Associate Artist of the RSC wouldn't answer this point, but that was his verdict as he made a rapid exit from the ongoing drama.

And indeed the RSC were withholding their blessing – a curious decision as they had the slot available, would be more or less guaranteed against loss, and Stratford is a lifelong stamping-ground for me. However the Artistic Director, Greg Doran, was planning his own production of the play with – unsurprisingly – Antony Sher, two years hence to celebrate the four hundredth anniversary of Shakespeare's death, and it is as if the route were being cleared for some royal procession, its outriders charged with ensuring that Stratford was Lear-free for at least eighteen months before the event – and presumably afterwards as well, to avoid any unseemly comparisons. I may or may not be alone in finding it odd to contemplate a national company with a great deal of public money and a duty of care excluding the possibility of variety. Everybody knows in this industry that a glut of *Hamlet*s or *Lear*s can be very good for business, and we'd no more been hurt in Brooklyn by Langella's *Lear* than I had by Pryce's simultaneous *Hamlet* thirty-five years ago. The coded answer came soon after I got home in the form of a booby prize: a handwritten note declaring the RSC's poverty and offering me as compensation the ninety-nine-line part of the King of France in *Henry V*, by far the smallest I would ever have played at the RSC.

I knew in my bones that my Lear wouldn't make it to Stratford, and I don't suppose Shakespeare will spin in his grave in 2016. However, the door that I found closed on *Lear* has finished my business with a company with whom I've been intimately associated under every previous regime since Peter Hall founded it in 1961.

Pip listens to this with becoming modesty, a little like a very grown-up person about to be asked for a dance. The next thing that happens is I'm invited to the Press Night of *Wolf Hall* at the Aldwych. I see the celestial figure of James Dacre approaching across the foyer – a fine director for whom I once did an adaptation of *When We Dead Awaken* at the Print Room. He's heard all about *Lear*, as gratifyingly – since you can never be sure – have many people I've bumped into today. Hearing that the import is proving difficult, he points out that there is such a thing as an English production and also such a thing as a triangular co-production between three regional theatres, and that as the successful incumbent at Northampton, he's in a position to initiate one. Making rhapsodic mimes of phones to ears, we part.

Dacre will demonstrate his ability to make such a package a short while later when he contacts me on holiday in Sardinia, where I'm dedicated to washing that Lear right out of my hair. He explains that he's doing *Cat on a Hot Tin Roof* as a co-production between Northampton, Manchester Royal Exchange and Newcastle, and invites my Big Daddy. I almost spoil my holiday thinking about it, as this is normally a part I would have liked to do – the southern patois, the intoxicating rhythms of Tennessee Williams – but I must be suffering from a pleasant post-traumatic disorder: anything remotely smelling of Lear I don't want, just the real thing. In particular I don't much fancy playing an unredeemable brute so soon after playing a redeemable one. Thinking it might set back his thoughts of doing *Lear* with me later (human nature being what it is), I decline even after he's offered me the revised version of the play Williams, in defiance of Elia Kazan, used for the first major revival, which actually makes Big Daddy a bigger part but presents him in an even worse light. However, as events would prove, Dacre is a gentleman – not least because, although like most directors he must have a *Lear* on his mind for some future time, he would never raise a cavil about my existing partnership with Philip.

As light relief, while still in Sardinia I'm offered Kuragin in Timberlake Wertenbaker's day-long adaptation of *War and Peace* for BBC radio. The part is particularly reduced in the adaptation, but still worth doing. We crunch some dates. Then it turns out John Hurt can only record Bolkonsky on certain days. And they have changed, to ones that I'm not free on. So I'm dumped. A certain kind of big name has become as important in radio, where you don't see anyone's face, as it is to guarantee a movie. So I miss the chance of playing with a much-admired acquaintance the very funny scene when Kuragin arrives at Bolkonsky's house to discuss marrying his son to Bolkonsky's daughter Marya; Bolkonsky is so incensed that his servants have cleared the driveway of snow in exaggerated respect for the visitor that he demands it is all shovelled back again, giving the approaching carriage some difficulties. Pity.

## *Wednesday, May 14th, 2014*

I sit down with Kurt, my branch manager at Lloyds, in an oak-panelled office that transports me immediately to a long-gone age when you could visit your bank manager, drink a cup of coffee, and after a small pleasant overture discuss in quiet tones what can be done about your overdraft. Kurt is in fact a woman but I have my own affable reasons for giving her that name. My nostalgia might have something to do with the fact that this is the thirtieth anniversary of my father's sudden death, and a little over fifty years since he set me up with this bank. I've been there ever since, as I keep pointing out, somewhat meaninglessly, to its employees.

Outside the window it's late spring, in a part of London I know well, in fact grew up near. The atmosphere, considering what we are discussing, is sweet and English. We've talked over the entire sequence of fraudulent events and indeed begun to put it right. We've also paused from time to time, like tennis partners between sets; in one such breather, she's told me there used to be a little hatch in the wall, which, depending on the position it was set at, told the outside world that the manager should not be disturbed, could be disturbed, or – most intriguingly – could be disturbed as long as you knocked on the door first. Odd that you wouldn't knock on the door anyway. We agree, without quite knowing what we mean, that those were the days. She points out where the little hatch has been boarded over.

Kurt is fixing everything fast; a brand-new account, a full refund of the stolen money, all of it, all with a metaphorical flick of the wrist. And a little *ex gratia* payment for my trouble. Then something more difficult – and intensely interesting – happens. As if all the foregoing was only a means of delaying the inevitable, she has, with an air of resignation, picked up her phone and called Fraud.

Twenty-five minutes later she is still held on the line unconnected, though I think without muzak. Once or twice during this time she has had to nip out of the office and has left me with the phone in case we suddenly get through: and in fact we finally have been, so that I found myself asking someone slightly friendlier than Brooke or Charlotte to stay on the line until Kurt got back. Which she did almost immediately, thank God, as further small talk with Fraud might have been tricky.

From then on, I hear only her side of the conversation. She is guaranteeing that the customer is to be trusted, that the new account we have established should be acknowledged, and that all monies are to be transferred to it, including what was stolen.

Then, answering one question, Kurt says in a simple, direct tone that contains just a hint of seniority:

> "I have no idea how it was done, but you know that there are many ways this could happen."

There's something at the other line. She interrupts.

> "No, I'm not putting words in your mouth but you know as well as I
> do that there are many ways this could happen."

Oddly enough, she seems to be having a tough time of it, even being subjected to questioning. Everybody wants to be a cop in this game, it seems. She says the same thing twice more, and I think this is as close as anyone's going to come to admitting that this whole business could be an inside job.

As Kurt hangs up, with a little long-suffering *moue*, I look her in the eye and ask her if there could be such a thing as a bad apple in the bank. Of course, she says. Do the police get involved in these cases, I ask. No, she says, but there may be an internal enquiry, though neither she nor I will ever know the outcome of that. There is a depth of understanding that is almost Chekhovian beneath this exchange. Perhaps, I say, the villains have been promoted. She laughs. She's already told me she'll be retiring next year.

As for the other threats to peace, it will be some time before I get to the point of not thinking that if anything has gone missing in my life someone has stolen it. Or that every piece of spam that comes in on the computer is sinister. Soon after coming home I find that the money Santander instantly credited back to me in New York has – an exquisite touch – been debited again, by them. The reason is that a disclaimer form attesting the legitimacy of my claim arrived in London while I was still in New York, and because I wasn't there to complete and return it within the requisite ten days the money has been taken back.

Fortunately I have the number of my original contact there – the equivalent of Kurt at Lloyds – and that's soon fixed. It's not her fault that, nevertheless, there follows a summer-long game of telephone tag – or rather, one that keeps breaking down as Santander lumbers along in pursuit of the distant criminals. A variety of operatives call, asking me the same questions, promising to call back but never doing so. It's quite fishy: even the best lack all conviction. I am told with a mediocre consistency that any of my own acquaintance could be guilty – at one point, enraged, I ask if they're implying that my fifteen-year-old granddaughter might have taken the train from Oxford, picked the lock, disabled the alarm, found my bank statements, deduced the pin numbers and emptied my bank account. Underneath most of it I sense drift, the blame subtly being shifted back to the customer. I'm constantly warned to be careful and check my account: me be careful, mind you, not the banks be careful not to let people walk out of their branches with large quantities of cash belonging to their customers and in their care.

A James thinks that it might be possible to look at the CCTV at a certain branch where the fraud was done. Hallelujah, James, what branch is that? He won't tell me.

A Des comes on the line. He doesn't really introduce himself; when I ask him if he's from Fraud he says unrevealingly that there are many elements in the Fraud Department. He says he's heard I am a "Shakespeare actor" and asks if I've ever lived in Sheffield. He promises to get back with some news after the weekend but then disappears forever; I hope I won't go online one day and find the money gone and no answer from his phone. Then I hear a rumour of Santander losing the proceeds of a house sale that was immediately needed for a purchase. And another, of a bereaved daughter trying to clear her mother's bank account after her sudden death, armed with birth certificates and all, being told that she must find her long divorced father, now in his 80s, and bring him into the bank to prove proximity of kin.

As for Orange, I end up going to CISAS – that is, the Communications and Internet Services Adjudication Scheme, approved by Ofcom to "help you with unresolved complaints with a telecommunications company". Their tag is 'Independence, Integrity and Impartiality'. I prepare a case, at enormous length, to be submitted to an independent adjudicator; EE, as Orange now are for these purposes, present a defence which suggests I am making it all up and there is no claim to answer. Asked in my application form what compensation I want if I win, I enter "up to" £1000: I say that though that's the approximate damage incurred in my bills, I'd be happy enough with something approaching it.

Having implicitly acknowledged in this request that I have some responsibility for not having read some section of my contract with sufficient care, I find the Adjudicator replies in kind. Although my statement and Orange's defence together run to the length of a novella, within an hour of its submission – not, I should have said, time enough for due consideration – I am notified of his verdict: I have no claim, for lack of evidence. Since I can't prove that I did not make a hundred phone calls, any more than I could prove that I do not have any weapons of mass destruction, I'm stuffed. To rub it in, he has misread the claim for compensation and says simply that I should not receive the £1,000 I've asked for. He's judged the wrong case, I complain to CISAS, but in their pro forma reply they say there is no right of appeal. Meanwhile I am still with EE because they seem no worse than most, and I sense that Data Roaming Charges are becoming a thing of the past. I bask in the utterly unreal fantasy that I can take some credit for this, as if I were the straw that broke the Blackberry's back.

However, I suggest you have nothing to do with CISAS, for all their claims to represent your interests in a complaint. You're far better off with Social Media.

❖

The summer of 2014 yields a number of jaunts and some short-order work: you'd think I was waiting for something to happen. First World War poetry at the Ledbury Festival with Harriet Walter; then to Urbino to direct a five-day workshop on *Romeo and Juliet* with a clientele that includes a woman who saw *Lear* in Brooklyn and a widower in his mid-eighties who's come specially all the way from Melbourne. He's the only one of our group happy to walk the steep hill back from our local restaurant to the hotel, rather than take a cab with the young ones. I got hold of Franco Zeffirelli's film and Baz Luhrmann's (I think) much better one, and I based quite a lot of the sessions on Caravaggio, who lived at exactly the same time as Shakespeare and revolutionised what we expect from realistic art much as Shakespeare did in the theatre. So much so that all the designers on the TFANA *Lear* acknowledged him as an influence.

I read Siegfried Sassoon poems at Heytesbury for the Sassoon Society: the organiser thanked all the participants for their generosity in giving their services to the charity, forgetting for the moment that she was paying me quite a fat fee. On to Cheltenham, to promote my new book about Shakespeare, which the interviewer, John Miller, declared to be the best such he'd ever read; as I was sitting on the platform next to the very nice Jonathan Bate, a true Shakespearian scholar of real bite and insight, it seemed only courteous for me to shout with melodramatic self-effacement "from an actor, that is". On a first ever visit to Glyndebourne I was reminded of *Last Year at Marienbad* or perhaps *The Draughtsman's Contract*, having the feeling that if I glanced round quickly to look at the scene in the gardens, there would just be the *bric à brac* of a film unit on location, and if I then turned back fully for a second look the whole vision would have gone. During the intervals of the opera I had a somewhat heated email exchange with the director of the Cameri Theatre in Tel Aviv as I wasn't sure I wanted to go through with a date I had with them shortly to do a week of my *Sweet William* solo show. Israeli-Palestinian hostilities had broken out again, and her first assumption was that I was scared: she immediately boasted about the effectiveness of the Israeli ground-to-air Iron Dome defence system that, she insisted, made Tel Aviv the safest place on earth. When she then detected that some part of my feeling was disapproval of Netanyahu's policies, she informed me that I didn't understand and I had to come there to learn; I tartly replied that I've been often to Israel, starting in 1983, but this rolled off her back. And of course when the time came, to be there with a Shakespeare evening was a powerful thing: the possibility of the Montagues and Capulets beginning to talk peace when they've been fighting for hundreds of years drew a spontaneous round of applause. So – liberal writer, liberal audience; and it was as ever quite shocking to meet several men and women at dinner implacably out of patience with the West's "sentimental" view of Palestinians. But then when I went thirty years ago, a doctor, one of the most cultured and liberal people I met, described all Arabs as animals.

In the autumn I played Anthony Blunt in Alan Bennett's *Single Spies* at the Rose Theatre in Kingston and came to believe that Blunt wasn't only the most incompetent but also the most unlucky of the Cambridge Spies. The moralising news clips at the time of his outing by Thatcher were nauseating, and the loyalty of his former pupils – Neil MacGregor, Anita Brookner – who understood that his Marxist sympathies in the Thirties were an entirely respectable response to Fascism (Bernard Shaw made a particular ass of himself over this) was accordingly very moving.

For the first time my grip on the lines was a little bit uncertain; this had never happened before and despite its horrible implications, I'm glad to say it passed as soon as it arrived. I learn a part well in advance now, but that's my only concession to the passage of time. In the weeks to come I would cross the paths of various Bennett veterans, all of whom said he was very difficult to learn. A comic genius who is difficult to learn? This is not a criticism of the writer of course – Judi Dench found David Hare's *Amy's View* hard, Lucky in *Godot* is obviously hard, a one-man show can be hard, though if most of the material is by Shakespeare it does make it easier. I think my difficulty was a little to do with Bennett's style, which like Shaw's often uses multiple clauses to similarly great effect. However the logic can be tricky to catch without the aid of private mnemonics. At the outset Bennett sent us a cartoon of himself looking morose, as he said he would be if he came to rehearsals; it was I think the same one he'd sent when I did *The Madness of George III* a few years ago and had no greater success in catching his attention.

During rehearsals Donald Sinden dies. Donald Sinden, who seduced me into joining the Garrick Club, a thing I'd thought I'd never want to do; Sinden, who said to me when I played Edgar – and he would listen carefully on the tannoy each night to everything between his scenes – that what was wrong with my performance was that I had never seen anybody die, as Edgar does his father. At the time this was true, and an obstacle I could do little to overcome, but it did help me to think a bit more closely about it. Donald, who was so pleased to get his knighthood that he kept telephoning Buckingham Palace even after sending back his acceptance, so afraid was he that it might have got lost in the post.

Prue and I went to Portland Oregon with *Sweet William* again, and there, deep in a leather armchair in the hotel, was Patrick Stewart, on a break from shooting an indie movie called *Green Room* in which he was playing a very bad guy, the leader of a white supremacist group. We muse on the RSC under its new management. Back to London to do an utterly remarkable piece by the great David Rudkin about the last days of Euripides for that Radio 3 eleven pm Sunday slot that ensures culture but possibly not high ratings; to Cordes sur Ciel in the Tarn for another *Sweet William*.

And then, like another rap on the door, Richard Pasco dies at 88 after a long struggle with Alzheimer's.

I last saw him just before leaving for New York, and the experience was like an overcast day in which the sun occasionally came dazzlingly out. Richard would throw his head back and laugh: a full-throated joyousness burst out from behind his repeated questions, his stalling and uncertainties, the puzzlement in his gaze. Then of course we were back in the Dirty Duck in 1980, and for his wife Barbara Leigh-Hunt and myself – that is, his constant helpmeet and his very inconstant but sincere friend – it was worth everything.

Sitting in the church at the funeral in Aston Cantlow I find Patrick Stewart slipping into the pew beside me. Greg Doran is on the other side of me, but Patrick and I decide this might not be the moment to test the theories we developed in Oregon. Richard's is the first wickerwork coffin I've seen – you can sense the weight of the body inside and it creaks gently. His son William, looking exactly like him, reads Donne's prayer that we will all be united

> in that house where there shall be no darkness nor dazzling, but one equal light; no noise nor silence, but one equal music; no fears nor hopes, but one equal possession; no ends nor beginnings, but one equal eternity…

with difficulty: it's the grown-up children for whom this is the worst, I think, and I wonder how I can forewarn my own son.

### February 2015

Watching *King Lear* is like being cast adrift and looking for help. Where wisdom is normally found in Shakespeare – in the old, in the women – it is horribly absent. We turn to the rank outsiders, most of whom profess no wisdom at all. There we find fools of all kinds: fools by nature, blind fools, and one professional who is then supplanted by a man who pretends to be a lunatic. For the first half of the play the image of the benighted old King with his wise Fool at his side is particularly enduring, like Hamlet with his skull or the two tramps under their tree in *Waiting for Godot*. I recently saw a colleague with dementia being helped along the street by his son and thought of Lear; they looked as if they'd been doing it for years. Junius Brutus Booth used his young son Edwin (later to become a yet greater actor) as his dresser, purveyor of brandy in the wings and general saviour: demented after playing Shakespeare, Junius had to be chased around the New England countryside or along the Baltimore waterfront by this old child of his, trying to calm him down and bring him home. It is one of the great Shakespearian ideas – the elderly as a threat to himself and the guardian child old before his time.

Michael Pennington, Sweet William

In Le Pain Quotidien with Pip Franks again. Although my daisy chain of short commitments last year always left space for it, I couldn't say that *King Lear* had haunted me, not really, any more than he would in the year to come, but he kept grumbling and cursing in the background, like an old grizzling dog. On the way to Pip I've seen Poor Tom – a beggar leaping about in the street for no evident reason, howling and roaring and also looking very dangerous, ready to do plenty of damage. He was so aggressive that rather than give him anything I crossed the road to avoid him. But then, Jacob Fishel in New York sometimes mercilessly begged for money from the patrons in the first row of the stalls, who couldn't escape.

This time, Pip advises me to take another look at Andrei Tarkovsky's *Stalker* – for its sense of Armageddon, its brown monotones, its puddles and its fog; also to think of Mr Dick in *David Copperfield* (but not *Nicholas Nickleby*'s Smike) when considering a young oddball Fool. He talks about the movie *The Book of Eli*, another post-apocalyptic tale in which one man fights his way across America in order to protect a sacred book that could save the human race; of a flapping tarpaulin that could represent the storm and then collapse in on itself to make the Hovel. Regardless of whether any of these things survive, I could weep with the pleasure of it. It seems the gods do love old men after all.

In turn I'm able to tell him that there are signs that in the cut-throat world of commercial theatre the idea of a re-thought *Lear* with an English company is beginning to get a better reception than in the subsidised Shakespeare centre. And sure enough, in Buenos Aires a couple of weeks later (*Sweet William* again) I get an email from Howard Panter, Joint Chief Executive of Ambassador Theatre Group. So begins a correspondence of notable candour with him and Michael Lynas, his Business Affairs Director, and an equally supportive one with Danny Moar of the Theatre Royal Bath as well as with James Dacre again. This will resolve itself nine months later in the triangular co-production model James first mooted, with one partner, ATG, owning four of the theatres we visit; and for me the prospect of doing twelve eight-performance weeks of the part all round the country – ninety-six *Lear*s in a row. The auditoria we play will range from four hundred and fifty to two thousand.

So be careful what you wish for. Eyebrows are raised among my nearest and dearest: Robin Ellis thinks I must be completely mad. Certainly it could make a strong man blench, but it also makes me think with some satisfaction of the oldest of traditions: Anthony Quayle did the same thing at around my age, and probably Wolfit too. If it were to prove to be a bowing-out, in one way I can't think of a better one.

Also in February, Alan Howard dies. My neighbour as well as one of the great co-ordinates of the classical theatre of these last forty years or so, an absolute hero in both tragedy and comedy; I would say along with Scofield the supreme vocalist of my lifetime, whose uniqueness lay in his simultaneous evocation of a great tradition of heroic acting and a form of lyrical intelligence that was entirely his own. Alan was literally his own masterpiece, and like all masterpieces somewhat inexplicable. In due course there would be a full-blown memorial service to celebrate him; meanwhile my pleasure at being asked by Sally Beauman, his widow, to come to the tiny immediate ceremony at the crematorium – his friends Terry Hands, Bill Paterson and Julian Barnes and only three or four others – and to read a Shakespeare sonnet didn't make up for his dying, but was extreme. Alan was in a wicker coffin too and as I stood alongside it with Sonnet 60 I wondered if I couldn't hear it creak in protest; it reminded me of Richard Griffiths's funeral a couple of years back, when a mobile phone went off during the tenderest moment of the ceremony. Mindful of Richard's famous objection to such a thing happening during a performance, the entire congregation – I promise – turned to look at the coffin. For a moment it seemed that death might have no dominion after all and that we were about to witness a miracle.

Then in July, while I'm in technicals for *She Stoops to Conquer* at Bath, Roger Rees follows Alan. I can't go to the funeral in New York: instead I work out the time difference and sit in silence in a remote part of the theatre, remembering him pulling a succession of toy mice and other knick-knacks out of his Restoration wig when we did *The Way of the World*.

All in all, it's been a hell of a year. And now the father of a Syrian migrant has lost his wife and two small sons trying to get to Europe: the tragic image of one of his boys being recovered from the sea has shaken the world better than words and has even threatened to move the government an inch or two towards human decency. It may yet bring out the best in the British: but the fact is that this is uniquely moving because we never knew the poor man before – he is a stranger, someone we would never have heard about otherwise. In time he'll recede too. Meanwhile the single image of his suffering, like Lear battling the storm, has become indelible.

### *January 2016*

> Even so quickly may one catch the plague. A minor incident over a garden fence can lead to a man decapitating his neighbour with an electric saw; an imagined slight inflames the mind more than a calculated insult; the very fact of unchecked power makes the idea of genocide quietly entertainable. By the twenty-first century, we have learned how fragile our restraints can be, how we can be sent to hell in a second. On the day that I'm writing, the television news tells of a man who raped both his daughters repeatedly for twenty years, causing them eighteen pregnancies. In the next item, it is reported that aid to Somalia, one of the poorest nations on earth, may have been stolen wholesale by aid workers en route. So what is so strange about *King Lear*?
>
> Michael Pennington, *Sweet William*

And now Alan Rickman dies. I barely knew him, though I spent one season at Stratford with him, before his glory days, when he was markedly unhappy; success brought him great content and I wish I'd run into him then. Like Roger, Alan was a flame that wasn't supposed to go out. Some people should surely have an exemption, and the huge public response to his death has been marked with a sort of incredulity.

I'm writing this in a restaurant, eavesdropping as usual. There's a man with a dangerously short fuse next door, playing the fool as a means of not speaking to his wife, whose views he does not feel he needs, let alone those of his daughter. As for me, I often forget what I've just said, and names are an increasing problem. I take longer to learn my lines but, thanks be, once they're in, they're in. I do think about death most days, even if only *en passant*. I know about people occasionally looking at me enquiringly, needing an answer and my not having one. I sometimes make a note to be sure to tell Prue something, and then forget it. I take offence increasingly easily, and have tidal waves of paranoia (as you may have noticed). But I'm surprisingly strong considering how little exercise I take except on the stage.

I'm afraid of losing my mind, but I'm reasonably philosophical so far about having to pause and recollect facts, as everyone over the age of seventy has to. I'm afraid of losing control of myself and nonsense coming out of my mouth, or of seeing something that's not there, or of my own temper. Of others looking blankly at me; of overstaying my welcome, especially amongst the young. All these things make me fearful, but also irritated by the people who cause it, albeit unwittingly. Don't they know what awaits them? I sometimes say biscuits instead of bread, or Chinese rather than shiny. When I encounter the bits of Lear that seem outside of me, such as sexual horror, I have to remember the times I've been harshly judged by a woman, for Lear's daughters are all three of them condemning him in their own way. When Cordelia refuses to oblige in the first scene he rages that he'd rather keep company with the "barbarous Scythian" who eats his own children than ever see her again. Apart from the hyperbole, it's a confused idea since he's choosing a father who eats his daughter rather than a daughter her father, as he feels she has done. By the very next scene in the play, he is thinking clearly again and seeing what a mad mistake he made. Impossible? Well, when I'm thwarted I often do Barbarous Scythian immediately, usually in the privacy of my own home, then calm down and begin to think more clearly. Or turn on the TV, where I might see a politician defied by a TV interviewer having to suppress a Barbarous Scythian moment, saying instead something like "That's a good point, Jeremy"… or that pally, we-understand-each-other "Look… we both know…" Lear's insane Barbarous Scythian – intolerant, vengeful, cruelly excessive – is only an extension of something most people have felt.

So why would I not be good as King Lear?

❖

I'm sad to say that four men have been indicted for picking up two thirteen-year old girls on our former route home to Classon Avenue from Franklin Avenue subway, gang-raping and then attempting to prostitute them. They were then foiled by a concerned relative who texted one of the teenagers and apparently received a text in return – "Want a date?" – from the defendants, who had taken control of the girls' phones. The relative then replied, "Yes" and asked for the price and the location. He went to the apartment, paid for the alleged services and retrieved the girl. For some reason I think of the flophouse window I heard the yelling come from before I fell down in the street, almost two years ago to the day.

Back in Blighty, our tour is booked, all three producers are ready to go. Pip casts the play with style and relish; he has repeated sessions with the designer Adrian Linford and the composer Matthew Bugg. We agree (as fans of the PR officer played by Jessica Hynes in John Morton's wonderful *W1A*) that at last we're sucking sauerkraut, and we should nail this puppy to the floor, yeah? I promise that when we do, I'll never mention what we did in the New York production; after all, if you want to upsize your footprint you better change your shoes or you'll be drinking from the fire extinguisher.

Then Pip is taken ill. He needs major surgery and a longish recovery process afterwards, enough for his doctors to advise him firmly to leave the project. It's heartbreaking. My own regret is necessarily combined with the need to keep the production together if possible, now that we have a tour and a cast booked. This means a new director who's prepared to jump on a bus that's already begun to move off. It can slow down a bit – the design can be adjusted as he or she wants – but it can't stop. The actors are contracted.

As can happen in our profession, a dark and hopeless week turns suddenly around – for me, not for Pip. It becomes apparent that Max Webster, an Associate at the Old Vic and the director of their Christmas hit *The Lorax*, bubbles with ideas and has no difficulty accepting the parameters. On the day he says yes, Pip is in the operating theatre. On the day Pip comes home, Max and I meet to discuss how to cut *King Lear* before going to see a first night at the Old Vic – Ralph Fiennes in *The Master Builder*.

As an actor, it's sometimes nice to be compared to a chameleon, for the obvious reasons. But a chameleon has another talent: it is able to look in two directions at once, and its brain can process the information from each eye separately. So I can now get on with profoundly commiserating with my friend, simultaneously wishing he could do the show and rejoicing that

Max can instead, visiting both of them in turn, thinking of something else Pip and I could do together in the autumn or spring, learning my lines for Lear and finishing this book in time to start rehearsals in a couple of weeks' time. As I look across a table in the Leafy Greens and Beans Café in North London at Max, discussing whether we should cut the know-all Gentleman in Act Three Scene One, it's like coffee with Arin Arbus all over again.

# INDEX